Beating the Financial Futures Market

Founded in 1807, John Wiley & Sons is the oldest independent publishing company in the United States. With offices in North America, Europe, Australia and Asia, Wiley is globally committed to developing and marketing print and electronic products and services for our customers' professional and personal knowledge and understanding.

The Wiley Trading series features books by traders who have survived the market's ever changing temperament and have prospered—some by reinventing systems, others by getting back to basics. Whether a novice trader, professional or somewhere in-between, these books will provide the advice and strategies needed to prosper today and well into the future.

For a list of available titles, please visit our Web site at www.Wiley Finance.com.

Beating the Financial Futures Market

Combining Small Biases into Powerful Money Making Strategies

ART COLLINS

Foreword by Robert Pardo

WILEY

John Wiley & Sons, Inc.

Published by John Wiley & Sons, Inc., Hoboken, New Jersey.
Published simultaneously in Canada.

For general information on our other products and services or for technical support, please contact our Customer Care Department within the United States at (800) 762-2974, outside the United States at (317) 572-3993 or fax (317) 572-4002.

Wiley also publishes its books in a variety of electronic formats. Some content that appears in print may not be available in electronic books. For more information about Wiley products, visit our web site at www.wiley.com.

Library of Congress Cataloging-in-Publication Data:

Collins, Art.
    Beating the financial futures market : combining small biases into powerful money making strategies / by Art Collins ; with a foreword by Robert Pardo.
      p. cm.—(Wiley trading series)
    Includes indexes.
    ISBN-13 978-0-470-03865-9 (cloth)
    ISBN-10 0-470-03865-9 (cloth)
    1. Financial futures.   2. Futures market.   I. Title.   II. Series.
    HG6024.3.C63   2007
    332.63'2—dc22   2006011072

Printed in the United States of America.

10 9 8 7 6 5 4 3 2 1

For my wife Pat and daughter Maggi,
to whom I am especially biased

Contents

Foreword   xi

Preface   xvii

Acknowledgments   xxi

About the Systems and Studies in This Book   xxiii

CHAPTER 1   The Problem with Non-Mechanical Trading   1

CHAPTER 2   Understanding the Numbers Game   5

CHAPTER 3   But Why Doesn't Spontaneous Trading
             Work? Why Is It So Hard for Someone to
             Profit by Merely Using His Head?   7

CHAPTER 4   Identifying Simple Biases   10

CHAPTER 5   Close versus Closing Averages   14

CHAPTER 6   The Four Rules of Prudent Optimization   16

CHAPTER 7   Two-Day versus Five-Day Averages   25

CHAPTER 8   Fifty-Day Order of Extreme Highest/
             Lowest Closes   29

CHAPTER 9   Combining the First Three
             Basic Indicators   31

CHAPTER 10   Cuing Off Relative Range Sizes   35

CHAPTER 11   Fifteen-Day High/Low Averages   38

CHAPTER 12   Combining All Five Indicators   39

CHAPTER 13   Other Combinations of the Five
             Basic Indicators   43

CHAPTER 14 Two More Open-to-Close Biases   **47**

CHAPTER 15 Cups and Caps   **49**

**CHAPTER 16 Three-Day 20 Percent
Support-Resistance Indicator**   **56**

**CHAPTER 17 The Eight Indicator System
(Plus a Discussion of Outliers)**   **58**

CHAPTER 18 Entering on Stops   **65**

CHAPTER 19 Entering on Limits   **69**

**CHAPTER 20 Some General Observations about Stops
(and an Actual Application)**   **72**

**CHAPTER 21 The Pros and Cons of Price Targets
(Featuring Another Effective System)**   **76**

**CHAPTER 22 Other Applications of the Two High/Low
Exit Technique (Live! As It Happens!)**   **82**

**CHAPTER 23 On Further Optimization, Market Drift,
and Virgin Data**   **85**

**CHAPTER 24 "The Best System in the World"—
(If Only!)**   **96**

CHAPTER 25 Targeting Sectors   **103**

**CHAPTER 26 Index Biases Part One—Days of
the Week**   **110**

**CHAPTER 27 Index Biases Part Two—Days of the Month
(Or How to Beat the Stuffings out of the
Bellwether S&P Indicator)**   **115**

**CHAPTER 28 Index Biases Part Three—Month of the
Year Indicator**   **120**

**CHAPTER 29 Index Biases Part Four—Combining Day
of Week, Monthly, and Previous
Eight Indicators**   **124**

CHAPTER 30 The Dow-Spoo Spread—"Told You So!"   **127**

CHAPTER 31 Intraday Day Trading Part One:
            The Most Significant Price in
            Your Arsenal   138

CHAPTER 32 Intraday Part Two—The Switch
            (Can Promising Trading Environments
            Be Anticipated?)   143

CHAPTER 33 Intraday Part Three—An Effective
            Index Switch   148

CHAPTER 34 Intraday Part Four—A Financial Switch   151

CHAPTER 35 Intraday Part Five—Four Combined
            Entry Signals in the Indexes   153

CHAPTER 36 When It Gets Extreme—What to Do after
            Five Closes in the Same Direction   158

CHAPTER 37 Some Additional Fade Ideas   163

CHAPTER 38 Another Look at N Day and an
            Alternative Stop Approach   165

CHAPTER 39 Taking On the Axioms Part One—
            The RSI Indicator   171

CHAPTER 40 Taking On the Axioms Part Two—
            The Reversal Day Indicator   174

CHAPTER 41 Potpourri—Systems as I Discover and/or
            Rediscover Them—In No Particular Order   176

  200 Percent Range Expansion—Four Days in Trade   176
  The Continuous 66 Percent Momentum System   177
  Contracting Ranges—Buying Off Lower Closes—
   Selling Off Higher Ones   179
  Five- versus 15-Day Closing Averages   181
  A Soybean Play That Has Worked 70 Percent of the Time
   over the Last 40 Years   181
  Yet Another Moving Average Crossover—The 3-Day
   30-Day System   186

The 15–30 Day Close Indicator   186
The Bonds Lead the Indexes   187

CHAPTER 42 A Final Step-by-Step System
                    Construction—The Six Signal Indicator   190

CHAPTER 43 Combining the Non–Either-Or Indicators   193

CHAPTER 44 Six Signals Plus Non–Either-Or—
                    Putting It All Together   195

CHAPTER 45 Know It When You See It—What Is
                    Mechanical, What Isn't—(A Quiz)   198

CHAPTER 46 Embrace Mechanical Trading in Your Gut
                    on a 100 Percent All-or-Nothing Basis:
                    That's the Only Way It Will Work   200

CHAPTER 47 Final Observations   203

APPENDIX   TradeStation Formulas   205

Index   239
About the Author   245

Foreword

I first met Art Collins when he contacted me to see whether I would be interested in being included in his book *Market Beaters*—which, by the way, is a very good book with a not so good title.

Always happy to get some press and always equally happy to do what I can to help traders of all sorts understand what it takes to be successful at the difficult art of trading, I expressed my interest.

Since that time, I have taken Art under my wing—as an informal student trading system developer work in progress, so to speak. I did so for a number of reasons.

When Art asked me to write the foreword to his newest book, I was both honored and glad to be able to help bring a book as interesting and unique as this one before the trading public.

First, I found Art to be refreshingly honest and forthright in a business, which—to say the least—does not always exemplify these qualities. It was also striking to me that—even as a middle-aged man with years of real-time trading experience and as a man who has interviewed a number of highly successful traders for his various books—Art was possessed of an almost childlike curiosity and enthusiasm for trading system research. It was a refreshing contrast to the know-it-all-ism, cynicism, and hypocrisy that one can find among those who vend information to the trading community. I was further impressed by Art's objectivity and lack of bias. If I had a nickel for every time that Art asked me to puncture the balloon of his latest and greatest trading idea . . . And, last, but far from least, I have been—and continue to be—impressed by Art's persistence and diligence. Art is not a quitter, nor do I expect that to change.

We all know about the flim-flam guys and the snake oil salesmen, so enough about that. Fewer know—or understand—about those honest vendors who just don't know enough or are not rigorous and/or realistic enough to really deliver the goods on a trading product that can produce trading profits in real trading and over the long haul. Fewer yet know much about those who actually are the real deal—for example, the folks talked about in the *Market Wizard* and *Market Beater* type books—who know how to develop trading systems and to trade effectively but are so tight-lipped that they will say nothing about how they do it for fear that they are "arming" future competitors.

I have been in this business a long time—as a software developer, trading system expert, trading consultant, and money manager to mention a few hats that I have had the pleasure to wear—and, as a result, have had the opportunity to deal with a lot of very successful traders from all walks of life, a variety of vendors of different trading products, and a cross-section of trading "pundits."

I can tell you that to be successful in trading is difficult—and not strictly because it is difficult to find and validate a successful trading methodology. For while that process can be rather daunting—especially for the neophyte—it is not the most difficult part of the trading equation. Trading system development is a skill that can be acquired if one works at it hard enough. And this book will most certainly be a valuable asset in that process.

The most difficult part of successful trading is that it demands steely self-discipline and a tremendous confidence—if not in one's self, at least in one's trading system. Discipline and confidence both emerge—in the most healthful way—from a clear, objective, compassionate and penetrating self-knowledge. But that is a story for another time.

Suffice it to say, that if you were to take a survey of successful traders, you will find some things in common. First among those will be discipline, next confidence, and last but not least, you will also find honesty, passion, enthusiasm, curiosity, and objectivity.

I think that you will also find that successful traders share another trait in common—an insatiable curiosity about what makes the markets tick and an equally insatiable urge to learn and to continuously improve their skills.

So, for the trader—beginner to expert—education is an ongoing and continuous process. Of course, books on trading are a big component of this process. However, in fairness, there aren't that many great books out there about trading. I would even be so bold as to say that there aren't even that many good books written about trading. If you have read many trading books, you will probably agree with me that there are a lot of really poor, redundant, and undocumented books out there clamoring for your dollars.

I am glad to say, that Art's book is *not* one of those books. In fact, this is a very good book. If it were not a good book, friend or not, I would not and could not write this foreword.

However, because I say this book is a very good book does not mean that I agree with everything Art says in it, for I do not. Nor does it mean that I would not do things differently if I were writing it, because I would do some things differently.

However, this should in no way diminish your view of this book, because it is a book that has a lot of information packed into it—in fact, if one were to price Art's book in the same way that some of these "lesser" trading books are priced, it would be costing you a great deal more—and it is a book that looks at these ideas in some new and interesting ways.

Suffice it to say, that as a reader of many a trading book, a developer of countless trading systems and a successful trader, I can assure you that this is a book that can teach you something, whether beginner, intermediate or advanced trader. In truth, it is will probably prove more helpful to the beginner-to-intermediate trader, but even the advanced trader will probably find something useful in this book.

This book reads a bit like a mystery novel. Art's passion and enthusiasm for the "hunt" for the "perfect" trading system is infectious. He takes you through the process of discovery that he followed in the exploration of these trading ideas.

As I have said, this book is pretty well loaded when it comes to trading ideas. I know—both from my years as a vendor of trading system software and from some comments about my book—that people (especially beginners) are really looking for trading ideas. In fact, what they are really looking for is trading system that will turn $10,000 into $1,000,000 in one year . . . and all in a book that costs $49.95. I would suggest that if this is the goal, keep looking. It will be a long search.

I have always found this emphasis to be rather ironic because it doesn't take all that much digging to come up with decent trading ideas. A lot of really good trading ideas are out there in the public domain. The irony comes in, in that people generally don't recognize them when they see them, or discard them as "old-school," or they set the "profit bar" way too high. And, even when they do settle on trading ideas, they do not know how to test and evaluate them. For the trader who has gone even that far, in the end, most cannot follow the trading system with the consistency required when it is winning (enter greed) or when it is losing (enter its sidekick, fear).

When asked the question "Do trading systems work?" Larry Williams once said "Trading systems work, traders don't."

How does this book help with all of that? Well, first, it provides ten different trading ideas. I will say that in my career as a trading system developer and trader, I have encountered and explored just about every one of the ideas Art researches in this book. I won't comment further on their relative merit—so as not to "spoil the story" nor relieve you of your responsibility to make your own informed decision. Read the book and make up your own mind based on the evidence Art has so painstakingly presented.

Secondly, Art takes an approach to the integration of these different ideas into one trading system that I have not seen discussed too often—if at all—in the trading literature. That is, he creates various indices or indicators out of various configurations of these different indicators, triggers or trading ideas. It is an idea that I have had occasion to employ myself over the years and—ironically—I am currently exploring an application of this indexing approach to one of my new trading systems. Suffice it to say that indexing can be very powerful if it is done correctly. It can be a very effective way to "summarize" large amounts of complex information. Art handles this well, but do remember that there is a lot of information that is presented in this book and that there are even more complex and useful ways to interpret and index it.

Part of the fun and the uniqueness of this book is that there are enough tools in here that can be configured in so many ways that it is possible that any number of people—if they exercise their creativity and the required effort—will be able to come up with unique trading systems of their own.

Third, Art demonstrates a sound methodological approach to this process. If one wants to know what it really takes to have a shot at developing a profitable trading system, read this book and see the work that it does take.

Certainly, there are more advanced methodologies. But Art's methodology is sound and sufficient for what he sets out to accomplish. And, once again, there are developers of trading systems who dig even more deeply that Art has done. However, do keep in mind that, as in all arenas, there are many levels of skill and experience. Trust me, however, Art digs a lot deeper than many authors of similar books that address the same audience as this one.

I feel safe in saying that if everyone searching for a trading system made as much effort to be as exhaustive and thorough as Art has in this book, the fruits of their labor would be far sweeter.

What is the bottom line here? Trading is difficult. Developing a trading system that has a positive expectancy is the first step to success in trading. To develop a successful trading system takes a lot of blood, sweat and tears. To develop a trading system and to trade it successfully requires objectivity, discipline, and honesty.

Art has delivered a very honest book. Does he provide you with a "get rich quick scenario?" No. Do I believe that you will be able to develop a successful trading system? I cannot promise that you will, for that is up to you, but I do think that the effort will prove fruitful in many ways.

Will you learn some new trading ideas? Unless you already have a very extensive background in trading systems, I am pretty sure that you will.

Will you get a sample of how much effort it really takes to develop a trading system? You bet.

Will you see an effective application of a somewhat unknown but effective approach to trading data application—indexing? Yes, you will get that as well.

You will find within these pages the blow-by-blow account of an honest and sincere man's effort to develop a reliable and effective trading system.

In the end, if you are one who considers himself to be a serious student of trading system development, will you be better off for having read this book? I can honestly tell you that even though I have seen and explored just about every idea in this book individually, I personally have not put them together the way that Art does in this book. I learned a few new tricks. Perhaps you will as well.

As a matter of fact, to demonstrate our commitment to these trading ideas, Pardo Group Limited—in conjunction with Art—will be responsible for the creation of a web site that will serve as an idea and information exchange and clearing house regarding various incarnations, refinements and developments of and from these trading ideas.

For more information, please visit us at www.pardocapital.com.

Enjoy the hunt . . .

Bob Pardo
President
Pardo Capital Limited
Pardo Group Limited

Preface

I used to bet professional football in a strictly technical fashion. I was not a true fan. I knew next to nothing about the players and how they matched up. In fact, I've seldom watched a game I didn't have money on. I did, however, recognize the true significance of professional betting lines. They had nothing to do with a sports book's opinions about the outcome. Their only purpose was to entice half the gamblers to bet one way, and half the other. If the bookies achieved that ideal, they were automatic risk-free winners because the losing side paid an additional 10 percent "vigorish" (or "juice") of their betting amount.

Such logistics convinced me that any fundamental information about the players, the teams, the coaching, the weather, the stadium, or anything else was going to be reflected in the lines. You weren't likely going to out-Einstein the odds makers or come up with something brilliant that they didn't consider.

There seemed to be only one potential winning path, and it's the same one I follow in markets. The path of past performance. How did the teams do against the lines and under what circumstances? You'd get these little imbalances, like home teams covered a greater percentage on Monday nights than during the season at large. Home underdogs tended to reward more than average during most years. Some teams covered more on grass, others more on Astroturf. Many small groups of stats. Sometimes, the tendencies held up into the future, and sometimes they became anti-stats.

It was all one big win-loss hopper, and when the smoke cleared, I had overcome the 5 percent bookie edge. That it wasn't by much should hardly be surprising. Five percent over many trials is huge. Ask Vegas.

This is part of where I learned about the beauty of simplicity. I wasn't great, but I tended to do no worse than the season ticket holder who knew everything about the rosters—much to their annoyance. Fan-oriented analysis too often comes more from the heart than the head. Besides, it didn't seem too attentive to the only thing that mattered—the lines.

Stats are fascinating but elusive little animals. If you put too many biased trials together, you can lessen your sample size to unreliable levels. Combining raw elements doesn't automatically make them better, nor even commensurate with what the sum of the individual parts would suggest.

Complexity usually implies advancement—higher levels, but markets are frequently unlike the world at large. I got an inkling of that as a 20-something trading hopeful in the precomputer age, noting the dozens and dozens of trend lines a chartist had meticulously penciled in. He had filled his page almost to the point where every tick was on a support or resistance line—the whole sheet was almost solid gray. I think of that image when some giant like Elaine Garzarelli (or even the Fed for that matter) makes their pronouncements. What is behind these master mechanisms? Automated rotating compass points and belching computers? Labs that look like a James Bond villain lair? Obviously, I'm oversimplifying the point, but not by much. How much more right can Alan Greenspan be if he has an extra dozen computers backing him? Certainly not 12 times as accurate as before. In market analysis, you see near instantaneous application of the law of diminishing returns.

When I wrote *Market Beaters* and interviewed 13 mechanical and technical experts, I asked each of them to give me one mechanical system for promo purposes—just one system no matter how simple. Not one complied, so I abandoned the idea. In looking back, maybe I was asking for something unreasonable. It's too easy for even a well performing system to look bad. It could hit an air pocket just as it's printed and released. There will always be debatable points even about good performance summaries. Nothing gives you a smooth perfect return.

Winning systems depend on many things, including money management and the temperament of the trader himself. (A system loses if the operator loses his nerve prematurely—"woulda-shoulda" doesn't count.) The more you break something down into a basic component, the less extenuating circumstances you'll have.

I offer raw stats the same way Al O'Donnell does in his fabulous *Point Spread Playbook*—my bible during my football involvement. Like O'Donnell, I'll suggest you use it as a tool in conjunction with whatever else suits you. You might want to consider whether to take a trade fighting against some given bias, for example, or maybe you'll decide that your own input overrides that. On the other hand, I will be presenting several complete effective stand-alone systems. My only caution there is, follow them 100 percent exclusively as they're designed.

The choice is yours. Regardless, you certainly can't object to having the facts made available.

Acknowledgments

I want to thank the following people, without whom this labor of love would have been a lot more laborious.

David Mecklenburg, editor of Tiger Shark Trading (www.tigershark trading.com) for the media exposure, good advice, and tireless assistance he's extended.

Tony Blumberg, my soon-to-be son-in-law, for alleviating my computer woes.

Master Bill Cho, for being a great inspiration.

My fellow Cleaning Ladies, John, Scott and Dan, for periodically shaking up my cloistered writer-trader existence. (www.cleaningladys.com).

Ditto for Hatman and Landis—I appreciate your market input even though I'll still stubbornly follow my systems regardless of how "wrong they are this time."

All the e-mail respondents who have offered feedback on my writings and online commentaries. It's gratifying to know you're out there.

My cousin, Bob Zeman, for reading all my books, even though he isn't market-oriented.

My mother and father, for standing by me as always.

My trading partner, Mark LaSarre, for keeping me on the straight and narrow.

The people in Japan who bought my last book. I look forward to someday meeting you.

About the Systems and Studies in This Book

I treated the enclosed studies as though they were nitroglycerine. I'd like to think I always do that—what's normally at stake, after all, are my own finances. If my signals are inaccurate due to faulty testing, transposing, or order placement, I stand to lose money. Why would one need more incentive than that to be careful? Still, somehow I manage to make periodic, sometimes costly mistakes while trading. I am not alone in this. My partner has made errors when he's taken over the order execution helm, and he's a professional computer programmer. Floor traders make errors. You'd think they'd be bearing down constantly and yet out-trade issues are part of the everyday landscape of the exchanges.

I don't excuse mistakes in any of my market-related endeavors, but somehow, presenting an accurate book feels like the greatest pressure of all. I guess it comes down to this—if I lose money, I'll be wounded, but I'll recover. If I get something wrong in my book, it will be in stone for the ages, for all the world to see, at least until the next printing. I don't wish to take grief from my peers or my readers.

Nevertheless, I have to admit to the possibility that not everything within these pages is 100 percent virtually guaranteed error-free. Sheer volume dictates that, combined with a great deal of copying and recopying. Furthermore, I know that there are more streamlined, less clumsy ways to code some of the enclosed Trade Station formulas. (And I'll probably be hearing all about them. As I'll reiterate, I'm not all that mathematical.) Some of my contentions may be arguable and others may even ultimately prove unsupportable. Overall, though, I feel confident in the validity this work because I know it has been motivated by a desire to tell market truths as best as I understand them.

Again, though, logistical issues kept popping up here and there in the course of the writing and research. Believe anyone who tells you it's the little things that drive you crazy. I spent hours and hours in "crazy."

Let's start with TradeStation—a software server for which I have a high regard overall. I have recommended it to many people asking how to get started in research. But there are these little inconsistencies—maybe true of all software—maybe just unavoidable programming realities but, nonetheless, real irritants to anyone trying to keep stats straight.

Within TradeStation, given the same formulas, the same charts and the same testing time periods, one of my computers will spit out slightly different results than the other. I'm not sure why. Maybe it has something to do with open trades being counted differently depending on when you first accessed a data stream. Also, sometimes different procedures within the same time frame in the same market on the same computer will give you slightly different results with two different studies—say a performance chart verses an optimization report. Or the difference between a performance summary and an annual periodical return chart, which I used in two successive charts in this book. The yearly total sums should be equivalent to the performance summary totals, but they aren't. They're slightly different—not enough to induce panic, but certainly enough to irritate.

And, yes, I did recheck these numbers several times. I used a January 4 start date in some fields rather than January 2 because it was the only way I could then synch up a periodical study—showing exactly the number of years I wanted—with a performance summary page. I'd get different results if I were testing in a single data stream versus one in which another market was inserted. I'd go back two weeks after first constructing a table, and get the same results everywhere except in two of the markets. Obviously, there had been some erroneous ticks down the line that were subsequently readjusted. Can't beat fun at the ol' ballpark.

I'm not implying any TradeStation results are wrong—merely that computations from different points of origin are apparently producing dissimilar results. TradeStation has always given me plausible (albeit convoluted) explanations when I've questioned similar discrepancies during my personal trading research. I could make it my quest to fully understand everything they're doing and why to the point where I could explain it, but then this book would be coming out about three or four years past my deadline. And again, it is a good company overall and life is short.

So there were logistics I had to work around. For some reason, daily data in the mini indexes sometimes only goes back about four years; consequently, full contracts were used in daily charts. The software's bias leans in the other direction when it comes to intraday trading—therefore, mini contracts were used there. The two contracts should be roughly interchangeable for practical trading purposes.

All testing was done on day session bars only—never overnights. For daily bars, I used @ and then the market symbol followed by a dot d suffix, which is usually "P" for pit session. For intraday continuous bars, I used only the @ symbol followed by the market—no P or D dot suffixes. (You'd get more history that way.) The intraday market had to then be formatted in the "view/customize" function to make it reflect the day session time frame. For indexes, the trading hours are 8:30 A.M.–3:15 P.M., Central Standard Time. The remaining targeted financials trade from 7:20 A.M.–2:00 P.M. CST.

I invite any serious reader to duplicate my posted results. You don't need to rely on the veracity of these printed pages. You merely need the proper controlled environment (i.e., the same setup) I have. Hopefully, not all of the following will prove absolutely necessary for identical results, but just for the record, here are my lab tools.

1. I'm testing in TradeStation, version 8.1, Build 2826. The company's frequent updating of versions and builds will presumably not impact the data fields.

2. The beginning and ending dates of the testing periods are always noted. Sometimes, it's a little hard to synch up a first date, especially in longer term studies. It seems that x amount of run-up bars are required before a first trade date can be generated. For the daily five-year continuous data studies, 10-18-00 was inputted into "first date" which then pinpointed January 2, 2001, as the first possible entry date. The "last date" input was 11-19-05.

3. Unless otherwise noted, strategies should be formatted as follows:
   a. Commission: 0
   b. Slippage: 0
   c. Maximum contracts per position: 1
   d. Fixed shares: 1

4. Type in the appropriate TradeStation formula (see Appendix) exactly as it appears. It will be referenced by the appropriate table or figure number (Table 5.1, Figure 6.2, and so forth).

The necessity of personal involvement in system development from the ground up will be a frequently cited theme of the book—ergo the invitation to verify my studies. You won't be able to consistently profit by blindly following advisors. I have access to some of the most talented people in the industry, and I haven't been able to prevail in such a fashion. What is it President Reagan used to say about the Soviets?—"Trust but verify." I'm not sure how much I'd concur with the "trust" part.

Finally, to respond to an anticipated question of probable general interest, yes I do personally trade various incarnations of some the enclosed methodologies.

CHAPTER 1

The Problem with Non-Mechanical Trading

You can't go broke taking a profit.
Let your profits run.

Dr. Discretionary

Chances are you've encountered the adage that markets aren't right or wrong—they just "are" and that if you're losing, you're somehow arguing with them rather than heeding what they're telling you. As a mechanical trading advocate, I have come to appreciate the precariousness of that position. I've seen traders drive themselves crazy day after excruciating day, trying to retrofit reasons for their failure. "I thought I was buying the start of a fifth Elliot wave, but it was really a reaction in an extended fourth." "I thought I was selling away from the value area, but I should have seen that it was setting up a new higher value area."

Their new "insights" never seem to move them forward. Why?

The answer primarily lies in the nature of the playing field itself. Markets are overwhelmingly random noise with a small trend component. The latter is what mechanical traders largely hang their hopes on, but it's not perceivable on an individual trade basis. You need many trials to expose biases the same way Vegas needs many bets to exemplify the fact that their long-term edges are ultimately insurmountable.

Follow your convictions.
Don't get married to an idea.

Dr. Discretionary

The trade in progress is the only focus of the gut trader. "How do I turn this loser into a winner? How do I maximize this profit, and where do I decide that it's given all it's going to?"

Since the trend component can't be exploited over one trial in a small trading horizon, gut traders are almost by definition attuned to the noise. Despite the rare gifted individual who grows prosperous as the exception to the rule, most of us can't hear what the market is saying any more than we can perceive subsonic reverberations. We aren't hearing because the markets ain't talking.

What we are inputting, however, is random intermittent feedback, which is not necessarily a good thing. Researchers have scientifically demonstrated that the hardest behavior to break or modify is that which is rewarded in an arbitrary fashion. A lab rat that only occasionally receives food, a drug rush, and so forth when he pushes a lever will continue to hit it until his paw is raw. This is the phenomenon behind compulsive gambling. Note the robotic behavior of people hooked on slot machines—the spell stays unbroken until the last coin is gone.

Furthermore, there's the problem of what is actually being reinforced. In nearly every other life situation, repeated experience results in learning. Trading doesn't conform because good ideas (whatever they are) won't necessarily produce winning trades any more than bad decisions will become losses. People get frustrated trying to form rules around an overload of information, and the result is like trying to see the forest for the trees. The other hand ("I should have been short, not long") is omnipresent and could always be theoretically argued in hindsight. Something clearly compels us to continue making such trades, but the hoped-for underlying revelations never seem to materialize.

> *Stay long unless the 8500 support level is taken out.*
> *Why did you get out?! It was only penetrated by a tick!*
> Dr. Discretionary

There's a weird déjà vu that runs through the discretionary world. We remember soybeans hanging on a bottom for months just before exploding into a weather market—let's buy them! Did we forget that even when the charts played out almost exactly according to plan, there were periods where the heat was too much for us and we got stopped out prematurely? How about the times we were just flat out wrong and the market almost immediate plunged through the support? And how we held on too long? Or we kept chopping ourselves up—frantically exiting and then re-entering?

There's always a sense of "this time I'm right—this is a trade I can't afford to miss." It's a powerful feeling that seems to have an intrinsic logic.

Why, after all, would we make a trade we didn't strongly feel was going to work? But again, more often than not, such impulses are wrong.

Some of the most accurate clichés in the industry apply to the chances of our success or failure. Ninety to ninety-five percent of traders lose money to the remaining minority. Let's review the resulting walk-through:

1. Most people are neither systematic nor mechanical.
2. Most people trade according to whatever whim strikes their fancy at the moment.
3. Most people lose.
4. It therefore stands to reason that you do not want to do that which is psychologically gratifying if you don't want to be part of the big loser pool.

Probably every mechanical trader (and most traders in general) will affirm that the trades we fear the most are the ones that tend to be the greatest windfalls. This accounts for the timeless phenomenon of mechanical traders jumping ship on a system after a harrowing series of losses—only to watch from the sidelines as an over-the-top paper rebound occurs. It's a sickening feeling, one in which many traders affirm is worse than actually losing money. The other side, obviously, is that our comfortable trades tend to be our trouble spots.

This all makes a weird kind of sense when you think about it. If everyone were in synch and markets behaved in an intuitive manner, we'd all be making money—but of course, that can't be. Who, then, would be losing? Who would be providing the grist for our mill?

You have to be out of synch with the everyday trader to profit. It's incredibly difficult to maintain that position on a discretionary basis. Sooner or later, you'll start fooling yourself about what you really think is the incorrect pathway of the masses, and what is really the prudent contrarian alternative—and then all hell will break loose, as it always does. A mechanical system solves that problem by churning out signals completely independently of emotion.

> *Don't you have any market sense at all?*
> Dr. Discretionary

You can advise people over and over about the discretionary dead end. They can even repeatedly experience the negative reinforcement (read losses) directly without an inkling that something has to change. It seems so right to do what's wrong, regardless of how many times you've been down the road.

To paraphrase trading legend Richard Dennis, successful trading depends on "doing the hard thing." Effective mechanical system trading is cut and dried, perfectly laid out, and readily fortifying. It's a series of mandates stemming from historic summaries. It involves no attempt to forecast the next market direction. Besides sufficient capital, your only requirement is that you maintain faith and determination.

This, of course, can be easier said than done. You have to follow your program all the time, 100 percent exactly as stipulated. Even one detour can completely skew your performance, which happens more often than one might imagine. Violations tend to occur the most during the worst pressure periods. Such times are often followed by the most unimagined turnaround windfalls.

You'd think our confirmed results would be enough to let us intellectually overcome our destructive impulses. You'd think a clear pathway would be more comforting than the nebulous, contradictory world of the rudderless impulse trader.

You'd think, but you'd be wrong. We're only human, after all, and that random intermittent response mechanism is tough to overcome.

Tough, but luckily, not impossible.

CHAPTER 2

Understanding the Numbers Game

Again, a discretionary trader has only one thing on his or her radar: the trade in progress. How does one maximize the ongoing profit? Where is the point where the move is losing steam—where is a reversal is likely? How about the loss in progress—is it liable to come back as part of the natural market ebb and flow, or is it going to get bigger? How and when does one decide that? Where does one cry uncle?

A mechanical trader, by contrast, acts off what has been demonstrated over an entire data field—a series of trials. A simple example—(not necessarily an actual effective system)—the trader buys any time the market trades at or above yesterday's high plus yesterday's range. He does this because he has observed that over the last five years, doing so at every possible opportunity would have produced $36,000 in net profit. He has other fortifying stats at his disposal also—he knows that 53 percent of the trades were winners, 46 percent losers and 1 percent broke even. He knows that his average trade netted $486. He knows that his wins and losses were fairly consistent over the whole time period—there was only one small losing year out of the five, and no outstanding (fluky?) runaway winners.

He is also aware that his idea tested well in related markets, and even netted small profits in most of the not-so-related data fields he routinely examined. Testing software pops out pages of such simple results, alongside more complicated features such as standard deviations, Sharpe ratio, and coefficient variation.

Like a lot of mechanical trading advocates, I have found that the simpler a methodology is, the more trustworthy it's likely to be. We'll be breaking many concepts down into elemental basics in the pages to follow. For now, we're saying that whether we're talking easy, hard or something in between, all kinds of stats are instantly accessible to any and all committed people. This truly is the information age!

This stream of data is the driver behind the numbers game. Simply put, a numbers game is a series of trials that has a positive mathematical expectancy.

Vegas is an ultimate numbers game. It features several games—each offering a variety of potential bets. Some bets figure to be won, some lost. Overall—guaranteed—Vegas will triumph.

There is no doubt about that outcome over any kind of reasonable long run. Slot machines are so deterministic that even the sequence of wins and losses is completely preordained. Each machine is programmed to pay on this roll, then another 14 spins further down, then 10 later, and so forth. The total payoffs will always be less than what is taken in. With table games, the house does have to sweat the short run—the occasional high roller on a hot streak—to get to its inevitable long-run payoff.

Historically, there has actually been one pathway to reversing Vegas odds—blackjack card counting. Some select people profited by knowing when a deck favored them. They were able to change their betting units and playing strategy according to the deck's composition. This one-time-only anomaly could have only originated in the precomputer era, and the only reason the casinos haven't completely closed the loophole is because of the number of noncounter cash cows who might stop playing if the game were changed. In other words, gaming lore has stuck the casinos with their glitch, but they manage their players well enough—barring them if necessary. Their kazillion lights, lavish fountains and ornate palaces and entertainment extravaganzas aren't threatened.

Vegas prevails by exploiting an edge—often miniscule—over a sheer volume of trials. Many trials—wins and losses—are added together producing a positive result for the operator. That's the nature of a numbers game.

The Vegas numbers game is more perfect than our trading models can ever be. For us, the element of luck is never going to be completely quantified. There are methods to mitigate the fluke factor in our testing, which we'll discuss. There are ways to be confident that one tested prudently rather than carelessly. We won't, however, ever be able to say with exact certainty that the future is going to resemble the past to the degree that we can absolutely ensure a profit. If you're a stickler for guarantees, you might consider giving up your trading aspirations. There is no methodology that will give you Vegas's assurance that a seven will turn up on the craps table one time out of every six. As a noted Market Wizard once observed, however, it's amazing how much money you can make being imperfect.

CHAPTER 3

But Why Doesn't Spontaneous Trading Work?

Why Is It So Hard for Someone to Profit Merely by Using His Head?

The trading world is a magnet for people who have triumphed elsewhere. It takes money to play the game, which obviously tends to screen out the unsuccessful. Movers and shakers understandably think they can apply their skills in the same fashion to this brave new world. They call on their instincts and common sense. Perhaps even a gambling mentality served them well in their more familiar arenas—a cobra-like sense of knowing when to strike.

Being astute people, they are perhaps not surprised when their first few trades lose money—they'll concede they're still neophytes. As they make their adjustments, however, and time passes without any perceivable change in the outcome, they are faced with something unfamiliar. Persistent failure. Despite the occasional profit here and there, the overall outcome is relentlessly negative. Why?—they wonder—doesn't one find the trading key by cracking the code of the world at large?

No. The trading world is like the overall world in some respects. It is a business. The number one cause of general business failings is underfunding. Trust that the markets will be no more forgiving than your store, your corporation, and so forth. You need sufficient startup capital to weather inevitable short-term storms.

Like other businesses, there are applicable adages. Don't let losses get out of hand. The trend is your friend. These are axioms that you almost inevitably will confirm and validate within any successful system you create.

The fine points or intangible elements of non-mechanical trading, though, are another story. How do you make enough in your profitable

7

trades to overcome the debit of your inevitable losses? This, you won't find in your reference books, and you probably won't even be able to learn it from other traders—even good ones. Anyone sufficiently capitalized and determined can make mechanical systems work. Spontaneous reactive trading success however—the stuff of commodity trading legend—is down to personal wiring. If you're not born with it, you're almost certainly never going to acquire it. Furthermore, if it is in your DNA, you probably aren't going to have to endure much of a learning curve. Market Wizards tend to hit their strides pretty much immediately.

An astute trader once observed that markets are like an opponent who is trying to defeat you by teaching you to make bad moves. Obviously, there is not an actual malevolent consciousness behind the markets, but in some ways, it's prudent to act as if there were. It is our psychological nature to tend to be out of synch with markets because they so often confound our normal expectations. To reiterate:

1. The trades we fear the most tend to pay off the most.
2. Our biggest problems are going to come out of the trades with which we're the most comfortable, complacent, and confident.

You see example after example of markets completely flying in the face of apparent conventional wisdom or common sense. This is being written just after the summer of 2005, and people living anywhere near the Chicago commodity exchanges might have sworn that they had just witnessed the biggest drought in at least a quarter century. (My lawn resembled something out of Arizona.) The soybean market obviously disagreed. On September 30, the bellwether November contract closed at $5.73 1/4—the same general level it was at in the previous mid-February timeframe. Between those dates, there was a spike up to $7.70. It wasn't that high, and it was extremely short-lived. Overall, there was more opportunity on the short side that season. Drought, schmought.

How about the aftermath of Hurricane Katrina, supposedly the second or third greatest natural disaster in American history? That *had* to be a financial negative, right? Wrong! The first trading opportunity after the event (Monday, August 29) saw the December S&P futures finish the day 850 points higher. The ensuing carnage, botched government response, and so forth were all completely shrugged off. By the September 9 close, another 2750 points had been tacked on.

It's not just singular events that confound. Mini-S&P day traders have largely been singing the blues for at least the last two years. There's little follow-through to help you gauge probable direction. Even a decisive up day is likely to be followed by a down one and vice versa. There have been intraday air pockets—rallies and breaks out of nowhere. Support-resistance levels are routinely breached before the market makes another assault on the opposite daily extreme.

Day after day, my partner voices one of his favorite observations: "How could you possibly spontaneously trade this market?" He then goes on to lament, "How could you possibly have seen that rally [break] coming?"

I've done exercises where I've scrolled through intraday bar by bar of data, trying to latch onto something—anything. If reactive spontaneous trading were possible, life would be easier. Clean slate every day. Fewer drawdowns with less intensity.

But I haven't found anything, unless I could get really objective about fading myself. I seem to have created ingenious antitrading techniques, but of course, that's deceptive. Both sides of quick, abundant intraday trades would lose because there's so little give relative to trading costs. I don't like to say never, and I am told that some people are navigating those waters successfully. So far, there are no breakthroughs to report from this particular lab.

The mechanical trading approach isn't perfect, but it's the best thing most of us will have. Again, if most traders lose and you can position yourself in the 5 to 10 percent winning minority, should you really be complaining about the cumbersome, sometimes painful nature of your approach? It's still 180 degrees afield of being in the huge loser pool.

CHAPTER 4

Identifying
Simple Biases

If Vegas didn't have the green zero and double zero on the roulette table, all players would enjoy true odds. The black even money bet would feature 18 ways to win and 18 to lose. Say you could bet on an individual number and get today's 35-to-1 payoff. Thirty-five times you'd lose one unit and on the 36th, you'd win it all back. The two green slots exist for a reason—Vegas wants an edge.

In trading, we don't create the green slots so much as we discover them. Let's look at one of the most basic.

In my first book, *Market Rap: The Odyssey of a Still-Struggling Commodity Trader*, I demonstrated a few biases in the futures markets. One fell into a category for which I have an especial interest—the "either-or" indicator. Specifically, on a daily basis, a market will, more often than not, close higher than its open following a down close (close-to-close) and vice versa after an up close. (Down close projects a higher open-to-close, up close indicates a lower one.)

This produced a win-loss ratio leaving little doubt that something was going on beyond mere chance. Fifteen major markets were posted, and the test period was 1989 through 1997. Out of 16,350 trials, 53.7 percent resulted in the anticipated direction. That may not seem like much compared to what the pit wizards might enjoy, but keep the following in mind.

1. The concept was raw, robust and simple—not jerryrigged in any way.
2. Bookies enjoy roughly a 53 percent edge, and Vegas settles for even less on many of their frontline bellwethers.

The bias is actually not holding up well lately. It's offered as a mere illustration of what will be uncovered and divulged—the actual "system" is not the point. Furthermore, I'm neither surprised nor disheartened by the shift. My experience is that markets do drift, and part of the optimization process (to be discussed later) is periodically adjusting for that fact without overdoing it, so that you become a dog chasing its tail. (Some of the interviewees in my most recent book, *Market Beaters*, said they reoptimize their systems as frequently as once a year.)

My success as a mechanical system trader has hinged on simple concepts. I used to knock them dead with a daily 30 year T Bond system that keyed off the basis points. Bonds trade in full points and 32d increments, so you see prices that are 110 and 23 32ds (11023), 114 and no 32ds (11400), and so on. My focus was on the full numbers (113xx, 114xx, etc.). If the market opened in a point different than the point of the previous close (such as 11203 open verses 11129 close), I'd enter the market on a stop as soon as it crossed 00 back into the original basis point (i.e., 01 was always the stop entry for longs, 31 was the short entry). Figure 4.1 shows two examples from the good old days of 1986.

I'd hold the trade over one night. On Day 2, if I were short, the Day 1 low would be my profit objective, and the high plus one tick would be the stop loss. If neither side was filled, I'd exit on that close. Everything was vice versa for longs.

This may be a lot of verbiage to describe a rather simple concept. The bond basis point methodology was little more than an overnight

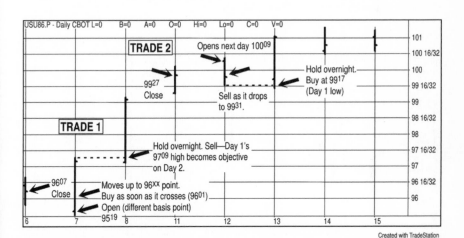

Created with TradeStation

FIGURE 4.1 Basis Point System: Daily 30-Year Bonds (*Source:* © TradeStation Technologies, Inc. 1991–2006. All rights reserved.)

momentum play keying off obvious psychological price levels. It was my first actual system, and its success begat more success and more desire for success. I was propelled into a 20-plus year research frenzy.

Alas, some things are not meant to last forever. The Chicago Board of Trade moved their financial openings from 8:00 to 7:20 CST. This was done to enable pit traders to react just as 7:30 government reports were hitting. That also had the effect of killing my driver—the necessity of frequent gaps which you'd get if openings were held off until after reports were digested. My premier system was unceremoniously retired (but fondly remembered).

For another similar example, I'd use a dual entry setup on soybeans, always fading the direction of the previous day's close. Following a down close, if the market opened below the previous low, the close would be the stop entry. If it opened at or higher than the low, but lower than the close, the order would be placed at the high. Once in the trade, I used the same rules of the above bond system. Again, simple technique, very satisfying results. I got many wild rides in the drought of 1988 (see Figure 4.2).

I had my second most successful day on Black Monday, trading the S&Ps. The concept was to merely subtract the previous daily range from the low to determine a sell stop entry. Accordingly, I was positioned short the preceding Friday. My biggest windfall was another S&P short—this time, entering on momentum off an opening toward the direction of the previous five-day average. While I wish I were a better programmer, I

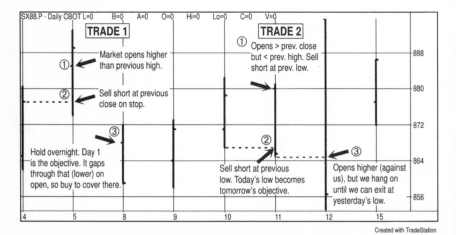

FIGURE 4.2 Fading Closes—Dual Entries: Daily Soybeans (*Source:* © TradeStation Technologies, Inc. 1991–2006. All rights reserved.)

haven't achieved better performances in my more esoteric ideas verses my dumb bunny ones despite contrary initial expectations. If anything, the opposite has been true.

Let's start with basic either-or indicators. By isolating elemental building blocks that signal every day—a long or a short—we can then assign each unit a plus or minus one value. The values can then be combined into something that will offer a whole greater than the sum of its parts.

CHAPTER 5

Close versus Closing Averages

I f a close is higher than a given closing average, the market bias tends to be upward and vice versa if it's lower. Let's turn this into a day trade rule.

If the close is greater than the 40-day closing average, then buy the next day on the open and exit on the close.

If the close is less than the 40-day closing average, then sell short the next day on the open and buy to cover on the close.

We'll discuss how we arrived at 40 as opposed to some other number in a moment.

The above formulas demonstrate a trading edge or bias. How big? Not surprisingly, fairly miniscule. (Were that not the case, trading would be easy and no one would have to work at producing goods and services for society.) Slim or not, though, it can only help to know as much as possible about the exact nature of our tools. It's absurd to leave anything to chance when answers are so readily available in the information age. If "up" portends continued "up" more often than "down," why not be aware of it? The concept conforms to a rational driver. As you'll discover early on in your testing, momentum persists. Nothing is as readily apparent.

Table 5.1 shows the results of optimizing the full sized S&P from 5 to 50 in 5-point increments (10 total tests). We're seeking theoretical biases to serve as future system components, so at this time, we're not concerned with slippage/commission. (In actual trade, you should figure you'll give up about $100 average per round turn on a full sized contract—more if the market is unusually volatile or illiquid.)

TABLE 5.1 Optimizing Simple Averages—Full-Sized S&P—01-02-01 through 11-19-05

N	Net Profit	# Trades	% Profit	Profit/Trade	Max. DD	ROA
5	($34,263)	1,227	48	($27.92)	$97,775	NA
10	($81,063)	1,228	47	$66.01	$100,000	NA
15	$39,688	1,228	49	$32.32	$51,700	76.8
20	$122,788	1,228	50	$99.99	$45,225	271.5
25	$128,888	1,228	51	$104.96	$42,000	306.9
30	$128,688	1,228	51	$104.79	$52,900	243.3
35	$34,388	1,228	50	$28.00	$69,000	49.8
40	$53,187	1,228	50	$43.31	$66,000	80.6
45	$36,088	1,228	50	$29.39	$83,525	43.2
50	$15,038	1,228	49	$12.25	$96,675	15.6

TABLE 5.2 Close versus 40-Day Closing Averages—01-02-01 through 11-19-05

	Net Profit	# Trades	% Profit	Profit/Trade	Max. DD	ROA
NASD (Full)	$59,850	1,226	50.73%	$48.82	$69,450	86.2
Russell (Full)	($62,700)	1,226	50.00%	($51.14)	$129,975	NA
30-Yr. Bonds	$21,688	1,221	52.09%	$17.76	$11,906	182.2
10-Yr. Notes	$24,938	1,221	52.58%	$20.42	$5,578	447.1
5-Yr. Notes	$12,000	1,223	51.76%	$9.81	$4,922	243.8
Japanese Yen	($5,988)	1,221	49.14%	($4.90)	$27,500	NA
Euro Currency	$9,063	1,220	49.10%	$7.43	$13,763	72.8
Swiss Franc	$63	1,222	49.26%	$0.05	$17,425	0.4

As you can see, most numbers are positive. (The negative ones are in parentheses.) The best performer here is 25, but as we should expect, other numbers are optimal in other markets. Again, even sheer chance could predict that.

This is where you get into the inexact science of comparing, contrasting, and weighing biases across multiple fields. What is good in the market(s) where you want to trade and is also serviceable in related ones? Here we're looking for relative uniformity throughout. ("Relative" is key, "exact" being so difficult.)

The number 40 perhaps best serves us overall, which is why it is now a part of our formula. Table 5.2 shows us what that yields in our other markets.

CHAPTER 6

The Four Rules of Prudent Optimization

S ince we're going to be applying the same testing rules to subsequent ideas, this is probably a good place to define them. You need a methodical step-by-step testing approach to mitigate the problem of tapping into results that are merely random. It is astonishingly easy to come up with good summaries through arbitrary number crunching. (We'll illustrate a doozy of a "don't let this happen to you" result at the end of this section.)

The key is *robustness*—a word that crops up frequently in mechanical testing. You want not only good numbers, but also some indication that there was heartiness or durability to them—that they will likely persist (more or less) into the future. This brings us to optimization—one of the main tools of mechanical testing. Optimization is the process of identifying the best-performing variables within your formulas.

Variables are simply numbers that could assume different values. You might discover, for example, that buying the highest high of the last 20 days on a stop and similarly short selling the lowest low is something that produces positive numbers. You haven't even applied stops, filters, or other qualifiers yet, so you're feeling you have something pretty solid.

But is 20 a magic variable of some sort? (We could justify it as a month's worth of trades I suppose.) But would maybe five work better, one week's worth of trades, or perhaps 50 or 100?

When you optimize, you set a lowest variable (say 5) and a highest (200) and a minimum increment (5). Your optimization test then spits out the full results of every permutation—in this case 5 through 200 in increments of 5, or 40 total tests. We're inevitably going to get a variety of results—perhaps ranging from the negative to the truly eye-popping. There will be a single worst result and a single best, but logic should tell us that this would also be true with a merely random series of tests that were known to have no biases. What to do? Do you just go with the best and hope you haven't stumbled upon something fluky that doesn't figure to persist into the future?

A better decision would be weigh and balance according to the four rules of optimization.

1. **Make sure your best outcome resides in a neighborhood of similarly good numbers. You don't want to act off a stand-out diamond in the rough.**

Say that over your 10-year testing period, your best variable turns out to be 35. It produces a net profit of $90,000, a worst drawdown of $9,000, and a return on account (net profit divided by worst drawdown times 100) of 1,000 percent. That means that if you had started trading with an account equal to the worst historic drain from high to successive worst level ($9,000), the amount the system ultimately yielded ($90,000) would be a percentage of that initial stake—(10 times, or 1,000 percent).

Let's also imagine that the numbers surrounding that variable were from so-so to negative. The variable of 40 produced $12,000 with a $17,000 drawdown; 45 yielded $3,500 with a $24,000 drawdown. When we go lower than 35, we get negative net results.

Meanwhile, another clump of our optimized numbers—say between 75 and 110—all produce solid return on accounts of at least 350 percent. Let's say the median number, 90, has a $70,000 net profit with a $15,000 drawdown. While those numbers don't show as much profit as the 35 result, they're more reliable. You're getting confirmation from the neighborhood. As one of my interviewees, Murray Ruggiero, observed in *Market Beaters*, "if you don't like the neighboring numbers, you've got a problem because odds are, you will wind up with the neighboring set of parameters."

2. **System results should hold up in other markets, especially those closely related to your original testing field.**

You don't want to see a barn-burning S&P idea become an anti-system loser in the Dow or the NASDAQ. Related fields don't all have to be tradable like your primary one, but there should at least be some confirmation in most and hopefully very good numbers in some. At the very least, you should not be getting an array of negative net totals before you even apply your slippage/commission projections.

3. **Profits and losses should be dispersed somewhat evenly throughout your data field.**

Statistically speaking, a single or small series of trials means nothing. Again, the numbers game concerns itself with small edges exploited over many trials. One big event, plus or minus, could impact your results dramatically, but that portends nothing for the future. You're just as likely to be long or short, right or wrong, during the next extreme event.

Therefore, if you have a system that is struggling along, putting and taking over many years until two abnormally huge winning trades dramatically increase your overall results—should you be fortified? What if you could trace the trades to historic anomalies—Black Monday or 9/11? I came in the right way during the former and wrong during the latter. I wasn't more likely to be right than wrong in either case—*single trials are meaningless.*

You mitigate the problem by avoiding the profit bunch-up. If your best variable depends too much on your most extreme results, think about settling on second or third best or lower if necessary.

4. **Understand your drivers. Test only in support of theories or concepts you believe to be true about the markets.**

Virtually every interviewee in *Market Beaters* concurred: You want to have some idea of what you're testing—what you're hoping to confirm. Otherwise, you're merely trolling for best numbers, and you'll find them whether or not there's a legitimate bias behind them. A large enough sample of coin tosses would produce some periods—perhaps lengthy—of extreme results far afield of the expected 50–50 outcome. In statistics, there is a mean, but also a sometimes wide deviation from it.

There are market tendencies that will occur to you over the course of your work. It's possible you could enumerate some before you even begin research. Most traders are aware of the phenomenon of momentum, for example. Momentum, or the tendency for moves to persist, is the cornerstone of most mechanical systems. Anything I uncover is encouraging if it's validating the concept, and suspect if it isn't.

It is imperative that your testing field encompass a full array of market environments. Five years' worth of data is the conventional minimum requirement for most inter-day systems, but you have to be conscious of logical exceptions. Someone testing S&Ps from 1996 to 2000 might conclude that the market is eternally volatile with an explosive bias to the upside. The time frame represents nothing more than the bubble years. Your sample should also encompass bear markets, choppy eras, times of low volatility, and so forth.

At my lectures, I present a system that has never had a losing trade in over 100 trials. I perform some mock theater of how I deserve a Pulitzer prize because I have conquered THE trader nemesis—losses! (I'm such a ham.)

The results are real—throughout a 23+ year history, there is a market that has conformed to one concept time and time again. (Actually, more than one market!) Nobody gets too excited, though, over the prospect of running out and actually trading it. Despite a unanimous win/loss record, future performance is immediately suspect, and that's a major relevancy. We are not interested in popping out numbers that make us feel good. We want past results that strongly suggest future profits.

Here's the concept, developed in full-sized daily S&Ps over the contract's entire history—mid-1982 through 11-19-05. As always, we're looking at regular pit session hours only—in this case, 8:30 A.M.–3:15 P.M., CST.

If yesterday's close was lower than the previous 37 closes, then buy today at yesterday's low on a limit order—assuming, of course, we get the opportunity. Once we're in the trade—*we don't need no stinking stops!* The market will always bail us out! Isn't that what we heard forever from the buy-and-hold crowd?

Of course, it is psychologically gratifying to periodically ring the cash register, so we'll apply a five point profit—$1,250 per contract, or $250 if we select the minis. There is no corresponding short selling— something that ought to make us head for the hills with any futures trading idea. Again, though, we just want to see spectacular numbers in this demonstration.

Here are the results. (See Table 6.1.) What can we conclude? If our perspective is narrow and limited, we could deduce we have an unprecedented loss-free system. Obviously, alarm bells should be ringing immediately unless we are the most naïve of pipe dreamers. Ding DONG, what's the CATCH?

The catch is we've rigged the system to be buy-oriented in a data field we know has an historic upward slope. With no stops in place, a paper loss can be held indefinitely until it's bailed out. So far, that has always happened. Do you want to bet that it always will? Could you sleep nights while holding an open loss totaling tens of thousands of dollars just because it figures to eventually close out at a $1,250 profit? (Someday . . . who knows when? Maybe 20 years after you're dead.)

This is an obvious sham demonstration that likely won't tempt any reasonable traders. Sometimes, though, similar fallacies are not so obvious. Again, good numbers are not difficult to uncover—the challenge lies in ascertaining their future reliability.

Suppose you couldn't instantly recognize the pitfall of Forever Long

TABLE 6.1	Forever Long S&P—Full-Sized—Daily—Contract Inception through 11-19-05		
Total Net Profit	$130,125.00	Profit Factor	n/a
Gross Profit	$130,125.00	Gross Loss	$0.00
Total Number of Trades	102	Percent Profitable	100.00%
Winning Trades	102	Losing Trades	0
Even Trades	0		
Avg. Trade Net Profit	$1,275.74	Ratio Avg. Win:Avg. Loss	n/a
Avg. Winning Trade	$1,275.74	Avg. Losing Trade	$0.00
Largest Winning Trade	$2,650.00	Largest Losing Trade	$0.00
Max. Consecutive Winning Trades	102	Max. Consecutive Losing Trades	0
Avg. Bars in Winning Trades	13.18	Avg. Bars in Losing Trades	0.00
Avg. Bars in Total Trades	13.18		
Max. Shares/Contracts Held	1	Account Size Required	$0.00
Return on Initial Capital	130.12%	Annual Rate of Return	3.56%
Return Retracement Ratio	0.14	RINA Index	177.91
Trading Period	23 Yrs, 4 Mths, 17 Dys	Percent of Time in the Market	20.91%
Max. Equity Run-up	$149,437.50		
Max. Drawdown (Intraday Peak to Valley)		**Max. Drawdown (Trade Close to Trade Close)**	
Value	($36,250.00)	Value	$0.00

S&Ps? The first three rules of prudent optimization would not have exposed it.

1. *Your best optimized numbers should reside in a neighborhood of similarly good numbers.*

Not only are the surrounding numbers good, but the *entire optimization field* yields unanimous winners. It would have to—a trade is not closed out until the profit objective is hit. Granted, a few of the individual trials in Table 6.2 contain gargantuan hidden open losses, but so what? The theory is that the market always comes back. We don't throw in the towel until a trade is closed, and by definition, every closed trade earns at least $1,250—more if you get a favorable gap opening.

2. *Your concept should work in an array of markets, particularly closely related ones.*

TABLE 6.2 Forever Long S&P Optimized for Number of Days Referenced—
8-9-82 through 11-19-05

No. Days	Net Profit	# Trades	% Profit	Profit/Trade	Max. DD (Close-Close)
1	$253,750	194	100	$1,307.99	$0
2	$228,100	175	100	$1,303.43	$0
3	$211,825	164	100	$1,291.62	$0
4	$214,200	166	100	$1,290.36	$0
5	$187,588	145	100	$1,293.71	$0
6	$178,913	138	100	$1,296.47	$0
7	$166,425	128	100	$1,300.20	$0
8	$167,550	129	100	$1,298.84	$0
9	$166,963	129	100	$1,294.29	$0
10	$161,975	125	100	$1,295.80	$0
11	$150,850	117	100	$1,289.32	$0
12	$140,825	109	100	$1,291.97	$0
13	$146,425	113	100	$1,295.80	$0
14	$146,863	113	100	$1,299.67	$0
15	$139,375	107	100	$1,302.57	$0
16	$128,863	99	100	$1,301.65	$0
17	$119,013	92	100	$1,293.62	$0
18	$117,463	91	100	$1,290.80	$0
19	$111,213	86	100	$1,293.17	$0
20	$105,888	82	100	$1,291.32	$0
21	$99,650	77	100	$1,294.16	$0
22	$95,675	74	100	$1,292.91	$0
23	$92,550	73	100	$1,267.81	$0
24	$90,050	71	100	$1,268.31	$0
25	$90,125	71	100	$1,269.37	$0
26	$84,950	67	100	$1,267.91	$0
27	$83,963	66	100	$1,272.17	$0
28	$74,313	59	100	$1,259.54	$0
29	$70,563	56	100	$1,260.05	$0
30	$69,313	55	100	$1,260.24	$0
31	$76,813	61	100	$1,259.23	$0
32	$75,563	60	100	$1,259.38	$0
33	$139,063	109	100	$1,275.81	$0
34	$137,800	108	100	$1,275.93	$0
35	$136,375	107	100	$1,274.53	$0
36	$131,450	103	100	$1,276.21	$0
37	$130,125	102	100	$1,275.74	$0
38	$130,125	102	100	$1,275.74	$0
39	$127,625	100	100	$1,276.25	$0
40	$122,625	96	100	$1,277.34	$0
41	$124,100	95	100	$1,306.32	$0

(continues)

TABLE 6.2 *(Continued)*

No. Days	Net Profit	# Trades	% Profit	Profit/Trade	Max. DD (Close-Close)
42	$125,375	96	100	$1,305.99	$0
43	$121,625	93	100	$1,307.80	$0
44	$121,625	93	100	$1,307.80	$0
45	$120,375	92	100	$1,308.42	$0
46	$120,888	92	100	$1,314.00	$0
47	$118,388	90	100	$1,315.42	$0
48	$115,888	88	100	$1,316.91	$0
49	$113,263	86	100	$1,317.01	$0
50	$108,263	82	100	$1,320.28	$0

TABLE 6.3 Forever Long NASDAQ—Daily—Contract Inception through 11-19-05

Total Net Profit	$101,175.00	Profit Factor	n/a
Gross Profit	$101,175.00	Gross Loss	$0.00
Total Number of Trades	79	Percent Profitable	100.00%
Winning Trades	79	Losing Trades	0
Even Trades	0		
Avg. Trade Net Profit	$1,280.70	Ratio Avg. Win:Avg. Loss	n/a
Avg. Winning Trade	$1,280.70	Avg. Losing Trade	$0.00
Largest Winning Trade	$2,200.00	Largest Losing Trade	$0.00
Max. Consecutive Winning Trades	79	Max. Consecutive Losing Trades	0
Avg. Bars in Winning Trades	4.46	Avg. Bars in Losing Trades	0.00
Avg. Bars in Total Trades	4.46		
Max. Shares/Contracts Held	1	Account Size Required	$0.00
Return on Initial Capital	101.18%	Annual Rate of Return	7.43%
Return Retracement Ratio	0.38	RINA Index	173.01
Trading Period	9 Yrs, 4 Mths, 28 Dys	Percent of Time in the Market	11.40%
Max. Equity Run-up	$109,120.00		
Max. Drawdown (Intraday Peak to Valley)		**Max. Drawdown (Trade Close to Trade Close)**	
Value	($33,600.00)	Value	$0.00

Here are the NASDAQ results, using the original 37-day parameter. (See Table 6.3.)

Here's the Russell. (See Table 6.4.)

Here's the Dow. (See Table 6.5.)

As for the third qualifier:

3. *Your profits should be distributed relatively evenly throughout your data field . . .*

. . . well, how could they *not* be? There is nothing but winners throughout the history!

There is only one thing that Forever Long S&P does not conform to. *A rational driver.* We avoid the pitfall simply by knowing ahead of time that it is a crackpot idea. *Know your drivers.* It's a crucial concept in system analysis.

TABLE 6.4 Forever Long Russell—Daily—Contract Inception through 11-19-05

Total Net Profit	$62,025.00	Profit Factor	n/a
Gross Profit	$62,025.00	Gross Loss	$0.00
Total Number of Trades	47	Percent Profitable	100.00%
Winning Trades	47	Losing Trades	0
Even Trades	0		
Avg. Trade Net Profit	$1,319.68	Ratio Avg. Win:Avg. Loss	n/a
Avg. Winning Trade	$1,319.68	Avg. Losing Trade	$0.00
Largest Winning Trade	$3,250.00	Largest Losing Trade	$0.00
Max. Consecutive Winning Trades	47	Max. Consecutive Losing Trades	0
Avg. Bars in Winning Trades	27.04	Avg. Bars in Losing Trades	0.00
Avg. Bars in Total Trades	27.04		
Max. Shares/Contracts Held	1	Account Size Required	$0.00
Return on Initial Capital	62.02%	Annual Rate of Return	3.84%
Return Retracement Ratio	0.07	RINA Index	16.64
Trading Period	12 Yrs, 6 Mths, 30 Dys	Percent of Time in the Market	38.79%
Max. Equity Run-up	$131,425.00		
Max. Drawdown (Intra-day Peak to Valley)		**Max. Drawdown (Trade Close to Trade Close)**	
Value	($84,400.00)	Value	$0.00

Source: © TradeStation Technologies, Inc. 1991–2006. All rights reserved.

TABLE 6.5 Forever Long Dow—Daily—Contract Inception through 11-19-05

Total Net Profit	$52,500.00	Profit Factor	n/a
Gross Profit	$52,500.00	Gross Loss	$0.00
Total Number of Trades	42	Percent Profitable	100.00%
Winning Trades	42	Losing Trades	0
Even Trades	0		
Avg. Trade Net Profit	$1,250.00	Ratio Avg. Win:Avg. Loss	n/a
Avg. Winning Trade	$1,250.00	Avg. Losing Trade	$0.00
Largest Winning Trade	$1,250.00	Largest Losing Trade	$0.00
Max. Consecutive Winning Trades	42	Max. Consecutive Losing Trades	0
Avg. Bars in Winning Trades	14.48	Avg. Bars in Losing Trades	0.00
Avg. Bars in Total Trades	14.48		
Max. Shares/Contracts Held	1	Account Size Required	$0.00
Return on Initial Capital	52.50%	Annual Rate of Return	5.33%
Return Retracement Ratio	0.40	RINA Index	71.04
Trading Period	7 Yrs, 11 Mths, 2 Dys	Percent of Time in the Market	28.61%
Max. Equity Run-up	$52,850.00		
Max. Drawdown (Intra-day Peak to Valley)		**Max. Drawdown (Trade Close to Trade Close)**	
Value	($23,850.00	Value	$0.00

Source: © TradeStation Technologies, Inc. 1991–2006. All rights reserved.

CHAPTER 7

Two-Day versus Five-Day Averages

L et's return to the task of identifying biases.

If the average 2 day close is less than the average 5 day close, then buy the next day on the opening. If the average 2 day close is greater than the average 5 day close, then sell short the next day on the opening. Exit all positions on the close.

Table 7.1 shows results in the S&Ps.

The related NASDAQ produces similar figures (see Table 7.2).

Table 7.3 shows performances in our other financials.

To summarize, we've demonstrated that a close above a 40-day average creates a long bias, and vice versa if the close is below the average. We've also isolated a tendency for five-day closes to point a market direction relative to two-day closes. Traditionally, the opposite is true, that is, a smaller average shows a direction relative to a larger one. (The smaller one is more sensitive; changing direction more quickly.) Two days worth of concerted strength/weakness, however, can be shown to indicate a short-term overbought/oversold condition. Most of us would probably intuit that two up days would tend to be followed by a down day and vice versa. (How many of us have sweated such wins—"I like my longs, but what chance do I have tomorrow after two decisive up days in a row?")

Table 7.4 confirms the idea in five years of daily full-sized S&P trades. After two like closes in a row, enter on the next day's open in the opposite direction. Exit on the close.

TABLE 7.1 Two-Day versus Five-Day Average Closes—Daily—01-02-01
through 11-19-05

Total Net Profit	$100,137.50	Profit Factor	1.08
Gross Profit	$1,284,787.50	Gross Loss	($1,184,650.00)
Total Number of Trades	1,226	Percent Profitable	52.28%
Winning Trades	641	Losing Trades	583
Even Trades	2		
Avg. Trade Net Profit	$81.68	Ratio Avg. Win:Avg. Loss	0.99
Avg. Winning Trade	$2,004.35	Avg. Losing Trade	($2,031.99)
Largest Winning Trade	$16,500.00	Largest Losing Trade	($10,125.00)
Max. Consecutive Winning Trades	9	Max. Consecutive Losing Trades	7
Avg. Bars in Winning Trades	1.00	Avg. Bars in Losing Trades	1.00
Avg. Bars in Total Trades	1.00		
Max. Shares/Contracts Held	1	Account Size Required	$65,625.00
Return on Initial Capital	100.14%	Annual Rate of Return	14.20%
Return Retracement Ratio	0.32	RINA Index	0.00
Trading Period	4 Yrs, 10 Mths, 19 Dys	Percent of Time in the Market	0.00%
Max. Equity Run-up	$138,575.00		
Max. Drawdown (Intraday Peak to Valley)		**Max. Drawdown (Trade Close to Trade Close)**	
Value	($69,625.00)	Value	($65,625.00)

Source: © TradeStation Technologies, Inc. 1991–2006. All rights reserved.

Table 7.5 shows corresponding results in our other targeted financials.

In short, we're probably driver-consistent with the two–five day system. Five days is a relatively small range suggesting a go-with bias. Two days is demonstrated to be a perhaps too small of a range—a logical fade side.

TABLE 7.2 Two-Day versus Five-Day Average Closes—Daily—01-02-01 through 11-19-05

Total Net Profit	$27,150.00	Profit Factor	1.02
Gross Profit	$1,207,800.00	Gross Loss	($1,180,650.00)
Total Number of Trades	1,225	Percent Profitable	49.47%
Winning Trades	606	Losing Trades	605
Even Trades	14		
Avg. Trade Net Profit	$22.16	Ratio Avg. Win:Avg. Loss	1.02
Avg. Winning Trade	$1,993.07	Avg. Losing Trade	($1,951.49)
Largest Winning Trade	$41,450.00	Largest Losing Trade	($21,250,00)
Max. Consecutive Winning Trades	9	Max. Consecutive Losing Trades	13
Avg. Bars in Winning Trades	1.00	Avg. Bars in Losing Trades	1.00
Avg. Bars in Total Trades	1.00		
Max. Shares/Contracts Held	1	Account Size Required	$129,900.00
Return on Initial Capital	27.15%	Annual Rate of Return	4.91%
Return Retracement Ratio	0.09	RINA Index	0.00
Trading Period	4 Yrs, 10 Mths, 19 Dys	Percent of Time in the Market	0.00%
Max. Equity Run-up	$127,400.00		
Max. Drawdown (Intra-day Peak to Valley)		**Max. Drawdown (Trade Close to Trade Close)**	
Value	($136,150.00)	Value	($129,900.00)

Source: © TradeStation Technologies, Inc. 1991–2006. All rights reserved.

TABLE 7.3 Two-Day–Five-Day Indicator—01-02-01 through 11-19-05

	Net Profit	# Trades	% Profit	Profit/Trade	Max. DD	ROA
Russell (Full)	$59,100	1,226	50.49%	$48.21	$65,450	90.3
30-Yr. Bonds	$48,531	1,219	51.03%	$39.81	$19,344	250.9
10-Yr. Notes	$33,234	1,220	51.23%	$39.81	$19,344	171.8
5-Yr. Notes	$20,813	1,221	49.96%	$17.05	$4,500	462.5
Japanese Yen	$8,825	1,221	48.65%	$7.23	$16,775	52.6
Euro Currency	$33,213	1,220	51.72%	$27.22	$19,588	169.6
Swiss Franc	$19,188	1,217	50.29%	$15.77	$13,325	144.0

TABLE 7.4 Fade Two Same-Directional Open-to-Closes—Daily—01-02-01 through 11-19-05

Total Net Profit	$49,400.00	Profit Factor	1.09
Gross Profit	$579,900.00	Gross Loss	($530,500.00)
Total Number of Trades	568	Percent Profitable	51.76%
Winning Trades	294	Losing Trades	273
Even Trades	1		
Avg. Trade Net Profit	$86.97	Ratio Avg. Win:Avg. Loss	1.02
Avg. Winning Trade	$1,972.45	Avg. Losing Trade	($1,943.22)
Largest Winning Trade	$16,500.00	Largest Losing Trade	($10,350.00)
Max. Consecutive Winning Trades	7	Max. Consecutive Losing Trades	9
Avg. Bars in Winning Trades	1.00	Avg. Bars in Losing Trades	1.00
Avg. Bars in Total Trades	1.00		
Max. Shares/Contracts Held	1	Account Size Required	$51,225.00
Return on Initial Capital	49.40%	Annual Rate of Return	8.21%
Return Retracement Ratio	0.30	RINA Index	0.00
Trading Period	4 Yrs, 10 Mths, 19 Dys	Percent of Time in the Market	0.00%
Max. Equity Run-up	$90,225.00		
Max. Drawdown (Intraday Peak to Valley)		**Max. Drawdown (Trade Close to Trade Close)**	
Value	($53,150.00)	Value	($51,225.00)

Source: © TradeStation Technologies, Inc. 1991–2006. All rights reserved.

TABLE 7.5 Fading Two Like Closes In a Row 01-02-01 through 11-19-05

	Net Profit	# Trades	% Profit	Profit/Trade	Max. DD	ROA
NASD (Full)	$63,800	587	49.23%	$108.69	$36,450	175.0
Russell (Full)	$47,450	598	50.50%	$79.35	$83,325	57.0
30-Yr. Bonds	$3,031	601	48.92%	$5.04	$13,875	21.9
10-Yr. Notes	$2,344	616	51.62%	$3.80	$9,063	25.9
5-Yr. Notes	$2,172	584	49.66%	$3.72	$4,516	48.1
Japanese Yen	$8,700	584	48.46%	$14.90	$5,338	163.0
Euro Currency	$18,875	571	52.54%	$33.06	$10,825	174.4
Swiss Franc	$6,038	554	51.44%	$10.90	$10,175	59.3

Fifty-Day Order of Extreme Highest/Lowest Closes

How about the order of extreme high/low closes? Could we theorize about whether we'd expect to see a highest close before or after a lowest within a given number of days if we were trying to buy?

Again, with a numbers game, we're working off many potential outcomes. Overall, perhaps we could expect a slight buying edge if an extreme low was more recent than an extreme high. It's kind of saying the up leg is close to its inception rather than long established—we'd be getting in earlier. Which seem more promising?

Results confirm buying if the low is more recent, short selling if the extreme high is closest. (Again these are day trades—in on the open, out on the close.) What number of days are we talking? It's a pretty good optimization spread as Table 8.1 reveals.

The best variable in the S&Ps is 5, although as usual, others are better elsewhere. Table 8.2 demonstrates that 50 works well overall.

We now have three basic building blocks that we'll set aside for later use. Keep in mind that all are either-or indicators, all are designed for day trades—in on the open, out on the close, and all can be assigned +1/–1 values that would correspond to the buy/sell signals. Let's see what happens when we combine them.

TABLE 8.1 Optimizing for Number of Days—Extreme Highest/Lowest Close—
01-02-01 through 10-19-05

M	Net Profit	# Trades	% Profit	Profit/Trade	Max. DD	ROA
5	$130,388	1,228	52	$106.18	$58,025	224.7
10	$112,863	1,228	20	$91.91	$72,350	156.0
15	($12,238)	1,228	20	($9.97)	$111,963	NA
20	$11,613	1,228	49	$10.11	$73,838	15.7
25	$12,413	1,228	49	$10.11	$82,563	15.0
30	$49,013	1,228	49	$39.91	$88,463	55.4
35	$27,763	1,228	50	$22.61	$81,413	34.1
40	$87,113	1,228	51	$70.94	$65,675	132.6
45	$117,813	1,228	52	$95.94	$58,450	201.6
50	$93,113	1,228	52	$75.82	$58,450	159.3

TABLE 8.2 Extreme Highest/Lowest Fifty-Day Close Order—01-02-01
through 10-19-05

	Net Profit	# Trades	% Profit	Profit/Trade	Max. DD	ROA
NASD (Full)	($35,550)	1,226	48.78%	($29.00)	$128,600	NA
Russell (Full)	$154,700	1,226	49.84%	$126.18	$66,500	232.6
30-Yr. Bonds	$23,187	1,220	48.85%	$19.01	$14,688	157.9
10-Yr. Notes	$10,469	1,221	48.40%	$8.57	$13,063	80.1
5-Yr. Notes	$7,813	1,223	48.98%	$6.39	$9,625	81.2
Japanese Yen	$23,113	1,221	50.45%	$18.93	$9,825	235.2
Euro Currency	($3,450)	1,220	49.51%	($2.83)	$27,313	NA
Swiss Franc	($1113)	1,222	48.94%	($0.91)	$23,763	NA

CHAPTER 9

Combining the First Three Basic Indicators

I n Table 9.1, the first three rows under each market are the original three indicators.

1. Whether the close is above (+) or below (–) the 40 day average close.
2. Whether the two-day average close is below (+) or above (–) the average five-day close.
3. Whether the highest close of the last 50 days is before (+) or after (–) the lowest close of the last 50 days.

The fourth row shows the three signals combined. If the sum of the three is greater than zero, buy on the next open, if less, sell short. Exit all trades on the close.

How does the concept pan out? How do we judge our final step in relation to our individual component performance? What exactly are we looking for?

Ideally, we'd like to see our fourth line combined net profits exceed each of the first three individual ones. It's unlikely our results will comply across the board, but what we especially don't want to see is one indicator conspicuously carrying most of the load. That would imply that maybe some or all of the remaining indicators had a "Stone Soup" deceptiveness. You probably remember the fable about the chef trying to impress the king with his stone in boiling water, which became a delicacy only after

TABLE 9.1　Three Basic Components Individually and Combined—01-02-01 through 11-19-05

	Net Profit	# Trades	% Profit	Profit/ Trade	Max. DD	ROA
S&P (Full)						
40-Day Average	$53,188	1,228	50.98%	$43.31	$66,000	80.6
2-Day 5-Day	$100,138	1,226	52.28%	$81.68	$65,625	152.6
50-Day Close Order	$53,263	1,228	52.28%	$43.37	$65,925	80.8
3 Combined	**$147,338**	**1,228**	**53.75%**	**$119.98**	**$63,863**	**230.7**
NASD (Full)						
40-Day Average	$59,850	1,226	50.73%	$48.82	$69,450	86.2
2-Day 5-Day	$27,150	1,225	49.47%	$22.16	$129,900	20.9
50-Day Close Order	($35,550)	1,226	48.78%	($29.00)	$128,600	NA
3 Combined	**$69,550**	**1,226**	**50.08%**	**$56.73**	**$115,500**	**60.2**
Russell (Full)						
40-Day Average	($50,150)	1,226	50.16%	($40.91)	$131,100	NA
2-Day 5-Day	$39,350	1,226	50.16%	$32.10	$79,450	NA
50-Day Close Order	$154,700	1,226	49.84%	$126.18	$66,500	232.6
3 Combined	**$43,800**	**1,226**	**49.76%**	**$35.73**	**$116,875**	**37.5**
30-Yr. Bonds						
40-Day Average	$21,938	1,220	52.21%	$17.98	$11,906	184.3
2-Day 5-Day	$48,531	1,219	51.03%	$39.81	$19,344	250.9
50-Day Close Order	$23,188	1,220	48.85%	$19.01	$14,688	157.9
3 Combined	**$60,188**	**1,220**	**51.80%**	**$49.33**	**$15,063**	**399.6**
10-Yr. Notes						
40-Day Average	$24,938	1,220	52.21%	$20.42	$5,578	447.1
2-Day 5-Day	$33,234	1,220	51.23%	$27.24	$6,234	533.1
50-Day Close Order	$10,468	1,221	48.40%	$8.57	$13,063	80.1
3 Combined	**$51,938**	**1,221**	**52.91%**	**$42.54**	**$5,672**	**915.7**
5-Yr. Notes						
40-Day Average	$12,000	1223	51.76%	$9.81	$4,922	243.8
2-Day 5-Day	$20,813	1,221	49.96%	$17.05	$4,500	462.5
50-Day Close Order	$7,812	1,223	48.98%	$6.39	$9,625	81.2
3 Combined	**$34,719**	**1,223**	**52.82%**	**$28.39**	**$3,859**	**899.7**
Japanese Yen						
40-Day Average	($5,963)	1220	49.18%	($4.89)	$27,500	NA
2-Day 5-Day	$8,425	1,220	48.61%	$6.91	$16,775	50.2
50-Day Close Order	$23,113	1,221	50.45%	$18.93	$9,825	235.2
3 Combined	**$16,437**	**1,221**	**49.88%**	**$13.46**	**$8,813**	**186.5**

TABLE 9.1 *(Continued)*

	Net Profit	# Trades	% Profit	Profit/ Trade	Max. DD	ROA
Euro Currency						
40-Day Average	$10,025	1,220	49.10%	$8.22	$13,763	72.8
2-Day 5-Day	$32,850	1,220	51.72%	$26.93	$19,588	167.7
50-Day Close Order	($3,450)	1,220	49.51%	($2.83)	$27,313	NA
3 Combined	**$31,175**	**1,220**	**50.90%**	**$25.55**	**$18,550**	**168.1**
Swiss Franc						
40-Day Average	$3,938	1,223	49.30%	$3.22	$13,550	29.1
2-Day 5-Day	$17,513	1,218	50.25%	$14.38	$15,000	116.8
50-Day Close Order	$513	1,223	48.90%	$0.42	$23,763	2.2
3 Combined	**$21,738**	**1,222**	**50.41%**	**$17.79**	**$16,163**	**134.5**

more conventional ingredients (seasonings, vegetables) were added. We want none of our components to be the non-contributing "stone."

We have an encouraging distribution. The S&P fourth line is clearly superior to the other three. This is also true of the Swiss franc and all the bond contracts. The Euro combined is about the same as its two-day five-day component. The remaining three markets have stand-outs in different places. For the NASDAQ, the simple 40-day average beats the composite. For the Russell and the yen, it's the order of the 50-day extreme high/low closes. So far so good. We have no evidence that any of our ideas are superfluous statistical flukes.

There's something else to bear in mind when comparing net profits in the combined system to the sum of the individual ones. To do a true apples-to-apples evaluation, we must be mindful of the fact that we'd be trading one contract on each of the individual components (three total) versus only one contract on the combined line four system. That implies that we'd be taking roughly a third of the risk on the combined system relative to the individual ones, all else being approximately equal. Line four nets out profit roughly in the ballpark of the top three lines combined, and yet we arrived there with one third the exposure of the top three added together.

Consider the Japanese yen performance. If we had evidence that the order of the 50-day extreme highest/lowest close was going to consistently outperform the composite, that's obviously where we'd risk our single betting unit. (Let's assume for now that we're talking a one-lot.) In the absence of such a clue, our choice would be between trading one contract on each of the three individual lines or one on the fourth. We'd earn a $25,575 sum by trading three contracts. Would you rather achieve $16,437 with a $8,813 worst drawdown or $25,575 on three times the exposure? Those three drawdowns average $18,033 *apiece.*

Notice also that most of the profit per trades are superior in line four. This is another way of seeing payoffs in relative terms. Only the Russell and the yen post the biggest figures in individual indicator lines.

The composite systems tend to produce bigger bottom lines and significantly less drawdown if you compare the single contract combined line to the three contract individual ones. The return on account figures are clearly overall best in the combo lines. The "whole" vastly exceeds the sum of the parts. Hands down, our combined line four system is the better alternative.

Still, these are not the kind of solid results we'd like to see in order to actually trade a mechanical system. Let's see if we can boost our prospects by adding still more indicators.

CHAPTER 10

Cuing Off Relative Range Sizes

One technical trading adage has it that decisive momentum moves tend to spring out of tight ranges. There is even a technical term— coiling. Regardless of bar sizes, (daily, weekly, five minute), conventional charting wisdom has it that narrow consolidation channels are potential launching pads for significant directional moves. Naturally, we accept nothing, not even cherished maxims on mere faith, so let's run a variation through the lab.

If today's range is smaller than the x day average range, then on tomorrow's open, enter in the direction of the last closing net change. Exit on the close. X is optimized in Tables 10.1 and 10.2, NASDAQ and 30-year bonds respectively.

By settling on the number 10, we uncover a robustness that persists throughout our fields. (See Table 10.3.)

One of my partner's recurring questions is, if something ceases to meet a buy criterion, should it be considered a short candidate? If you're stopped out of longs because stats are getting negative, isn't that the same as saying you have a sell bias? (Should you be flipping around a certain percentage of the time as opposed to merely exiting?)

In this case, you can clearly do the opposite with opposite conditions. If your previous range is greater than the 10-day average, buy following a down close, sell short following an up one. The biases are pretty much in line with the previous. (See Table 10.4.)

When we combine both halves, we get another either-or indicator— something that signals nearly every day.

TABLE 10.1 Optimizing Number of Days in Range Averages—NASDAQ— 01-02-01 through 11-19-05

N	Net Profit	# Trades	% Profit	Profit/Trade	Max. DD	ROA
5	($20,050)	663	48	($30.24)	$115,800	N A
10	$53,850	674	50	$79.90	$88,200	61.1
15	$58,950	683	50	$86.31	$80,700	73.1
20	$11,400	689	49	$16.55	$108,000	10.6
25	$29,000	701	49	$41.37	$86,350	33.6
30	$25,700	703	49	$35.56	$84,650	30.4
35	$26,550	711	49	$37.34	$83,650	31.7
40	$41,600	711	50	$58.51	$69,750	59.6
45	$27,950	723	49	$38.66	$70,150	39.8
50	$46,250	737	49	$62.75	$62,400	74.1

TABLE 10.2 Optimizing Number of Days in Range Averages—30-Year Bonds 01-02-01 through 11-19-05

N	Net Profit	# Trades	% Profit	Profit/Trade	Max. DD	ROA
5	$8,781	654	49	$13.43	$23,250	37.8
10	$17,156	697	50	$24.61	$15,969	107.4
15	$8,844	694	49	$12.74	$19,750	44.8
20	$17,156	694	50	$24.74	$15,875	108.1
25	$17,469	700	50	$24.96	$12,500	139.8
30	$17,375	700	50	$24.82	$12,844	135.3
35	$12,938	705	50	$18.35	$13,594	95.2
40	$20,219	710	50	$28.48	$11,313	178.7
45	$16,969	709	50	$23.93	$10,719	158.3
50	$18,719	710	50	$26.36	$10,250	182.6

TABLE 10.3 Range Smaller than 10-Day Average Range—01-02-01 through 11-19-05

	Net Profit	# Trades	% Profit	Profit/Trade	Max. DD	ROA
S&P (Full)	$53,538	682	51.61%	$78.50	$52,950	101.1
NASD (Full)	$53,850	674	50.59%	$79.90	$86,600	62.2
Russell (Full)	($24,975)	658	49.70%	($37.96)	$108,025	NA
30-Yr. Bonds	$17,156	697	50.79%	$24.61	$15,906	108.0
10-Yr. Notes	$3,391	712	47.61%	$4.76	$10,719	31.6
5-Yr. Notes	$2,391	689	48.04%	$3.47	$6,063	39.4
Japanese Yen	$5,275	711	51.05%	$7.42	$11,650	45.3
Euro Currency	$5,262	707	49.22%	$7.44	$17,738	29.7
Swiss Franc	$12,338	716	50.28%	$17.23	$10,513	117.4

TABLE 10.4 Range Greater than 10-Day Average Range—01-02-01 through 11-19-05

	Net Profit	# Trades	% Profit	Profit/Trade	Max. DD	ROA
S&P (Full)	$135,025	534	54.31%	$252.86	$35,425	381.2
NASD (Full)	$34,050	538	51.86%	$63.29	$44,150	77.1
Russell (Full)	$47,375	561	51.16%	$84.45	$58,300	81.3
30-Yr. Bonds	$2,938	490	49.59%	$5.99	$11,625	25.3
10-Yr. Notes	($9,485)	490	49.18%	($19.36)	$12,656	NA
5-Yr. Notes	($5,703)	484	49.38%	($11.78)	$11,172	NA
Japanese Yen	$12,050	490	49.59%	$24.59	$4,588	262.6
Euro Currency	$22,625	498	53.41%	$45.43	$7,913	285.9
Swiss Franc	$8,325	489	52.15%	$17.02	$6,488	128.3

TABLE 10.5 Complete 10-Day Range Indicator—01-02-01 through 11-19-05

	Net Profit	# Trades	% Profit	Profit/Trade	Max. DD	ROA
S&P (Full)	$188,563	1,216	52.80%	$155.07	$57,200	329.7
NASD (Full)	$87,900	1,212	51.16%	$72.52	$107,600	81.7
Russell (Full)	$22,400	1,219	50.37%	$18.38	$105,275	21.3
30-Yr. Bonds	$20,094	1,187	50.29%	$16.93	$18,313	109.7
10-Yr. Notes	($6,094)	1,202	48.25%	($5.07)	$15,281	NA
5-Yr. Notes	($3,313)	1,173	48.59%	($2.82)	$11,328	NA
Japanese Yen	$17,325	1,201	50.46%	$14.43	$13,200	131.3
Euro Currency	$27,888	1,205	50.95%	$23.14	$21,750	128.2
Swiss Franc	$20,663	1,205	51.04%	$17.15	$7,363	280.6

If today's daily range was less than the average x day range—

Then buy tomorrow if today's close was higher or sell short if it was lower.

If today's range was greater than the average x day range—

Then buy tomorrow if today's close was lower or sell short if it was higher.

Exit on close.

For a 10-day range indicator, see Table 10.5.

CHAPTER 11

Fifteen-Day High/Low Averages

The next day trade concept is simplicity personified. Look to enter on the opening in the direction of a close relative to a 15-day high/low average. Instead of referencing off simple closing averages, take an average of the highs and lows; ((average (15,high) + average (15,low))/2). If your close is above it, buy the next day, if below, sell. This slight variation on the simple average theme does produce some fortifying numbers as Table 11.1 reveals.

TABLE 11.1 Fifteen-Day High/Low Average—01-02-01 through 11-19-05

	Net Profit	# Trades	% Profit	Profit/Trade	Max. DD	ROA
S&P (Full)	$94,588	1,228	49.92%	$77.03	$46,075	205.3
NASD (Full)	$166,050	1,226	51.63%	$135.44	$42,850	387.5
Russell (Full)	$15,300	1,226	49.18%	$12.48	$70,775	21.6
30-Yr. Bonds	$23,250	1,220	52.79%	$19.06	$20,406	113.9
10-Yr. Notes	$13,000	1,221	50.29%	$10.65	$12,016	108.2
5-Yr. Notes	$14,031	1,223	50.70%	$11.47	$5,453	257.3
Japanese Yen	$5,413	1,221	51.02%	$4.43	$12,813	42.3
Euro Currency	($22,675)	1,220	48.61%	($18.59)	$33,300	NA
Swiss Franc	($14,350)	1,222	48.45%	($11.74)	$17,138	NA

CHAPTER 12

Combining All Five Indicators

Table 12.1 depicts our obvious next step—combining all five indicators. The first lines of each are the three signals and the second are the five.

There is a slightly better combined net profit of $533,239 on five versus $476,883 on three. You could maybe argue that you clearly have a better five indicator S&P system that is not negated by the other market performances. That has some validity, considering the indexes are the only markets likely to give you both the volatility and liquidity you need for day trade profits. (The $169 per trade profit would be enough to overcome the $100 per trade slippage commission penalty we'd have to apply.) This is the result of 1,228 trades, which is somewhat fortifying.

It's not the quantum leap we were hoping for. On the other hand, five reliable indicators allow us to do something we can't do with three. We can act off a four-out-of-five-or-better majority.

Table 12.2 shows a simple majority of indicators on each top column. Underneath is what happens when at least four of five agree on direction. There are now many days that don't qualify for either the long or short side, so we're getting a significantly reduced number of trades. We're still seeing a combined market total in excess of 2,000 trials, however—still statistically significant. Furthermore, keep in mind that these numbers were pruned from bigger blocks of robust indicators. We tested each component properly, and each stood up on its own.

The return on account (ROA) is our best performance gauge. It shows profit in relation to money invested. The 30-year bond, for example, has a smaller bottom line with the filter, but you'd still be better off with it when

TABLE 12.1 Three versus Five Combined Indicators—Daily—01-02-01
through 11-19-05

	Net Profit	# Trades	% Profit	Profit/ Trade	Max. DD	ROA
S&P (Full)						
3 Combined	$147,338	1,228	53.75%	$119.98	$63,863	230.7
5 Combined	$207,938	1,228	53.34%	$169.33	$43,525	477.7
NASD (Full)						
3 Combined	$69,550	1,226	50.08%	$56.73	$115,500	60.2
5 Combined	$110,750	1,226	51.88%	$90.33	$104,550	105.9
Russell (Full)						
3 Combined	$43,800	1,226	49.76%	$35.73	$116,875	37.5
5 Combined	$35,400	1,226	50.24%	$28.87	$123,025	28.8
30-Yr. Bonds						
3 Combined	$60,188	1,220	51.80%	$49.33	$15,063	399.6
5 Combined	$52,125	1,220	52.13%	$42.73	$14,156	368.2
10-Yr. Notes						
3 Combined	$51,938	1,221	52.91%	$42.54	$5,672	915.7
5 Combined	$36,875	1,221	51.92%	$30.20	$10,500	351.2
5-Yr. Notes						
3 Combined	$34,719	1,223	52.82%	$28.39	$3,859	899.7
5 Combined	$31,000	1,223	52.49%	$25.35	$4,844	640.0
Japanese Yen						
3 Combined	$16,437	1,221	49.88%	$13.46	$8,813	186.5
5 Combined	$10,238	1,221	50.45%	$8.38	$7,275	140.7
Euro Currency						
3 Combined	$31,175	1,220	50.90%	$25.55	$18,550	168.1
5 Combined	$31,875	1,220	51.72%	$26.13	$17,875	178.3
Swiss Franc						
3 Combined	$21,738	1,222	50.41%	$17.79	$16,163	134.5
5 Combined	$17,038	1,223	50.70%	$13.93	$14,425	118.1

considering the impact of the drawdown. A worst giveback of only $4,063 was endured before achieving the ultimate $38,438. That was far preferable to making $52,125 after taking heat amounting to $14,156. You could have made more money trading twice as many contracts on the four of five indicator with less risk. ($76,876 net profit, $8,126 drawdown.) Six out of the nine of the filters improve the results—some dramatically. Three have numbers exceeding 500 percent—a fivefold or greater return over five years!

You can see significant jumps in the percent profit column. This may be where our greatest psychological fortification lies. How often are we right or maybe more importantly, how often are we forced to endure pain?

TABLE 12.2 Five Indicator—Simple versus Four Out of Five Majority—01-02-01 through 11-19-05

	Net Profit	# Trades	% Profit	Profit/ Trade	Max. DD	ROA
S&P (Full)						
Simple	$207,938	1,228	53.34%	$169.33	$43,525	477.7
4 out of 5	$135,213	288	60.07%	$469.49	$19,175	705.2
NASD (Full)						
Simple	$110,750	1.226	51.88%	$90.33	$104,550	105.9
4 out of 5	$102,350	255	54.12%	$401.37	$31,150	328.6
Russell (Full)						
Simple	$35,400	1,226	50.24%	$28.87	$123,025	28.8
4 out of 5	$57,050	263	52.09%	$216.92	$24,975	228.4
30-Yr. Bonds						
Simple	$52,125	1,220	52.13%	$42.73	$14,156	368.2
4 out of 5	$38,438	308	59.09%	$124.80	$4,063	946.0
10-Yr. Notes						
Simple	$36,875	1,221	51.92%	$30.20	$10,500	351.2
4 out of 5	$18,281	275	54.18%	$66.48	$2,906	629.1
5-Yr. Notes						
Simple	$31,000	1,223	52.49%	$25.35	$4,844	640.0
4 out of 5	$9,688	274	56.57%	$35.36	$2,517	384.9
Japanese Yen						
Simple	$10,238	1,221	50.45%	$8.38	$7,275	140.7
4 out of 5	$12,925	261	55.17%	$49.52	$3,638	355.3
Euro Currency						
Simple	$31,875	1,220	51.72%	$26.13	$17,875	178.3
4 out of 5	$10,825	301	50.83%	$35.96	$7,375	146.8
Swiss Franc						
Simple	$17,038	1,223	50.70%	$13.93	$14,425	118.1
4 out of 5	$6,325	265	50.94%	$23.87	$6,713	94.2

True, this may not be our best scientific evaluator. To paraphrase Warren Buffett, it doesn't matter so much if you're winning more often than you're losing or if your average gain is bigger than your average loss. The overall picture is all that counts. I have some systems that make money a third of the time with the profit column outdoing the loss column by several hundred percent. I've also employed techniques that had bigger losses than wins, but the 70 percent win/loss ratio more than compensated.

All that matters is that our total profits outpace our total losses. All other things being equal, though, we'd be happier ringing the cash register more often than not. Besides, that figure correlates with other returns. Look at the diminishing max drawdowns ($31,150 versus $104,550 in the NASDAQ).

Profit per trade also provides quick shorthand as to whether your system is sufficiently overcoming trading costs. Four out of the nine profit-per-trade figures exceed the slippage/commission hurdle. Even docking the standard $100 per trade would still leave us with a $369 figure in the S&Ps, $301 in the NASDAQ and $116 in the Russell.

We can now start thinking beyond mere bias. In at least the indexes, the four-of-five indicator deserves full blown mechanical trading status!

CHAPTER 13

Other Combinations of the Five Basic Indicators

L et's backtrack a moment and re-examine our indicators. By discovering other systems for our basic elements, we could accomplish a couple things. First, other profitable variations can only help our trading. There are many ways we can recombine, diversify, and re-allocate our portfolio using our basic either-or signals. Second, alternate positive results further justify our faith in the basic building blocks. Fortification is key to trading in a proper mechanical manner, that is, perfectly. You'll never do it if you have any doubts about your testing.

We've already seen results of combining the first three indicators. There are nine additional three-signal combinations that can be derived from all five. The five indicators are numbered as follows.

1. Close versus 40-Day Closing Average
2. 2 Day versus 5-Day Closing Average
3. Order of 50-Day Extreme High/Low Closes
4. 10-Day Range Indicator
5. 15-Day Average High/Low Indictor

They produce the following three digit combinations. 123, 124, 125, 134, 135, 145, 234, 235, 245, and 345. Use those numbers to refer to the results of Table 13.1.

Within each market, the return on account figures don't straggle far from their collective means. There are few outliers, or extreme numbers.

TABLE 13.1 Different Three Component Combos from Five Either-Or Indicators—01-02-01 through 11-19-05

	Net Profit	# Trades	% Profit	Profit/ Trade	Max. DD	ROA
S&P (Full)						
123	$147,338	1,228	53.75%	$119.98	$63,863	230.7
124	$143,988	1,228	52.77%	$117.25	$80,500	178.9
125	$83,588	1,228	51.22%	$68.07	$47,125	177.4
134	$241,838	1,228	54.40%	$196.94	$41,100	588.4
135	$96,288	1,228	50.57%	$78.41	$42,225	228.0
145	$154,637	1,228	51.55%	$125.93	$42,075	367.5
234	$221,688	1,228	54.07%	$180.53	$37,587	589.8
235	$185,438	1,228	53.26%	$151.01	$61,188	303.1
245	$205,838	1,228	52.77%	$167.62	$47,625	432.2
345	$162,388	1,228	52.93%	$133.24	$62,050	261.7
NASD (Full)						
123	$69,550	1,226	50.08%	$56.73	$115,500	60.2
124	$89,550	1,226	51.14%	$73.04	$129,200	69.3
125	$74,650	1,226	51.06%	$60.89	$72,250	103.3
134	$101,450	1,226	52.28%	$82.75	$101,050	100.4
135	$112,750	1,226	50.98%	$91.97	$43,850	257.1
145	$122,150	1,226	51.22%	$99.63	$65,250	187.2
234	$38,850	1,226	48.78%	$31.69	$140,050	27.7
235	$122,650	1,226	50.16%	$100.01	$71,700	171.1
245	$127,450	1,226	50.98%	$103.96	$116,150	109.7
345	$198,050	1,226	53.02%	$161.54	$83,950	235.9
Russell (Full)						
123	$36,400	1,226	49.59%	$29.69	$116,875	31.1
124	($32,950)	1,226	50.33%	($26.88)	$143,700	NA
125	$10,100	1,226	50.24%	$8.24	$105,100	9.6
134	$141,850	1,226	51.63%	$115.70	$95,675	148.3
135	$28,450	1,226	49.43%	$23.21	$70,775	40.2
145	($6,750)	1,226	50.08%	($5.51)	$92,425	NA
234	$86,800	1,226	50.24%	$70.80	$91,775	94.6
235	$71,450	1,226	48.78%	$58.28	$75,625	94.5
245	($14,500)	1,226	50.00%	($11.83)	$109,775	NA
345	$163,050	1,226	50.65%	$132.99	$76,275	213.8
30-Yr. Bonds						
123	$60,188	1,220	51.80%	$49.33	$15,063	399.6
124	$48,313	1,220	51.97%	$39.60	$15,844	304.9
125	$31,188	1,220	52.70%	$25.56	$10,156	307.1
134	$37,250	1,220	51.31%	$30.53	$23,781	156.6
135	$34,250	1,220	52.70%	$28.07	$19,219	178.2
145	$27,688	1,220	52.30%	$22.69	$13,156	210.5
234	$38,250	1,220	50.49%	$31.35	$18,375	208.2

TABLE 13.1 *(Continued)*

	Net Profit	# Trades	% Profit	Profit/ Trade	Max. DD	ROA
235	$68,250	1,220	52.13%	$55.95	$15,656	435.9
245	$45,938	1,220	52.05%	$37.65	$11,719	392.0
345	$47,813	1,220	51.89%	$39.19	$13,969	342.3
10-Yr. Notes						
123	$51,938	1,221	52.91%	$42.54	$5,672	915.7
124	$23,813	1,221	51.02%	$19.50	$8,797	270.7
125	$29,656	1,221	52.25%	$24.29	$8,453	350.8
134	$16,781	1,221	50.70%	$12.74	$11,375	147.5
135	$19,375	1,221	50.61%	$15.87	$8,266	234.4
145	$26,125	1,221	52.01%	$21.40	$8,000	326.6
234	$17,281	1,221	49.14%	$14.15	$10,328	167.3
235	$43,094	1,221	51.27%	$35.29	$7,797	552.7
245	$26,031	1,221	50.45%	$21.32	$7,156	363.8
345	$3,094	1,221	48.81%	$2.53	$15,063	20.5
5-Yr. Notes						
123	$34,719	1,223	52.82%	$28.39	$3,859	899.7
124	$14,187	1,223	50.86%	$11.60	$7,734	183.4
125	$18,688	1,223	51.59%	$15.28	$5,640	331.3
134	$17,875	1,223	51.84%	$14.62	$4,641	385.2
135	$13,156	1,223	50.45%	$10.76	$5,563	236.5
145	$16,063	1,223	51.68%	$13.13	$5,141	312.4
234	$4,156	1,223	48.90%	$3.40	$9,094	45.7
235	$30,188	1,223	52.17%	$24.68	$2,797	1,079.0
245	$17,938	1,223	50.45%	$14.67	$6,578	272.7
345	$15,156	1,223	50.45%	$12.39	$6,391	237.1
Japanese Yen						
123	$16,437	1,221	49.88%	$13.46	$8,813	186.5
124	($588)	1,221	48.24%	($0.48)	$13,100	NA
125	($6,213)	1,221	49.30%	($5.09)	$21,525	NA
134	$11,663	1,221	50.29%	$9.55	$12,275	95.0
135	$13,338	1,221	51.27%	$10.96	$10,025	133.0
145	$4,512	1,221	50.86%	$3.70	$16,488	27.4
234	$34,537	1,221	51.60%	$28.29	$9,850	350.6
235	$22,988	1,221	51.52%	$18.83	$12,338	186.3
245	$10,038	1,221	49.96%	$8.22	$15,225	65.9
345	$11,738	1,221	50.37%	$9.61	$10,188	115.2
Euro Currency						
123	$31,175	1,220	50.90%	$25.55	$18,550	168.1
124	$46,000	1,220	51.97%	$37.70	$12,375	371.7
125	$21,750	1,220	50.82%	$17.83	$17,963	121.1

(continues)

TABLE 13.1 *(Continued)*

	Net Profit	# Trades	% Profit	Profit/ Trade	Max. DD	ROA
134	$32,525	1,220	50.98%	$26.66	$29,738	109.4
135	($15,375)	1,220	49.18%	($12.60)	$24,925	NA
145	$4,775	1,220	49.59%	$3.91	$16,713	28.6
234	$27,450	1,220	50.74%	$22.50	$26,050	105.4
235	($4,100)	1,220	49.59%	($3.36)	$28,163	NA
245	$36,725	1,220	52.05%	$30.10	$11,863	309.6
345	$11,525	1,220	50.57%	$9.45	$24,588	46.9
Swiss Franc						
123	$26,013	1,223	50.45%	$21.27	$12,975	200.5
124	$33,788	1,223	50.86%	$27.63	$8,713	387.8
125	$63	1,223	49.22%	$0.05	$12,613	0.5
134	$13,588	1,223	51.10%	$11.11	$15,125	89.8
135	($10,513)	1,223	48.90%	($8.60)	$14,650	NA
145	($5,688)	1,223	49.22%	($4.65)	$13,088	NA
234	$12,713	1,223	49.98%	$10.39	$18,638	68.2
235	$11,487	1,223	49.96%	$9.39	$17,350	66.2
245	$20,438	1,223	50.38%	$16.71	$11,488	177.9
345	$4,213	1,223	50.12%	$3.44	$21,338	19.7

This is also true in the net profit and worst drawdown columns. Five out of the 10 markets post no negative results. Losers occur over the gamut of the combinations—not particular to a small number of them. We are not getting bunch-ups.

In short, there are no apparent stones in our soup, just active ingredients. Let's mush on.

CHAPTER 14

Two More
Open-to-Close
Biases

I t's not a new revelation that more often than not, an up close has historically led to a down close and vice versa. You've probably seen the stat
in some system book or periodical somewhere down the line, along
with the psychological ramifications of people getting over-aggressive in a
given direction and therefore blah blah. As mentioned earlier, the tendency has been mish-moshy at best lately—maybe a direct result of the
widespread publicity.

A slight variation on the concept is to fade the open to close. This is
not always as interchangeable as it seems, as anyone trading foreign
currencies might attest. The huge gap openings can make for night and
day differences regarding your perception of the market movement.
The news media might be touting a rout in the yen because it gapped
so far down overnight. Day traders, however, may have perceived an
unrelenting up day off the sharply lower open—closing much lower on
the day, but near its highs. At any rate, there is still a persisting albeit
rather small tendency in the open-close scenario. (Building blocks remember—possible harbingers of bigger things down the road.) See
Table 14.1.

Do we improve our edge if we get two days of the same open-to-
close direction? Table 14.2 says yes, hands down. We now have unanimous winners verse the previous five of nine. Virtually every return on
account has increased. Granted, we've decreased our sample, but only
by about half. We still have plenty of trials to fortify our theory that although momentum is the prevailing force in system development, there

TABLE 14.1 Fading Yesterday's Open-to-Close—Day Trade—1-02-01 through 11-19-05

	Net Profit	# Trades	% Profit	Profit/Trade	Max. DD	ROA
S&P (Full)	$158,338	1,226	53.26%	$129.15	$58,350	271.4
NASD (Full)	$147,950	1,212	50.91%	$122.07	$52,450	282.1
Russell (Full)	$85,125	1,215	50.45%	$70.06	$82,650	103.0
30-Yr. Bonds	($22,406)	1,206	48.18%	($18.58)	$40,938	NA
10-Yr. Notes	($12,297)	1,201	49.96%	($10.24)	$26,094	NA
5-Yr. Notes	($4,688)	1,187	49.37%	($3.95)	$10,828	NA
Japanese Yen	$1,975	1,196	47.32%	$1.65	$9,625	20.5
Euro Currency	$88	1,210	51.40%	$0.07	$20,863	0.4
Swiss Franc	($18,275)	1,202	49.25%	($15.20)	$24,175	NA

TABLE 14.2 Fading Two Same Directional Open Closes in a Row—1-02-01 through 11-19-05

	Net Profit	# Trades	% Profit	Profit/Trade	Max. DD	ROA
S&P (Full)	$142,725	570	55.96%	$250.39	$31,025	460.0
NASD (Full)	$198,850	581	52.50%	$342.25	$33,350	596.3
Russell (Full)	$74,925	590	50.85%	$126.99	$59,900	125.1
30-Yr. Bonds	$2,562	611	48.45%	$4.19	$14,031	18.3
10-Yr. Notes	$9,219	581	52.67%	$15.87	$7,219	127.7
5-Yr. Notes	$10,219	565	50.09%	$18.09	$3,547	288.1
Japanese Yen	$8,238	605	49.26%	$13.62	$7,438	110.8
Euro Currency	$14,613	577	52.69%	$25.32	$6,613	221.0
Swiss Franc	$2,113	591	51.61%	$3.57	$7,238	29.2

are logical points where it's going to be trumped by other influences. Short-term moves are especially psychologically driven. Traders believe that markets aren't likely to do the same thing many times in a row. The sentiment is prevalent enough to act as the occasional self-fulfilling prophecy.

CHAPTER 15

Cups and Caps

O ur next indicator is fairly well-known in one version or another. It's been called, among other things, cups and caps because of the visual image it suggests. The cup side is the buy projection, the cap is the sell. Both involve three bar formations—take your pick, daily, five-minute, whatever. The second bar has the extreme (lowest, highest) price. Sometimes the price in question is the low (or high for caps) and sometimes it's the close.

In this version of cups, both the lowest low and the lowest close have to occur in the middle bar. Also, the lowest bar must be lower than the three lows immediately preceding it. This is a rather arbitrary rule intended to limit the number of times the formation is occurring mid-range. Ideally, the cup should be a bottoming indicator, so think of the three-bar qualifier as a kind of running start setup.

Caps are the opposite. Bar 2 must have both a higher high and close than the surrounding two bars and a higher high than the previous three. Figure 15.1 highlights our version of cups and caps within a daily chart of the 30-year bonds.

We can use this formation as another tool in our daily arsenal. Buy the next opening after a cup has formed, sell short after a cap. Exit on the close. Table 15.1 shows the results.

There is another cups-caps application that has a more universal bias than probably anything we've uncovered to date. The formation's greatest predictive power lies in its overnight expectations. If you enter a cup on the close, you're likely to get a higher opening the next day for an exit

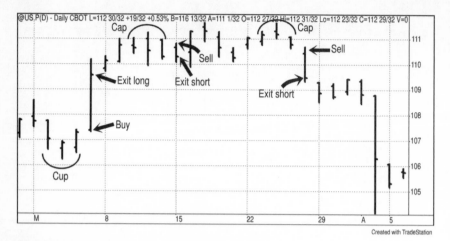

FIGURE 15.1 Cups and Caps—Daily 30-Year Bonds (*Source:* © TradeStation Technologies, Inc. 1991–2006. All rights reserved.)

TABLE 15.1 Buying/Selling Day after Cup/Cap Formation—01-02-01 through 11-19-05

	Net Profit	# Trades	% Profit	Profit/Trade	Max. DD	ROA
S&P (Full)	($3,000)	183	51.37%	($16.39)	$30,425	NA
NASD (Full)	$24,650	165	52.12%	$149.39	$36,150	68.2
Russell (Full)	($15,250)	174	51.15%	($87.64)	$31,050	NA
30-Yr. Bonds	$4,125	159	50.94%	$25.94	$9,594	43.0
10-Yr. Notes	$5,766	169	52.66%	$34.12	$5,797	99.5
5-Yr. Notes	$8,375	172	53.49%	$48.69	$2,438	343.5
Japanese Yen	($1,163)	263	46.01%	($4.42)	$10,263	NA
Euro Currency	$5,900	256	46.09%	$23.05	$11,625	50.8
Swiss Franc	$10,325	279	50.54%	$37.01	$5,250	196.7

Source: © TradeStation Technologies, Inc. 1991–2006. All rights reserved.

point and vice versa for a cap. Figure 15.2 is a visual sample typifying how, more often than not, the next openings will be favorable.

There will be occasional borderline circumstances where you won't be sure if the close is high or low enough to technically qualify, but such mistakes can generally be corrected quickly without a problem. The overnight sessions are now commencing shortly after the close of the regular markets.

As we've stated, the key to fortification of an idea is seeing it conform to a variety of environments. Usually we ask that a financial holds up to some degree in most other financials and fairly well in related markets. It's not generally a requirement that they also perform in agriculturals or

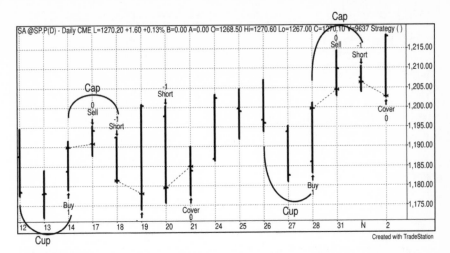

FIGURE 15.2 Cups/Caps—Entering on Close, Exiting Next Open—Daily S&Ps (*Source:* © TradeStation Technologies, Inc. 1991–2006. All rights reserved.)

exotics, for example. As always, though, we'll be happier with more corroborating evidence than less, and in that respect, cups-caps comes through indeed.

We're scanning many markets for this study as well as a lengthy history. The study encompasses entire contract histories for most markets. In the case of the longer-standing ones, 20 years are referenced. All have a last date of 11-19-05. (See Table 15.2.)

As you can see, out of 36 commodities tested, only the Euro currency posted a negative result. The vast majority of percentage profitability returns exceed 50. We've included thousands of trades in every major market sector over significant time frames. We've gotten consistent results—no bunch-ups anywhere we look. Talk about robustness!

Unfortunately, you may notice something else. The profit-per-trade figures are probably too skinny to lend themselves to a broad mechanical application. Almost none even approach the conventional $100 per trade we need to budget for. Most of my mechanical associates consider this to be the end of the story—if you can't overcome trading edges, you don't have anything. I just can't seem to let go of these broad robust biases, though. *If* opening-closing ranges were not prohibitively wide and uncertain and *if* you could average close to the posted opens and closes, undeniably you'd rule the world.

We're talking microns away here—is there no way to nudge it somehow? The obvious key would reside in the overnight sessions. I've done some research into how often you can get in a tick or two better than the

TABLE 15.2 Enter Cup/Cap on 3rd Day Close—Exit Next Open—20 Years through 11-19-05

	Net Profit	# Trades	% Profit	Profit/Trade	Max. DD	ROA
S&P (Full)	$35,587	708	53.39%	$50.26	$35,825	99.3
NASD (Full)	$18,835	294	52.72%	$64.06	$40,985	46.0
Russell (Full)	$26,850	425	47.29%	$63.18	$22,725	118.2
Dow (Full)	$1,210	280	45.36%	$4.32	$7,230	16.7
30-Yr. Bonds	$27,250	673	53.64%	$40.49	$5,313	512.9
10-Yr. Notes	$17,563	678	53.98%	$25.90	$3,359	522.9
5-Yr. Notes	$16,203	601	57.90%	$26.96	$1,266	1,280.0
30-Day Fed	$3,917	262	46.56%	$14.95	$1,250	313.4
Japanese Yen	$15,763	1,027	50.63%	$15.35	$12,538	125.7
Euro Currency	($3,113)	338	49.41%	($9.21)	$11,663	NA
Swiss Franc	$19,163	1,002	51.30%	$19.12	$11,450	167.4
Brit Pound	$41,369	982	52.14%	$42.13	$8,175	506.0
Canadian Dollar	$17,250	875	56.34%	$19.71	$2,410	715.8
Gold	$12,200	889	54.11%	$13.72	$2,900	420.7
Silver	$24,030	787	51.97%	$30.53	$3,390	708.8
Copper	$10,320	758	51.45%	$13.61	$8,075	127.8
Platinum	$30,100	857	54.84%	$35.12	$4,210	715.0
Crude Oil	$29,510	683	56.66%	$43.21	$4,890	603.5
Heating Oil	$3,482	753	53.65%	$4.62	$24,234	14.4
NY Hrbr Gas	$29,510	683	56.66%	$43.21	$4,890	603.5
Soybeans	$10,350	719	47.98%	$14.39	$8,625	120.0
Wheat	$10,031	618	55.99%	$16.23	$2,563	391.4
Corn	$9,375	629	55.33%	$14.90	$1,400	669.6
Oats	$14,356	598	58.53%	$24.01	$938	1,530.0
Soybean Oil	$6,510	697	53.08%	$9.34	$1,752	371.6
Soybean Meal	$320	668	46.71%	$0.48	$9,390	3.4
Live Cattle	$9,480	675	53.04%	$14.04	$1,160	817.2
Feeder Cattle	$18,465	658	56.99%	$28.06	$1,338	1,380.0
Live Hogs	$9,146	724	53.73%	$12.63	$6,762	135.3
Pork Bellies	$36,840	694	54.18%	$53.08	$4,290	858.7
Coffee	$37,463	680	55.74%	$55.09	$11,531	324.9
Cocoa	$9,090	805	53.29%	$11.29	$3,260	278.8
Cotton	$27,945	728	53.43%	$38.39	$2,750	1,016.0
Sugar	$12,645	648	55.09%	$19.51	$1,456	868.5
Orange Juice	$12,187	692	52.17%	$17.61	$2,565	475.1
Rough Rice	$12,400	567	48.85%	$21.87	$1,020	1,216.0

Source: © TradeStation Technologies, Inc. 1991–2006. All rights reserved.

TABLE 15.3 Cups-Caps—Overnight with Stops and Targets—01-02-01 through 11-19-05

	Net Profit	# Trades	% Profit	Profit/Trade	Max. DD	ROA
S&P (Full)	$43,413	183	55.19%	$237.23	$19,675	220.7
NASD (Full)	$15,150	165	50.30%	$91.82	$41,250	36.7
Russell (Full)	$11,075	174	57.47%	$63.65	$27,275	40.6
30-Yr. Bonds	$5,406	159	55.97%	$34.00	$7,938	68.1
10-Yr. Notes	$3,640	169	54.44%	$21.54	$5,359	67.9
5-Yr. Notes	$7,140	172	56.98%	$41.52	$3,031	235.6
Japanese Yen	($17,900)	263	47.53%	($68.06)	$19,238	NA
Euro Currency	$400	256	48.83%	$1.56	$13,725	2.9
Swiss Franc	$5,650	279	50.90%	$20.25	$11,038	51.2

official close, and how well that does to overcome the runaway evening where you can't. We'd need to somehow quantify how to deal with those missed trades. Do we just skip those trades, which obviously figure to be among our biggest winners—and hope we can make it up in our majority tick-or-two better days? Do we go to market after a certain time period? I don't have the answers, but I can't let go of the questions. Someday, I'll return to this full-force.

For now, there are alternative strategies that can get us even closer, at least in some of our key markets. Table 15.3 shows the results of an alternate of the original overnight strategy that keeps the trade alive beyond the next open. On the day after your entry-on-close, you're looking to exit at rather traditional profit targets and stop losses. If you're long, the objective is the highest three-day high plus a quarter of the three-day average range. The stop loss is one tick under the three-day lowest low. If neither side is hit, you exit on the next (Day 3) open. Vice versa for sells.

We've considerably improved our performance in the indexes to the point where we're knocking on the stand-alone system door. The S&Ps are beyond their $100 per trade threshold and the NASDAQ is just shy of it. All the other markets are confirming save the yen.

We've seen much overall persistence in the cups-caps concept, which justifies our spending extra time on it. For even further fortification, check out 10 year periodic breakdown in each of the index markets. As we've seen before, they tend to provide especial opportunity. What's more, they've been doing so for many years on a rather consistent basis. (Tables 15.4–15.6).

Table 15.7 summarizes the indexes' total 10-year performance. You might note that some of the profit-per-trades are sizeable. In this context, we could be thinking in terms of definite stand-alone systems. On the other hand, I tend not to get more enthusiastic just because further back

TABLE 15.4 Three-Day Cups-Caps—Yearly Performance—1996–2005—S&P

	Net Profit	% Gain	Profit Factor	# Trades	% Profit
1996	($1,150)	−1.15%	0.92	29	41.38%
1997	$20,913	21.16%	1.84	30	50.00%
1998	$25,275	21.10%	1.79	37	56.76%
1999	$18,850	13.00%	1.37	36	55.56%
2000	$16,875	10.30%	1.26	42	57.14%
2001	$34,213	18.93%	2.21	31	58.06%
2002	($6,675)	−3.11%	0.88	39	53.85%
2003	$26,425	12.69%	2.48	29	68.97%
2004	($11,650)	−4.96%	0.68	39	51.28%
2005	$1,100	49.00%	1.03	45	48.89%

TABLE 15.5 Three-Day Cups-Caps—Yearly Performance—1996–2005—NASDAQ

	Net Profit	% Gain	Profit Factor	# Trades	% Profit
1996	$5,590	5.59%	2.68	15	66.67%
1997	$5,155	4.88%	1.38	27	51.85%
1998	($720)	−65.00%	0.97	31	48.39%
1999	$7,930	7.21%	1.20	24	62.50%
2000	$117,415	99.54%	2.58	32	68.75%
2001	$13,300	5.65%	1.21	35	57.14%
2002	$15,150	6.09%	1.52	32	62.50%
2003	$3,450	1.31%	1.12	32	53.13%
2004	($7,650)	−2.86%	0.74	37	40.54%
2005	($9,100)	−3.51%	0.50	31	35.48%

TABLE 15.6 Three-Day Cups-Caps—Yearly Performance—1996–2005—Russell

	Net Profit	% Gain	Profit Factor	# Trades	% Profit
1996	$9,575	9.57%	1.74	40	50.00%
1997	$18,175	16.59%	2.35	29	72.41%
1998	($18,900)	−14.79%	0.61	35	37.14%
1999	($16,450)	−15.11%	0.55	31	45.16%
2000	$8,850	9.58%	1.16	33	51.52%
2001	$24,100	23.80%	2.34	28	67.86%
2002	($21,625)	−17.25%	0.62	38	50.00%
2003	$3,950	3.81%	1.12	33	60.61%
2004	$2,625	2.44%	1.06	37	54.05%
2005	$1,100	1.00%	1.02	38	57.89%

TABLE 15.7	Three-Day Cups-Caps—10-Year Summary					
	Net Profit	# Trades	% Profit	Profit/Trade	Max. DD	ROA
S&P (Full)	$124,175	357	54.06%	$347.83	$22,825	544.0
NASD (Full)	$150,520	294	54.08%	$511.97	$41,250	364.9
Russell (Full)	$11,400	341	54.25%	$33.43	$43,375	26.3

performance added to the mix creates overall better numbers, particularly given recent history. As we'll shortly discuss in more detail, good results will inevitably spring from the expansion and bursting of the millennial stock market bubble (98-01-ish). Since we don't know when the next anomalous wave of hysteria will hit, we should regard such over-performers with some skepticism. Still, it's always better to have earlier data affirm rather than contradict.

CHAPTER 16

The Three-Day 20 Percent Support-Resistance Indicator

I t's interesting how often pattern recognition techniques incorporate three bars. Here's another example, not too different from cups and caps. When three successive lows are close together, it's portending a support area—three bunched up highs suggest a resistance. Bear in mind that we're talking very rough figures, broad generalizations and skinny biases—but we're starting to see how even those have potential.

The idea seems consistent with driver theory. How many times have you hoped for a market to move through a given area, only to see it turn back two or three times and finally give up and move in the other direction? Peter Steidlmayer, developer of the market profile, likens a market to an auction. If the "auctioneer" can't unload her item (read sell order) at a certain level, she'll offer it lower. If one direction proves too hard, the market will explore the other one.

How do we quantify the idea of three bunched-together highs or lows? As usual, testing will reveal any existing workable numbers. Let's examine the distance between the highest versus lowest lows (or highs) as a percentage of the total three-day range. A robust result turns out to be 20.

If the highest low of the last three days minus the lowest low of the last three days is less than or equal to 20 percent of the entire three-day range, (highest high to lowest low), then buy the next day. For sells, the highest high to the lowest high must encompass not more than a fifth of the total range. Exit all trades on the close.

Figure 16.1 illustrates this on a daily bar chart of the Swiss Franc. Our array of results is shown in Table 16.1.

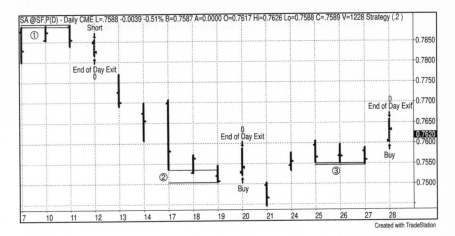

FIGURE 16.1 20 Percent Support/Resistance—Daily Swiss Franc (*Source:* © TradeStation Technologies, Inc. 1991–2006. All rights reserved.)

TABLE 16.1 Three-Day 20 Percent Support-Resistance Indicator—01-02-01 through 11-19-05

	Net Profit	# Trades	% Profit	Profit/Trade	Max. DD	ROA
S&P (Full)	$93,925	239	47.70%	$392.99	$16,875	556.6
NASD (Full)	$50,650	243	43.62%	$208.44	$17,250	293.6
Russell (Full)	$96,025	220	53.64%	$436.48	$24,250	396.0
30-Yr. Bonds	$10,968	239	52.30%	$45.89	$6,656	164.8
10-Yr. Notes	$10,031	202	52.97%	$49.66	$5,719	175.4
5-Yr. Notes	$1,578	205	47.80%	$7.70	$3,047	51.8
Japanese Yen	$3,350	131	48.85%	$25.57	$3,500	95.7
Euro Currency	($5,400)	156	44.87%	($34.62)	$10,950	NA
Swiss Franc	$4,513	151	49.01%	$29.88	$4,350	103.7

Source: © TradeStation Technologies, Inc. 1991–2006. All rights reserved.

CHAPTER 17

The Eight
Indicator System
(Plus a Discussion
of Outliers)

W e've independently tested and verified the validity of the following biases: For longs:

1. The close is greater than the 40-day closing average.

2. The two-day close is less than the five-day close.

3. The highest high of the last 50 days occurs before the lowest low of the last 50 days.

4. The range is smaller than the 10-day average range, and the close is higher *or* the range is bigger than the average 10-day range, and the close is lower. (Smaller ranges mean "go-with," bigger mean "fade.")

5. The close is higher than the average 15-day midpoints (15 highs plus 15 lows divided by 2).

6. The close was less than the open two days in a row.

7. Yesterday completed a cup formation.

8. Yesterday completed a three-bar congestion of lows—the highest low minus lowest low being equal to or less than 20 percent of the combined three-day range.

As always, vice versa for sells.

Let's once again give each indicator a +1/–1 value and add them together. We'll buy if the combined total is greater than zero, sell if it's less. In on the opening, out on the close.

Table 17.1 reveals trading results in the S&P that could justify full

TABLE 17.1 Eight Indicators Combined (Simple Majority)—S&P Daily—
01-04-01 through 11-19-05

Total Net Profit	$266,537.50	Profit Factor	1.34
Gross Profit	$1,057,812.50	Gross Loss	($791,275.00)
Total Number of Trades	908	Percent Profitable	56.28%
Winning Trades	511	Losing Trades	396
Even Trades	1		
Avg. Trade Net Profit	$293.54	Ratio Avg. Win:Avg. Loss	1.04
Avg. Winning Trade	$2,070.08	Avg. Losing Trade	($1,998.17)
Largest Winning Trade	$10,750.00	Largest Losing Trade	($10,125.00)
Max. Consecutive Winning Trades	11	Max. Consecutive Losing Trades	7
Avg. Bars in Winning Trades	1.00	Avg. Bars in Losing Trades	1.00
Avg. Bars in Total Trades	1.00		
Max. Shares/Contracts Held	1	Account Size Required	$38,675.00
Return on Initial Capital	266.54%	Annual Rate of Return	26.65%
Return Retracement Ratio	0.46	RINA Index	0.00
Trading Period	4 Yrs, 10 Mths, 14 Dys	Percent of Time in the Market	0.00%
Max. Equity Run-up	$284,375.00		
Max. Drawdown (Intraday Peak to Valley)		**Max. Drawdown (Trade Close to Trade Close)**	
Value	($42,700.00)	Value	($38,675.00)

mechanical system commitment. Our $293.54 per trade is significantly greater than the standard $100 slippage-commission threshold. This is over a more than adequate 908 trades. Dividing the $266,537.50 (net profit) by $38,675 (worst drawdawn) times 100 gives you a healthy return on account figure of 689.

We get more encouragement from the equity performance graph (Figure 17.1) and year by year breakdown (Table 17.2). So far, we see consistency as well as solid profitability.

We see similar results in the NASDAQ (Table 17.3): $147,250 total net profit, $163.43 per trade. Granted, the drawdown might dampen most stand-alone system aspirations, but we still haven't done much in the way of stops or other refinement. We're at least getting corroboration including a 161 percent return (100 times the net profit divided by max close-close drawdown) over our five-year testing period. Not bad.

This is probably a good time to reiterate the importance of understanding the environment you're testing. Table 17.3 represents a fairly normal

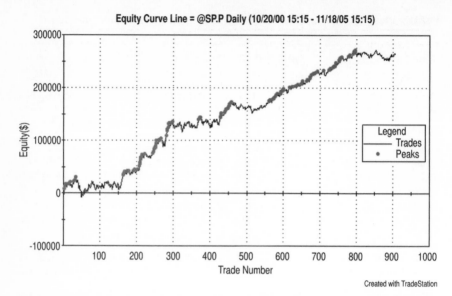

FIGURE 17.1 Eight Indicators—Equity Performance—Daily S&Ps—01-04-01 through 11-19-05 (*Source:* © TradeStation Technologies, Inc. 1991–2006. All rights reserved.)

TABLE 17.2 Periodical Returns—Eight Indicators—S&P—01-04-01 through 11-19-05

	Net Profit	% Gain	Profit Factor	# Trades	% Profitable
2001	$40,213	40.21%	1.16	191	51.83%
2002	$88,475	63.10%	1.49	176	60.80%
2003	$41,750	18.26%	1.27	190	57.37%
2004	$71,475	26.43%	1.77	184	57.61%
2005	$24,635	7.20%	1.21	167	53.89%

inclusive array of trading conditions. Bull markets, bear markets, volatile and sedate markets. Yearly analysis (Table 17.4) reveals a fairly steady return—two small losing years out of five. The average is not buffeted by any one over-performing year.

Table 17.5, by contrast, shows some dramatically improved numbers in the same market. What is different? One thing only—Table 17.5 has one extra year of data—the year 2000. It was the year of the dot.com bubble burst, and it skews just about any momentum-type idea you run through it. It represented a virtual system trading Nirvana. Just about any momentum-related idea you test will produce wildly profitable results in that era—prices moved in straight lines (pretty much straight down), and

TABLE 17.3 Eight Indicators—Daily NASDAQ—01-04-01 through 11-19-05

Total Net Profit	$147,250.00	Profit Factor	1.18
Gross Profit	$957,950.00	Gross Loss	($810,700.00)
Total Number of Trades	901	Percent Profitable	50.94%
Winning Trades	459	Losing Trades	431
Even Trades	11		
Avg. Trade Net Profit	$163.43	Ratio Avg. Win:Avg. Loss	1.11
Avg. Winning Trade	$2,087.04	Avg. Losing Trade	($1,880.97)
Largest Winning Trade	$18,850.00	Largest Losing Trade	($13,650.00)
Max. Consecutive Winning Trades	10	Max. Consecutive Losing Trades	7
Avg. Bars in Winning Trades	1.00	Avg. Bars in Losing Trades	1.00
Avg. Bars in Total Trades	1.00		
Max. Shares/Contracts Held	1	Account Size Required	$90,950.00
Return on Initial Capital	147.25%	Annual Rate of Return	18.58%
Return Retracement Ratio	0.45	RINA Index	0.00
Trading Period	4 Yrs, 10 Mths, 14 Dys	Percent of Time in the Market	0.00%
Max. Equity Run-up	$163,550.00		
Max. Drawdown (Intra-day Peak to Valley)		**Max. Drawdown (Trade Close to Trade Close)**	
Value	($95,350.00)	Value	($90,950.00)

Source: © TradeStation Technologies, Inc. 1991–2006. All rights reserved.

TABLE 17.4 Eight Indicators—Yearly Performance—NASDAQ—01-04-01 through 11-19-05

	Net Profit	% Gain	Profit Factor	# Trades	% Profitable
2001	$38,650	38.65%	1.11	195	48.21%
2002	$95,650	68.99%	1.70	179	55.31%
2003	($8,900)	–3.80%	0.93	188	49.47%
2004	$23,050	10.23%	1.24	189	52.91%
2005	($1,200)	–48.00%	0.98	150	48.67%

momentum was unprecedented. In addition to actually catching my share of the 2000 windfall, I've got dozens more shelved systems that would have theoretically made a killing.

You might be understandably convinced that given a long enough trading history, some market or other is going to give you a most unexpected over-the-top helping hand. It's not an unreasonable thought. Markets are unpredictable and occasionally wild.

TABLE 17.5 Eight Indicators—Daily NASDAQ—1 Additional Year—01-04-00 through 11-19-05

Total Net Profit	$440,415.00	Profit Factor	1.30
Gross Profit	$1,921,950.00	Gross Loss	($1,481,535.00)
Total Number of Trades	1,081	Percent Profitable	51.80%
Winning Trades	560	Losing Trades	510
Even Trades	11		
Avg. Trade Net Profit	$407.41	Ratio Avg. Win:Avg. Loss	1.18
Avg. Winning Trade	$3,432.05	Avg. Losing Trade	($2,904.97)
Largest Winning Trade	$31,950.00	Largest Losing Trade	($26,750.00)
Max. Consecutive Winning Trades	10	Max. Consecutive Losing Trades	7
Avg. Bars in Winning Trades	1.00	Avg. Bars in Losing Trades	1.00
Avg. Bars in Total Trades	1.00		
Max. Shares/Contracts Held	1	Account Size Required	$90,950.00
Return on Initial Capital	440.41%	Annual Rate of Return	28.68%
Return Retracement Ratio	0.35	RINA Index	0.00
Trading Period	5 Yrs, 10 Mths, 17 Dys	Percent of Time in the Market	0.00%
Max. Equity Run-up	$508,565.00		
Max. Drawdown (Intraday Peak to Valley)		**Max. Drawdown (Trade Close to Trade Close)**	
Value	($95,350.00)	Value	($90,950.00)

Source: © TradeStation Technologies, Inc. 1991–2006. All rights reserved.

Although such a possibility might occupy a corner of your awareness though, you'd better not plan for such an outcome when you're actually formulating your business plan. Instead, figure on the occasional devastating event, (9/11, Black Monday) catching you the wrong way. Guaranteed, it will happen sooner or later, given enough market history. The windfall might be almost as likely, but you can't afford to include that side of the coin in your projection.

Performance summaries will include results with and without outliers. An outlier is an extreme outcome. TradeStation defines it as a trade that does not fall within a standard three-deviation result—again it's an abnormally huge win or loss. You have to be especially cognizant of these kinds of profits. On the one hand, markets will continue to hand out huge surprises in the future, but again, you can't count on any outcome springing out of a single trial. As we've said, there's no likelihood that you'll be right rather than wrong during the next shock. Even a great system can't anticipate a single trade.

TABLE 17.6 Eight Indicators Combined (Simple Majority)—01-04-01 through 11-19-05

	Net Profit	# Trades	% Profit	Profit/Trade	Max. DD	ROA
Russell (Full)	$214,175	866	53.12%	$247.32	$36,500	586.8
30-Yr. Bonds	$60,875	899	53.50%	$67.71	$9,250	658.1
10-Yr. Notes	$39,344	899	52.84%	$43.76	$7,531	522.4
5-Yr. Notes	$26,813	926	52.81%	$28.96	$4,266	628.5
Japanese Yen	$5,575	953	50.47%	$5.85	$9,900	56.3
Euro Currency	$12,063	946	50.32%	$12.75	$17,725	68.1
Swiss Franc	$20,350	946	51.27%	$21.51	$14,813	137.4

In short, don't act on results that blow up without the inclusion of the outliers. You can keep it in the back of your mind—way in the back—that maybe the market might help you in unexpected ways down the road. You must also remember that you could just as easily get the flip side—instant devastation. Be very cautious any time you get a yearly breakdown that looks like Table 17.5. It is foolhardy to average one extreme anomalous timeframe into your whole data field and then plan around the higher averages. Always stay hard-nosed realistic. As the Boy Scouts say, be prepared.

Table 17.6 shows how the other 7 markets fared in 2001–2005.

Once again, if a simple majority works, we might wonder what kind of improvement we'll get by making a certain percentage point one way. Remember that now we're not talking solely either-or indicators. Up to three out of the eight could easily be neutral. Consequently, we return to the +/– 3 or better as a likely demarcation line. Table 17.7 shows the results.

We're starting to see a quantum leap in some of our numbers. Note that all three indexes are now well past the $100 slippage-commission barrier. Four out of five have return on accounts in excess of 500 percent.

TABLE 17.7 Eight Indicators—+/– 3 or Beyond—01-04-01 through 11-19-05

	Net Profit	# Trades	% Profit	Profit/Trade	Max. DD	ROA
S&P (Full)	$146,888	230	63.48%	$638.64	$20,800	706.2
NASD (Full)	$129,900	199	58.79%	$652.76	$16,900	768.6
Russell (Full)	$67,525	201	52.74%	$335.95	$30,100	224.3
30-Yr. Bonds	$25,563	235	59.15%	$108.78	$5,188	492.7
10-Yr. Notes	$23,656	244	58.20%	$96.95	$2,641	895.7
5-Yr. Notes	$16,125	238	59.24%	$67.75	$1,531	1,053.0
Japanese Yen	$8,438	236	52.54%	$35.75	$3,788	222.8
Euro Currency	$10,050	239	48.12%	$42.05	$6,138	163.7
Swiss Franc	$2,250	240	50.83%	$9.38	$11,037	20.4

One tops 1,000 percent. Keep in mind that this stat refers to the multiple by which the account would have increased over this particular five year period. Considering what most financial instruments yield, wouldn't even a decent percentage of these results be pretty phenomenal?

We've laid some pretty careful groundwork here. If the future isn't destined to cooperate, it won't be from our lack of planning.

CHAPTER 18

Entering on Stops

By focusing on trades that enter on the open and exit on the close, we're obviously looking at a small portion of the potential trading universe. Whether we're talking mechanical or discretionary approach, most traders are keying off intraday activity that is giving them further evidence of what decisions to make.

Momentum traders use stop orders as entries, which obviously flies somewhat in the face of the widely held "buy low—sell high" adage. A momentum trader wants to buy high, sell higher or sell short low, buy it in even lower. She's waiting for the market to tip its hand—nothing says strength like upward movement.

By stipulating alternate entry points, we can get a whole different array of results in the combined indicator systems. We'll focus on the eight indicators with the simple majority. Instead of entering on the open, we could buy a given amount above it on a stop, or sell short the same distance underneath. We still exit on the close.

As we'll discuss later, there are advantages to using dynamic triggers, that is, those that somehow key off market action. I'm partial to the average three-day range as a gauge. I used to think you needed nothing fancier than yesterday's range until I realized the impact the holiday-shortened days were having. They were skewing results—forcing arbitrarily quick entries. A three-day average smooths out such anomalies.

Some percentage of those averages can be turned into distances that resolve in stop entry triggers. Table 18.1 shows the results of optimizing the stop distance in the S&Ps. They range from zero times the average

TABLE 18.1 Optimizing Day Average Daily Ranges for Stop Entries—S&P—
1-04-01 through 11-19-05

X	Net Profit	# Trades	% Profit	Profit/Trade	Max. DD	ROA
0	$266,525	908	56%	$293.53	$41,800	637.6
0.25	$212,250	641	57%	$331.12	$24,050	882.5
0.5	$112,975	416	56%	$271.57	$20,775	543.8
0.75	$61,450	258	58%	$238.18	$22,350	274.9
1	$8,375	152	57%	$55.10	$18,275	45.8
1.25	$17,450	71	47%	$245.77	$5,175	337.2
1.5	$4,625	38	50%	$121.71	$5,025	92.0

three day range, (i.e., our previous opening price entry) up to one and a half times the amount in increments of .25. As you can see, the quarter range trial actually produces a higher return on account than our normal enter-on-open. The average profit per trade is also better.

The NASDAQ (Table 18.2) doesn't exactly support the idea, but it doesn't exactly refute it either. The quarter level is still holding its own fairly well. By contrast, the Russell convincingly argues for the new entries (see Table 18.3). The 25 percent line has a big return on account jump. The profit per trade is better. Even the net profit on the .25 line is larger, demonstrating that our weeded-out numbers weren't doing us any favors.

The other optimized results support the robustness, although subsequent testing tells us to keep our increments small. Actually, when we fine-tune our optimization a bit, we find that 33 percent of the three-day average range is a particularly good performer.

On a buy signal, enter at the open plus 33 percent of the previous three-day average range on a stop.

On a sell signal, enter at the open minus the same amount.

TABLE 18.2 Optimizing Day Average Daily Ranges for Stop Entries—Eight
Indicator—Simple Majority—NASDAQ—1-04-01 through 11-19-05

X	Net Profit	# Trades	% Profit	Profit/Trade	Max. DD	ROA
0	$147,250	901	50%	$163.43	$92,250	159.6
0.25	$65,300	628	52%	$103.98	$53,650	121.7
0.5	$62,400	385	53%	$162.08	$39,800	156.8
0.75	$29,550	231	53%	$127.92	$13,550	218.1
1	$15,450	134	52%	$115.30	$5,900	261.9
1.25	($5,600)	68	48%	($82.35)	($13,900)	NA
1.5	($1,600)	26	26%	($61.54)	($7,950)	NA

TABLE 18.3 Optimizing Three-Day Average Daily Ranges for Stop Entries—Eight Indicator—Simple Majority—Russell—1-04-01 through 11-19-05

X	Net Profit	# Trades	% Profit	Profit/Trade	Max. DD	ROA
0	$214,175	866	53%	$247.32	$39,350	544.3
0.25	$232,925	595	58%	$391.47	$23,500	991.2
0.5	$143,025	396	59%	$361.17	$16,000	893.9
0.75	$88,950	253	59%	$351.58	$10,825	821.7
1	$48,950	136	64%	$359.93	$10,575	462.9
1.25	$13,800	63	57%	$219.05	$7,225	191.0
1.5	$1,200	34	58%	$35.29	$10,600	11.32

TABLE 18.4 Eight Indicators—Simple Majority—33 Percent Entry Stops— 01-04-01 through 11-19-05

	Net Profit	# Trades	% Profit	Profit/Trade	Max. DD	ROA
S&P (Full)	$137,100	578	55.54%	$237.20	$29,625	462.9
NASD (Full)	$97,850	533	53.85%	$183.58	$38,300	255.5
Russell (Full)	$216,475	520	60.38%	$416.30	$15,050	1,438.0
30-Yr. Bonds	$31,219	534	56.55%	$58.46	$4,813	648.6
10-Yr. Notes	$27,781	526	55.70%	$52.82	$3,734	744.0
5-Yr. Notes	$18,188	521	54.13%	$34.91	$2,953	615.9
Japanese Yen	$8,688	520	45.77%	$16.71	$5,538	156.9
Euro Currency	$30,075	518	50.39%	$58.06	$5,888	510.8
Swiss Franc	$19,213	539	50.65%	$35.64	$4,638	414.3

You're obviously getting fewer trades with this variation. It stands to reason that the ones being lopped off would have been your biggest losers. (You never hit your entry because the market never went far enough in your favor.) What you're sacrificing in return, of course, is the difference between the new stop level and the more favorable opening price. (Now you're buying higher and selling lower.)

Table 18.4 shows how the 33 percent entry stop fared in our nine targeted markets.

Table 18.5 shows the results of not acting unless the +/–3 threshold is hit. As before, we have improved return on accounts and profit per trades. Look at how stratospheric the percentage winning trades is becoming in several of these markets. Granted, we've weeded out many trials, but you still have to take notice when your profitable trades are hovering around the two out of three realm.

TABLE 18.5   Eight Indicators—33 Percent Entry with +/–3 Qualifier—01-04-01 through 11-19-05

	Net Profit	# Trades	% Profit	Profit/Trade	Max. DD	ROA
S&P (Full)	$87,325	155	61.29%	$563.39	$10,425	837.6
NASD (Full)	$73,250	132	56.82%	$554.92	$10,450	701.0
Russell (Full)	$79,575	119	66.39%	$668.70	$11,450	695.0
30-Yr. Bonds	$12,125	149	61.07%	$81.38	$2,406	503.9
10-Yr. Notes	$18,625	153	66.67%	$121.73	$1,703	1,094.0
5-Yr. Notes	$13,547	139	66.91%	$97.46	$984	1,377.0
Japanese Yen	$5,338	127	48.03%	$42.03	$3,825	139.6
Euro Currency	$12,550	134	54.48%	$93.66	$3,868	324.5
Swiss Franc	$4,588	139	48.92%	$33.00	$5,763	79.6

CHAPTER 19

Entering on Limits

Given the robustness of the eight indicators, we might want to consider other possible entry points. As we've said, the downside of the stop entry is that it's at a worse level than the opening. What about if we were to initiate at a better level than the opening? Now, of course, we're talking limit rather than stop order which, as we'll see, has its advantages and disadvantages. Let's do the same run-through we did in the above section. Table 19.1 shows results of again optimizing the three day average range from 0 to 1.5 every .25 points in the S&P. We're now initiating the opposite of before—subtracting the number from the open for buys and adding it for sells.

Next, we look at the NASDAQ (see Table 19.2). The first thing to note in both is none of the limits are as good as the top enter-on-open lines. This doesn't prove true across all nine financials, but it does tell us a couple of

TABLE 19.1 Optimizing for Limit Percentages—Buying Lower, Selling Higher— S&P—1-02-01 through 11-19-05

X	Net Profit	# Trades	% Profit	Profit/Trade	Max. DD	ROA
0	$266,525	908	56%	$293.53	$41,800	637.6
0.25	$83,500	586	53%	$142.49	$57,800	144.5
0.5	$13,800	347	48%	$39.77	$28,325	48.7
0.75	($1,925)	198	45%	($9.72)	$20,800	NA
1	($8,050)	109	44%	($73.85)	$14,426	NA
1.25	($24,275)	48	35%	($505.73)	$24,375	NA
1.5	($12,525)	27	29%	($463.89)	$12,625	NA

TABLE 19.2 Optimizing for Limit Percentages—NASDAQ—1-02-01 through 11-19-05

X	Net Profit	# Trades	% Profit	Profit/Trade	Max. DD	ROA
0	$147,250	901	50%	$163.43	$92,250	159.6
0.25	$22,050	602	52%	$36.63	$78,600	28.1
0.5	($39,600)	357	46%	($110.92)	($60,800)	NA
0.75	($20,650)	212	45%	($97.47)	($38,400)	NA
1	($35,550)	108	40%	($329.17)	($38,550)	NA
1.25	($10,950)	60	51%	($182.50)	($21,650)	NA
1.5	($5,050)	25	36%	($202.00)	($19,850)	NA

things. One, when trying to do something roughly opposite to reliable ideas like momentum (enter on stops), you can probably expect flip-side results.

Second, though perhaps inferior, any persistent degree of success might prove valuable. For one thing, we may consider a sub-optimal idea to be a good portfolio addition—something that works in tandem, thereby helping with diversification. Also, you have the advantage of not being at the mercy of adverse fills. Again, we're setting our own entry prices.

So let's mush on. We're obviously not getting much encouragement in the way of buying/selling at sharply "better" levels. This probably shouldn't surprise us. The worst trades are obviously going to pass through our limit orders on their way to oblivion. Pit traders are aware of that phenomenon. It's the antithesis of "if I liked buying it at 7, I *loved* buying it at 4!" Veterans know the wisdom of assuming "bad" will likely to become "worse."

Our latest analysis has us finding a few winning percentages in the small end of the ranges; 25 being the best. Table 19.3 shows how it plays out in our targeted markets. Table 19.4 shows results with the +/–3 qualifier.

TABLE 19.3 Entering on 25 Percent Limit Orders—Remaining Markets—1-02-01 through 11-18-05

	Net Profit	# Trades	% Profit	Profit/Trade	Max. DD	ROA
Russell (Full)	($45,225)	560	46.96%	($80.76)	$77,075	NA
30-Yr. Bonds	$24,000	572	51.05%	$41.96	$9,188	261.2
10-Yr. Notes	$21,188	584	55.82%	$36.28	$5,125	413.4
5-Yr. Notes	$12,891	571	50.61%	$22.58	$2,921	441.3
Japanese Yen	$7,713	650	55.69%	$11.87	$6,513	118.4
Euro Currency	$14,638	642	53.43%	$22.80	$10,038	145.8
Swiss Franc	$3,538	614	51.14%	$5.76	$9,213	38.4

TABLE 19.4 Entering on 25% Limit Orders with +/–3 Qualifier—1-02-01 through 11-18-05

	Net Profit	# Trades	% Profit	Profit/Trade	Max. DD	ROA
S&P (Full)	$46,725	136	58.82%	$343.57	$21,325	219.1
NASD (Full)	$66,250	134	61.19%	$494.40	$22,350	296.4
Russell (Full)	($4,400)	128	46.88%	($34.37)	$27,450	NA
30-Yr. Bonds	$9,656	138	53.62%	$69.97	$3,343	288.8
10-Yr. Notes	$7,688	144	60.42%	$53.39	$2,453	313.4
5-Yr. Notes	$4,469	138	50.72%	$32.38	$2,734	163.5
Japanese Yen	$6,663	162	54.32%	$39.27	$2,350	282.3
Euro Currency	$15,750	170	57.06%	$92.65	$4,425	355.9
Swiss Franc	$1,400	157	52.23%	$8.92	$7,412	18.9

Some General Observations about Stops (and an Actual Application)

There are four basic types of stoplosses.

1. *Money management.* You risk a fixed dollar amount. When a price is hit resulting in that sized loss or greater, you're out of the trade. Period.

2. *A trailing stop.* You have an initial stop that acts the same as money management. If the trade goes bad immediately, you will be out if a certain adverse level is violated. If, on the other hand, the trade goes your way, you have an established threshold level, which, once hit, causes your stop to scale in the direction of your profit. If you're long, it trails upward, or downward if you're short. You're guaranteeing that you're either decreasing your potential loss or safeguarding a bigger portion of your profit as the market moves your way.

3. *A dynamic stop.* This is less arbitrary than the previous two because it adjusts according to market conditions. It's keyed off some market characteristic—most commonly, range averages. By risking, say, 50 percent of an average daily range from your entry price, you are keeping the percentage of times you'll likely be hit constant. By contrast, a $1000 money management stop would seldom have been hit in the 1980s full-sized S&P market but in 1999–2000, that barrier would likely have frequently fallen within minutes or less.

4. *A stop that unfolds directly out of your system principles.* The easiest example to imagine is no stop at all—just reverse signals. You're buying the highest high of the last 20 days on a stop, and you're sell-

ing short the corresponding lowest low. This is sheer momentum, the "stop" being part and parcel of the reversal. Obviously, this example would involve huge risks that one would be well-advised to mitigate, even if arbitrarily. Some systems achieve this level of purity even when there are stops that are separate from the reversals.

All varieties have their plusses and minuses, but as a rule, the less arbitrary you can make your stops, the better. Market environments do change, and your failsafe points should have some corresponding flexibility.

Let's refer back to Figure 17.3 which shows the original Eight Combined Indicator system (simple majority) in the NASDAQ. One stat we haven't considered is the biggest single losing trade. In the calm theoretical world where we find ourselves right now, that may not seem too relevant. If we one day suffer our largest losing trade amount of $13,650, so what? It doesn't seem so bad in the context of an ultimate $147,250 bottom line.

It feels different when you're trading—actually living the experience day by day. It's only natural to not want to surrender back big chunks of earned money regardless of what kind of ultimate bottom line you're weighing that against. Trading accounts are "marked to market" every day and that makes you "feel" givebacks as they happen. You're not as likely to be philosophical about Tuesday's $50,000 account equity if that has been discounted from Monday's $65,000 figure.

Even if you only manage to slightly improve your worst trade number, remember this: you haven't really seen the worst yet. The adage that says "your worst drawdown is always ahead of you" can apply to your biggest loser also. If you trade long enough, "bad" will inevitably become "worse." Having some sort of stop in place will significantly mitigate that eventuality.

Again, whenever possible, try to design stops that are dynamic rather than static. Table 20.1 shows S&P optimized stops created from percentages

TABLE 20.1 Optimizing Stop Exits on the Eight Indicator—S&P—01-04-01 through 11-19-05

U	Net Profit	# Trades	% Profit	Profit/Trade	Max. DD	ROA
No Stop	$266,538	908	56%	$293.54	$38,675	689.2
0.25	$183,038	908	33%	$201.58	$35,725	512.4
0.5	$252,738	908	49%	$278.35	$26,250	962.8
0.75	$268,463	908	54%	$295.66	$28,875	929.7
1	$274,588	908	56%	$302.41	$36,175	759.1
1.25	$290,813	908	56%	$320.28	$34,025	854.7
1.5	$279,063	908	56%	$307.34	$36,800	758.3

TABLE 20.2 Optimizing Stop Exits on the Eight Indicator—NASDAQ—01-04-01 through 11-19-05

U	Net Profit	# Trades	% Profit	Profit/Trade	Max. DD	ROA
No Stop	$147,250	901	51%	$163.43	$90,950	161.9
0.25	$125,200	901	30%	$138.96	$33,100	378.2
0.5	$186,850	901	45%	$207.38	$62,500	299.0
0.75	$167,900	901	49%	$186.35	$69,300	242.3
1	$182,800	901	50%	$202.89	$72,600	251.8
1.25	$158,200	901	50%	$175.58	$84,450	187.3
1.5	$152,300	901	50%	$169.03	$93,050	163.7

of the prior three-day average ranges. We're again entering at market, same as the original eight indicator system, but now we might exit before the close of the day. Our optimized range fractions (or multiples) are subtracted from long entry prices to create the sell stops. (Remember, here, the entry is the same as the daily opening.) For shorts, the figures are added to the entry (opening). Table 20.2 shows what testing produced in the NASDAQ.

We've settled on 66 percent as perhaps the best overall performer. (It's interesting how often thirds manifest themselves as robust performers. An argument for Fibonacci numbers perhaps?)

Table 20.3 shows our nine markets without stops (top line each) and with the applied 66 percent stops (bottom lines). The stops are dynamic. They behave in the same way whether you're talking relatively inert, narrow-ranged equities environments like the summer of 2005 or the wild bubble time frame around the turn of the millennium. They're always relative to the ranges of their immediate environment.

TABLE 20.3 Eight Indicator—Simple Majority With 66 Percent Stop—01-04-01 through 11-19-05

	Net Profit	# Trades	% Profit	Profit/Trade	Max. DD	ROA
S&P (Full)						
No Stop	$266,538	908	56.28%	$293.54	$38,675	689.2
66% Stop	$276,038	908	53.30%	$304.01	$25,725	1,073.0
NASD (Full)						
No Stop	$147,250	901	50.94%	$163.43	$90,950	161.9
66% Stop	$169,600	901	48.17%	$188.24	$59,100	287.0
Russell (Full)						
No Stop	$214,175	866	53.12%	$247.32	$36,500	586.8
66% Stop	$230,025	866	50.23%	$265.62	$31,025	741.4
30-Yr. Bonds						
No Stop	$60,875	899	53.50%	$67.71	$9,250	658.1
66% Stop	$56,469	899	50.83%	$62.81	$7,844	719.9
10-Yr. Notes						
No Stop	$39,344	899	52.84%	$43.76	$7,531	522.4
66% Stop	$34,813	899	49.72%	$38.72	$7,109	489.7
5-Yr. Notes						
No Stop	$26,813	926	52.81%	$28.96	$4,266	628.5
66% Stop	$23,313	926	49.46%	$25.18	$3,859	604.1
Japanese Yen						
No Stop	$5,575	953	50.47%	$5.85	$9,900	56.3
66% Stop	$6,113	953	47.95%	$6.41	$8,288	73.8
Euro Currency						
No Stop	$12,063	946	50.32%	$12.75	$17,725	68.1
66% Stop	$3,713	946	47.15%	$3.92	$17,325	21.4
Swiss Franc						
No Stop	$20,350	946	51.27%	$21.51	$14,813	137.4
66% Stop	$22,400	946	48.84%	$23.68	$10,100	221.8

The Pros and Cons of Price Targets (Featuring Another Effective System)

We touched on price targets, an enticing idea for many, me included. People love to ring the cash register and go "whew" before a windfall gets away. There are profitable systems that involve price targets, but as any researcher can tell you, most times the bottom line would have been better without them. Usually, we're not merely talking slightly better, which could justify diversification, but rather better to a degree that blots out the original target premise.

It's a vexing reality. I have several day systems, which all thrive best when keeping trades alive until the day's end or beyond. This is why, with all the different trading approaches we all swear by, we're often left with many systems traversing the same territory, trying to do more or less the same thing, slightly different entry points notwithstanding. It's also why momentum systems are such bellwethers despite the degree they chafe at our intuitive inclinations. We do have to give money back trading on a purely momentum basis, but from what level? It's frequently from a much better one than we would have anticipated, which defines the successful driver behind this particular numbers game.

We've noted that an advantage of using limit orders is that we won't get ripped on fills. The big disadvantage is that because of our insistence on a given price, we may not get the trade at all. Remember, whether we're talking pit or electronic trade, the forces of the opposing side are setting their own limits (bids and offers).

This is an issue not only in our actual trading life, but in our research world as well. It's critical that all hypothetical signals be doable exactly the same way in the real world, but this is clearly an area where that is not

76

the case. We have to adjust for the fact that software is crediting us with winning trades that wouldn't have occurred. Clearly, accurate projection is not as cut and dried as we'd hoped.

We'll illustrate the problem and how to compensate by using another system as an example. We'll call it the "second high/low exit" system. It incorporates our original five either-or indicators. For longs:

1. The close is greater than the 40 day closing average.
2. The two-day close is less than the five-day close
3. The highest high of the last 50 days occurs before the lowest low of the last 50 days.
4. The range is smaller than the 10-day average range and the close is higher *or* the range is bigger than the average 10-day range and the close is lower. (Smaller ranges mean "go-with," bigger mean fade.)
5. The close is higher than the average 15-day midpoints, (average of 15-day highs plus average of 15-day lows divided by 2).

As with earlier combo systems, a majority of the five indicators determines our direction. This time, a second qualifier has to be met as well. The close has to be greater than a 20-day average in order for us to be buyers. If that's true while the five indicators are also in bullish mode, we then buy the next day at the open minus 33 percent of the average three-day range on a limit order.

This is the first of our interday systems. We do not exit on the close.

After the completion of the entry day, note that high. We're seeking to take that out twice, the higher of which (regardless of the order) will become our profit target. However many days down the road it takes, that's our target unless our stop is hit first. The stop is a close under the 20-day average of the lows, which signals an exit on the next day's open. As always, the exact opposite scenario is used for short selling entrances and exits.

Figure 21.1 shows a profitable buy and a sell, both initiating on limit orders 33 percent of the previous three-day range better than the opening. On the first trade, the entry day high is taken out the next day. Seven days later, it is penetrated again, although the second day higher high is not. Still, this activates the setup for that second day high to become the profit target, which is realized two days later.

The second trade features a short. The Day 1 low is taken out on Day 2. The Day 2 low is taken out on Day 3, which sets up the objective that is filled the next day.

If the only controversial calls involve limit orders that are touched but not penetrated (and it would be acceptable to keep at least our unfilled entry orders working for subsequent days if necessary), then the odds are

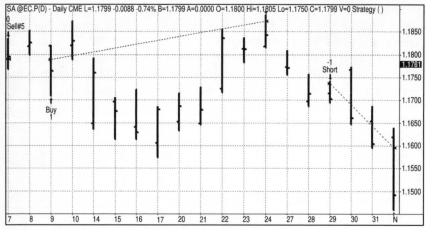

FIGURE 21.1 Second High/Low Exit: Daily Euro Currency (*Source:* © TradeStation Technologies, Inc. 1991–2006. All rights reserved.)

FIGURE 21.2 Second High/Low Exit—No Disputes—All Buy/Sell Levels Are Penetrated: Daily S&P (*Source:* © TradeStation Technologies, Inc. 1991–2006. All rights reserved.)

good we won't be trying to execute on an absolute high/low extreme. Figure 21.2 shows an array of indisputable entries and exits in the S&Ps, which is fairly typical of the whole field.

Table 21.1 are the across the board results for "second high/low exit." Pretty respectable. We're seeing some hefty average profit per trades although those are admittedly easier to churn on a multiday basis than intraday. Again, though, these are numbers that are by and large not susceptible to price skids. That should give us further fortification. Or should it? Let's look at Figure 21.3.

Note the highlighted trade in Figure 21.3. It's showing a sell on 10-16-02 in the December 02 five-year note contract at 11216—the high of the day. For the entire duration of the trade—seven trading sessions—that high was not seen again. The price steadily broke lower until 10-24-02 where, according to the chart, profit was taken at 11109.5. Coincidently, the exit price also happened to be at an extreme—the absolute low of the day, but we won't complicate the point by dwelling on that. Let's just stay with the fact that our software is showing a theoretical profit of $1,203.13 per contract. It's saying we actually pulled the entry trigger and were rewarded.

In reality, though, as any veteran can tell you, if your limit order is touched but not penetrated, it probably wasn't filled. Think of the order as being a mere fraction of a (sometimes huge) buy or sell pool. Some of the clamoring sellers will be filled but most will not. Most popular software considers all such questionable scenarios to be done deals.

What's especially troubling is, by definition, we can only be talking about disputed winning trades. Any time a trade goes negative, it has penetrated our limit threshold and would therefore (correctly) show up in our performance history. Such tallying of potentially bogus profit is not good if we want to maintain a hardnosed policy of—if anything—underestimating our probable success. What to do?

TABLE 21.1 Second High/Low Exit—Daily—01-02-01 through 11-19-05

	Net Profit	# Trades	% Profit	Profit/Trade	Max. DD	ROA
S&P (Full)	$221,475	199	54.27%	$1,112.94	$36,425	608.0
NASD (Full)	$113,100	198	50.51%	$571.21	$56,500	200.2
Russell (Full)	$228,650	204	57.35%	$1,120.83	$57,500	1,997.0
30-Yr. Bonds	$14,875	161	49.07%	$92.39	$14,906	99.8
10-Yr. Notes	$8,672	169	49.70%	$51.31	$8,641	100.4
5-Yr. Notes	$11,938	180	51.11%	$66.32	$5,766	207.0
Japanese Yen	($10,100)	181	45.86%	($55.80)	$17,188	NA
Euro Currency	$22,225	198	52.02%	$112.25	$18,313	121.4
Swiss Franc	($6,450)	204	41.67%	($31.62)	$18,475	NA

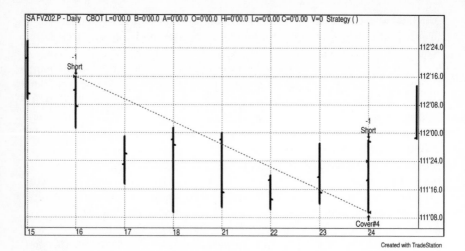

SA FVZ02.P - Daily   CBOT L=0'00.0 B=0'00.0 A=0'00.0 O=0'00.0 Hi=0'00.0 Lo=0'0.00 C=0'0.00 V=0 Strategy ( )

FIGURE 21.3 Daily Five-Year Notes: Would This Trade Have Been Executed? (*Source:* © TradeStation Technologies, Inc. 1991–2006. All rights reserved.)

We can set up a theoretical environment that is slightly more punishing than what we'll actually do in the real world. If we want to buy something at yesterday's low, we'll code it as yesterday's low minus one tick. If we want to sell yesterday's high, it's yesterday's high plus one tick. For any limit, decide the actual intended price, and then compensate in testing by "buying" one tick lower or "selling" one higher. The orders, however, will be placed at our original levels.

From here, there is no disputing any of the trades we'll actually execute. If we're showing a buy fill at one tick lower than the open minus 33 percent of the average three day range, then any order *right at* the open minus 33 percent of the range had to be filled. The exchanges guarantee penetrated orders. One exception is when the "fast market" sign is posted, and the other is the New York markets. For some reason, they don't seem to be held to certain industry standards.

Actually, we do continue to have a zone of uncertainty, only now it involves potential winners that are *not* showing. We're now witnessing only a portion of the original level orders that will be filled—all those that went at least a tick beyond (to our new levels). Failure to meet that criterion means the trade didn't register as a theoretical fill—software is regarding it as having fallen a tick short of the limit. Our actual order placement will be one tick "easier," however, and therefore, some of those touched-but-not-penetrated orders will be filled.

We're now not counting only the questionable trades that took off in the profit direction without ever looking back. Any other trade would

TABLE 21.2 Second High/Low Exit with Extra Tick/Slippage Penalty—
01-02-01 through 11-19-05

	Net Profit	# Trades	% Profit	Profit/Trade	Max. DD	ROA
S&P (Full)*	$221,475	199	54.27%	$1,112.94	$36,425	608.0
NASD (Full)**	$113,100	198	50.51%	$571.21	$56,500	200.2
Russell (Full)**	$228,650	204	57.35%	$1,120.83	$57,500	397.7
30-Yr. Bonds***	$14,875	161	49.07%	$92.39	$14,906	99.8
10-Yr. Notes***	$8,672	169	49.70%	$51.31	$8,641	100.4
5-Yr. Notes***	$11,938	180	51.11%	$66.32	$5,766	207.0
Japanese Yen****	($10,100)	181	45.86%	($55.80)	$17,188	NA
Euro Currency****	$22,225	198	52.02%	$112.25	$18,313	121.4
Swiss Franc****	($23,763)	200	40.50%	($68.81)	$24,988	NA

*Dock $50 **Dock $100 ***Dock $62.50 ****Dock $25

have, at some time, dipped below our theoretical buy or above our sell. They would have registered. This is a preferable scenario to having only tallied controversial winners. The performance summaries now have to be at least as good as they're showing, and probably better. It is consistent with our hardnosed skeptical aspirations.

We have to make one further adjustment, though, since we are claiming to enter one tick better than we actually will. We have to add the tick to our slippage commission line (that is, dock it from our profit). Also, since this system uses limits for exits (profit targets) as well as entries, we have to subtract another tick. Each trade is now docked two total ticks. Sometimes, stop exits will be involved, meaning two ticks are slightly more punishing than necessary, but we're close enough. It is now not as easy to come up with eye-popping numbers, but if we retain enough of our robustness, we should be on solid ground.

Table 21.2 shows the system can withstand the weight of the penalty. Given the relatively few trades involved, it's not surprising that our results aren't that different. There are, however, situations where the adjustment will be hugely significant, particularly in frequently-signaling intraday ideas we'll explore later. Many systems will blow up under the weight of the added scrutiny. Better to know it now before actual money is committed.

CHAPTER 22

Other Applications of the Two High/Low Exit Technique (Live! As It Happens!)

This book is kind of an organic exercise. I developed most of the enclosed techniques before I started writing it. Still, as I'm backtracking and retesting, I'm finding myself being drawn into new research pathways as one idea leads to another. (Just like any other time I'm sitting in front of testing software.) The book is feeding the research, which is feeding the book and back again. Therefore, as thematically incorrect as this might be, I want to sidetrack for a moment and further explore the exit techniques of the preceding section. Bear with me, I haven't done much with this to date, and I'm kind of getting swept up in the uncharted waters.

It never hurts to return to basics—in this case, a stripped-down momentum idea. Straight momentum ideas are at best an echo of what they once were. Maybe their relative ineffectiveness can be traced to the widespread publicity. (I still maintain that almost no one properly follows systems to the point where they could impact a performance pool, but perhaps I'll have to concede exceptions for some of the basic, hyperpublicized bellwethers.)

Maybe our new exit strategy is the driver that can re-energize the methodology. This does fly in the face of "profit-targets-reduce-bottom-lines" but maybe we've lucked into an exception. The pathway to effective mechanical system trading is seldom straight or unambiguous. We'll reiterate that profit is attainable in our imperfect world.

Now for the system, which we'll call "2d high/low exit #2." If the close is above the 25-day closing average, buy at the open plus 50 percent of the three-day average range on a stop. Again, if Day 1's high is penetrated twice, use a limit order to exit on the higher high. If the market closes below the 25-day average of the lows, exit the next day at market. Vice versa for sells.

Table 22.1 gives us further confirmation that the dual high/low exit is quite the contributing ingredient. (No stone here.)

The "2d high/low exit #3" has the following buy command: if the close is higher than both the previous high, and the 40-day closing average, then buy at market. Exit the next day if the close is below the 40-day low and use the same profit objectives. Vice versa for sells. Table 22.2 provides still more fortification for the dual high/low concept.

Could we apply the theme to some sort of limit order entry? The 2d high/low exit #4 (Table 22.3) says that if the close is above the 40-day closing average, then buy tomorrow at the opening minus 50 percent of the three-day average range. The exits and stops (40 days) are the same.

Some pretty impressive numbers—profits per trade ranging in the thousands, percentage profits hitting 60 percent or better . . . these aren't

TABLE 22.1　2d High/Low #2—Daily—01-02-01 through 11-19-05

	Net Profit	# Trades	% Profit	Profit/Trade	Max. DD	ROA
S&P (Full)	$166,250	234	43.59%	$710.47	$29,825	557.4
NASD (Full)	$88,650	229	43.67%	$387.12	$80,800	109.7
Russell (Full)	$174,500	241	43.15%	$724.07	$44,225	394.6
30-Yr. Bonds	$10,094	217	41.94%	$46.51	$15,094	66.9
10-Yr. Notes	$8,890	217	41.47%	$40.97	$13,438	66.2
5-Yr. Notes	$16,578	213	42.72%	$77.83	$4,641	357.2
Japanese Yen	($8,250)	188	40.96%	($43.88)	$19,750	NA
Euro Currency	$14,950	214	43.93%	$69.86	$23,713	63.1
Swiss Franc	($213)	208	41.83%	($1.02)	$16,338	NA

TABLE 22.2　2d High/Low #3—01-02-01 through 11-19-05

	Net Profit	# Trades	% Profit	Profit/Trade	Max. DD	ROA
S&P (Full)	$57,800	97	55.67%	$595.88	$33,525	172.4
NASD (Full)	$49,550	99	55.56%	$500.51	$43,750	113.3
Russell (Full)	$162,075	124	58.06%	$1,307.06	$31,650	512.1
30-Yr. Bonds	($7,625)	107	48.60%	($71.26)	$12,344	NA
10-Yr. Notes	$9,859	101	54.46%	$97.62	$7,531	130.9
5-Yr. Notes	$3,625	94	56.38%	$38.56	$4,422	82.0
Japanese Yen	$1,050	99	51.52%	$10.61	$21,563	4.9
Euro Currency	$35,125	95	55.79%	$369.76	$12,900	272.3
Swiss Franc	$7,225	100	52.00%	$72.25	$14,488	49.9

TABLE 22.3 2d High/Low #4—Limit Orders—01-02-01 through 11-19-05

	Net Profit	# Trades	% Profit	Profit/Trade	Max. DD	ROA
S&P (Full)	$183,775	99	63.64%	$1,856.31	$27,800	661.1
NASD (Full)	$187,650	94	64.89%	$1,996.28	$78,950	237.7
Russell (Full)	$146,500	140	58.57%	$1,046.43	$49,675	294.9
30-Yr. Bonds	($5,594)	101	52.48%	($55.38)	$18,656	NA
10-Yr. Notes	$16,359	83	59.04%	$197.10	$4,922	332.4
5-Yr. Notes	$13,969	98	59.18%	$142.54	$4,656	300.0
Japanese Yen	$10,900	118	57.63%	$92.37	$16,863	64.6
Euro Currency	$29,712	104	54.81%	$285.70	$11,400	260.6
Swiss Franc	$12,038	97	53.61%	$124.10	$10,550	114.1

the kinds of numbers you normally expect in limit order systems. A quick eyeballing tells us we'll be able to apply the earlier discussed tick/slippage handicap with no problem.

Buy lower, buy higher—it doesn't matter much. One can easily imagine entering in a variety of spots, taking some of the bunch-up out of our profit and loss streaks. This all helps make our trading world a little less scary, a little more affirming, and a little more doable. We'll take every little fortifying edge we can find.

CHAPTER 23

On Further Optimization, Market Drift, and Virgin Data

L et's re-examine some of the differences of prudent versus foolhardy testing. There's a reason I include nine financial markets in just about every test I run. (We'll view more specialized index-specific ideas later, but forget that for the moment.) Additional market confirmation supports the case for robustness. I want my primary trading markets, whether intended to be the S&Ps, the bonds, or whatever, to have stellar projections. Remember, you can only approximate through your summaries what you will ultimately generate. Normally, performance will fall short of projection.

I also want my idea to work reasonably well in related markets—I don't want to see a yen system lose in the franc, for instance, or a 30-year bond system blow up in the 10-year. I don't demand that all nine markets always confirm across the board, but I'd like to see at least some degree of success in most of them.

I'll always prefer to have a variable working well-to-very-well across the array than one working ridiculously well in one and not at all anywhere else. That wouldn't give me much confidence for the future. I always want more corroboration rather than less. All other things being equal, 20 markets agreeing are better than 10. Ten years of confirmation are better than five. If we're only targeting five years, it might mean that we don't consider all other things equal—market drift might get in the way, for example, if our testing field is too lengthy. But seeing something perform brilliantly over five years and also hold up okay in the prior five is preferable to recent spectacular performances preceded by years of losses. Any analyst will concede that.

One of the worst things we could do is custom fit our testing to each individual market. We'll always uncover standout numbers that way, but to what degree would random chance be entering the equation? We'll never be able to definitively answer that, but we can rest assured that we're increasing the chance element by specializing rather than universalizing our variables.

Imagine four different coin toss experiments taking place in different rooms. One uses a penny, one a nickel, one a dime and one a quarter. Each will involve 100 flips of the coin. We're going to pretend we don't know the logistics of any of the coins, we're ignorant about probabilities—in short, we're unaware that all the tests are equally random. (We'll just assume for the sake of argument that none of the coins are weighted.)

If we were like aliens, coming in cold, trying to find characteristics of coin tossing, might we erroneously conclude that the denomination of each coin is a big determining factor? Odds are that any given 100 flips will not come up exactly 50 heads and 50 tails. What if the penny yielded 52 heads and the nickel produced 57 tails? Would we be assigning unique and near opposite characteristics to each—in effect, making the penny a "long indicator" and the nickel a "short" one?

We'd be better off doing 400 flips and regarding all the coins as part of the same experiment. Then, after we maybe got slightly weighted results, we'd do better to run it again. A third time would make us even more fortified, a fourth better still and so on.

One of the points of contention I encountered in the course of writing *Market Beaters* concerned the eternal nature of markets, or lack of it. Some of the interviewees maintained that they were using systems they'd developed years earlier without modification. Their reasoning was, once you find the wheel, there is no point re-inventing it.

There is something to be said about system traders standing firm and rigid regarding their methodologies. To do otherwise would be to veer closer to typical spontaneous trader behavior—jumping back and forth among "hot" systems and advisors—a dog forever chasing its tail. Too much strategy change is another way of saying too little faith or fortification. If all systems have losing periods—often uncomfortably lengthy ones—what sense does it make to jump ship just because we're feeling market heat? Market pressure is everywhere, including within the systems we're likely to be drawn toward.

Chances are another system will tempt us because it is making money at the same time we are losing. "Let's go with the winner!" But again, everything is susceptible to drawdowns. If a losing streak gets you ever closer to your next breakout winner, the opposite is also true—

a hot hand is maybe the last thing you want to coat-tail. The drawdown may be more likely to hit the barn-burning system and cease on your faltering one.

There is a debate among system traders regarding the most logical times to press or to pull in the horns. Should you feel better entering a system trade after it racked up five winners in a row or five losers? Some portfolio managers eject systems that have been losing for the previous year or two. Others, by contrast, scale back on those that have been performing better than expected—the obvious reason being such systems are more likely to swing back to an underperforming norm. Some ventured still another viewpoint—that recent system performance can't provide any clues at all regarding portfolio allocation.

Just about everyone agreed that systems should be staying within certain bounds extrapolated from research, and that it was reasonable to jettison any that were exceeding the limits. The flip side is that a system shouldn't be considered broken if it is within the projected realm and tamper-prone traders would do better to manage their own anxieties.

That doesn't exactly answer the issue of market drift, though. In a macro sense, we're always playing the same game. There are eternally valid market forces such as momentum. Human psychology doesn't change in a broad sense—it's always the same fear and greed dance.

Finer system points, however, may be another story. Systems are optimized and certain variables are selected as logical robust choices. Time passes, and while the system is holding up in a broad sense, the operator might notice that substituting a "three" for the long-favored "five" would have doubled profits in the last year.

From 1982–1985, there was not one day in which the S&Ps had a range of ten points or more. In 1999, a mere ten trading days came in *under* that benchmark. Clearly, some conditions do change. The debate is over whether given aspects are at the heart of our market understanding, or merely superfluous irrelevancies.

Roughly half of the *Market Beaters* group advocated periodic reoptimization. Many retested annually. The rote nature of the process keeps it mechanical and different from the classic gut trading behavior of haphazardly retooling because of trading anxiety.

How well does periodic reoptimization work? Is there any kind of simulation we can do to answer that to our own satisfaction? The answer could be found within a resource we haven't yet discussed—the concept of virgin data.

Testing is a process of continuous retrofitting. We conceive an idea complete with mechanical rules. We write a formula for it and run it in a data field. From there, we constantly readjust so that our results go first from losers to winners, and then from winners to bigger winners. We're trying to be careful not to overuse hindsight, but we can't completely eliminate it, or we'd have no answers at all. Every variable that gets bigger or smaller is doing so because of how the formulas are responding to trades that would have happened in the past.

An acid test that often caps off a system study is to forward test through data that was not used as part of the optimization process. Usually, the most recent time frame is left out of the original testing sample. Say today is November 1, 2005. Someone might then test an inter-day trading system from January 1999 through December 2004. After doing all the expected testing steps and coming up with the final numbers, the researcher then runs the idea though 2005. Remember, this historical segment had no decision-related impact regarding whether to make this variable larger, this one smaller, etc. It's virgin data—a time frame that is, for all practical purposes, as unknowable as the future.

In the course of writing for online web sites such as TigerShark, I have presented hypothetical testing scenarios that have surprised me on occasion. One example is how consistently profitable results can be generated in one year's worth of virgin data off a previous five-year history. It seems to fly somewhat in the face of not getting overly cute and market specific with numbers. It's hard to argue, though, with what the following exercise is showing us.

Specifically, for illustrative purposes, we're looking at our original first three either-or indicators. Again, long biases result from the following (and as always, vice versa for shorts):

1. **The close being above the 40-day close.** We'll optimize this variable from 5 to 50 in 5-point increments. We'll assign this variable "E."

2. **The two-day average close being below the five-day.** We'll go from 2 to 4 on the smaller with a 1 increment. We'll do two tests on the larger—either 5 or 10. The variables are "N" and "P" respectively.

3. **The highest close of the last 50 days occurring before the lowest.** We'll again go from 5 to 50 in 5 multiples (variable "Q").

The above combination will yield 600 total tests for each data block. We're testing for best return on account. The top performers of the 1998–2002 time frame are then plugged into the virgin year 2003.

The 1999–2003 data is likewise optimized, and those numbers are applied to 2004. All testing blocks are five years long, and all resulting figures stem from the single-year virgin blocks. Table 23.1, in other words, contains nothing but results that occurred in a simulated "future." The left four columns show which numbers topped each optimization run.

This may not be a definitive result, but it sure seems to be giving weight to the "periodically reoptimize" argument. A key to this, though, is having robust indicators to start with. Let's re-cap what we've done.

We identified individual market biases. We ensured some degree of robustness by making the same idea positively perform over a reasonable time frame in an array of markets. We assembled the building blocks, careful not to muddy the waters with additional features we hadn't tested prior.

In an acknowledgement of market drift, we've allowed ourselves to change parameters within our principles without radically altering the principles themselves. We're not testing in a way that, for example, supports momentum in some places while refuting it in others. Part of the exercise's success may lie in the fact that whether we ultimately hit a best scenario or second, third, or maybe eighth best, nevertheless we'll see positive results. The system intrinsically has that kind of give.

It would be reasonable at this time to ask the following question.

"Okay, great. We can churn out positive virgin numbers by making them conform to our 'drivers' (understanding of market dynamics), keeping our tests pure and uncontaminated by extraneous components. But how do these results compare with, say, how we would have done had we never changed our optimized numbers from our original starting point?" (Year 2001.)

Good question. Table 23.2 shows how we would have done moving our 2001 variables forever forward.

"Holy Toledo!" you might say. "What's the point of reoptimizing every year? The original 2001 results across the board are far superior!" And that *would* be a terrific comfort—provided we knew ahead of time that 1996–2000 was the magical data bank to use.

This is part of what is deceptive about imagining in hindsight that we invented a wheel that we then let roll on forever. While it's true that we're still looking at virgin data summaries when we leave 2000 variables unaltered for four years, the "2000-as-Ground-Zero" part of the equation is arbitrary. What if 1998 was the year we developed our eternal variables off 1993–1997 data? Table 23.3 shows our 2001–2005 S&P results using 1989 optimized numbers (from the 1984–1988 data bank).

In this case, we would have done better had we updated every year. Other historical "constants" could be faring far worse. Reoptimizing annually may not produce the best numbers we can generate in hindsight,

TABLE 23.1 One-Year Virgin Data Results Off Five-Year Data Samples

S&P	E	N	P	Q	Virgin Net	# Trades	% Profit	Profit/Trade	Max. DD	ROA
2001	50	2	10	30	$83,063	248	52.82%	$334.93	$33,950	245.0
2002	50	2	10	30	$37,325	252	50.40%	$148.12	$59,600	62.6
2003	50	2	10	30	$20,425	252	52.38%	$81.05	$24,950	81.9
2004	50	2	10	30	($15,550)	252	51.59%	($61.71)	$30,850	NA
2005	30	2	10	25	$850	224	44.20%	$3.79	$29,150	2.9
Totals					**$126,113**	**1,228**				
NASD										
2001	40	3	5	30	($73,750)	248	47.98%	($297.38)	$145,550	NA
2002	15	3	5	15	$80,900	251	52.59%	$322.31	$14,250	568.0
2003	15	3	5	15	($19,200)	251	47.81%	($76.49)	$41,050	NA
2004	40	3	5	15	($7,900)	252	48.81%	($31.25)	$31,600	NA
2005	40	3	5	15	($41,700)	224	43.30%	($186.16)	$44,550	NA
Totals					**($61,650)**	**1,226**				
Russell										
2001	45	4	10	50	$28,950	247	51.82%	$117.21	$33,725	85.8
2002	20	2	5	10	$8,675	252	50.40%	$34.42	$39,325	22.1
2003	20	2	5	10	$20,125	251	49.80%	$80.18	$29,150	69.0
2004	25	3	10	10	$19,550	252	49.21%	$77.58	$36,125	54.1
2005	25	3	10	10	$51,000	224	53.57%	$227.68	$28,900	176.0
Totals					**$128,300**	**1,226**				
30-Year Bonds										
2001	10	4	10	50	$9,281	249	50.20%	$37.27	$10,625	87.4
2002	15	3	5	20	($3,563)	249	48.19%	($14.31)	$12,250	NA
2003	20	4	5	50	($5,125)	248	47.58%	($20.67)	$8,406	NA
2004	30	3	5	50	$5,938	249	50.60%	$23.85	$6,906	86.0
2005	30	2	5	20	($4,562)	221	48.87%	($20.64)	$6,125	NA
Totals					**$1,969**	**1,216**				
10-Yr. Notes										
2001	5	3	10	45	$6,594	249	51.41%	$26.48	$4,781	138.0
2002	15	3	10	45	$3,047	250	49.20%	$12.19	$7,781	39.2

Year										
2003	35	3	10	45	($125)	249	51.00%	($0.50)	$7,016	NA
2004	35	2	5	45	$8,250	249	55.82%	$33.13	$4,188	197.0
2005	35	2	5	45	$7,141	221	49.77%	$32.13	$1,781	401.0
Totals					**$24,907**	**1,218**				
5-Yr. Notes										
2001	5	3	5	45	$1,250	249	46.59%	$5.02	$3,188	39.2
2002	15	3	10	45	($31)	252	46.03%	($0.12)	$8,063	NA
2003	35	3	5	45	$10,563	250	55.60%	$47.00	$1,891	559.0
2004	35	3	5	45	($2,469)	249	53.82%	($9.91)	$4,891	NA
2005	35	2	5	45	$1,500	221	49.32%	$6.79	$2,563	58.5
Totals					**$10,813**	**1,221**				
Japanese Yen										
2001	40	2	5	45	($1,438)	250	47.60%	($5.75)	$9,175	NA
2002	40	3	5	45	($5,150)	250	47.60%	($20.60)	$12,225	NA
2003	30	2	5	45	$4,875	248	49.19%	$19.66	$6,750	72.2
2004	10	3	5	50	$7,388	249	50.60%	$29.67	$6,400	115.0
2005	25	2	5	50	$8,725	221	53.85%	$39.48	$4,138	211.0
Totals					**$14,400**	**1,218**				
Euro Currency										
2001	*									
2002	*									
2003	*									
2004	5	2	5	50	$3,475	249	50.60%	$13.96	$7,863	44.2
2005	5	2	5	50	$1,650	221	49.32%	$7.47	$8,063	20.5
Totals					**$5,125**	**470**				
Swiss Franc										
2001	15	2	10	45	($1,500)	250	45.60%	($6.00)	$5,913	NA
2002	15	2	10	40	($9,388)	251	43.43%	($37.40)	$10,838	NA
2003	5	2	5	10	($2,113)	249	49.00%	($8.48)	$8,825	NA
2004	5	2	10	10	$3,175	249	50.60%	$12.75	$6,213	51.1
2005	5	2	5	10	($5,125)	221	48.42%	($23.19)	$10,750	NA
Totals					**($14,951)**	**1,220**				

*Full data not available—contract was introduced in 1999.

TABLE 23.2 Using 2001 Optimized Numbers for Entire History

S&P	E	N	P	Q	Net	# Trades	% Profit	Profit/Trade	Max. DD	ROA
2001	50	2	10	30	$83,063	248	52.82%	$334.93	$33,950	245.0
2002	50	2	10	30	$58,275	252	50.79%	$231.25	$35,450	164.0
2003	50	2	10	30	$20,425	252	52.38%	$81.05	$24,950	81.9
2004	50	2	10	30	($15,550)	252	51.59%	($61.71)	$30,850	NA
2005	50	2	10	30	$850	224	44.20%	$3.79	$29,150	2.9
Totals					**$147,063**	**1,228**				
NASD										
2001	40	3	5	30	$500	252	48.79%	($243.75)	$92,750	NA
2002	40	3	5	30	$89,700	251	53.39%	$357.37	$16,550	542.0
2003	40	3	5	30	($8,700)	251	47.41%	($34.66)	$32,850	NA
2004	40	3	5	30	($7,900)	252	48.81%	($31.25)	$31,600	NA
2005	40	3	5	30	($41,700)	224	43.30%	($186.16)	$44,550	NA
Totals					**$31,900**	**1,230**				
Russell										
2001	45	4	10	50	$28,950	247	51.82%	$117.21	$33,725	85.8
2002	45	4	10	50	$22,925	252	51.19%	$90.97	$47,925	47.8
2003	45	4	10	50	($16,875)	251	46.22%	($67.23)	$44,275	NA
2004	45	4	10	50	$120,550	252	54.37%	$54.37	$31,825	379.0
2005	45	4	10	50	$18,625	224	52.21%	$82.41	$52,850	35.2
Totals					**$174,175**	**1,226**				
Thirty-Year Bonds										
2001	10	4	10	50	$9,281	249	50.20%	$37.27	$10,625	87.4
2002	10	4	10	50	$2,125	249	49.40%	$8.53	$12,750	16.7
2003	10	4	10	50	$10,438	248	50.00%	$42.09	$8,875	118.0
2004	10	4	10	50	$3,313	249	47.79%	$13.30	$9,000	36.8
2005	10	4	10	50	$1,563	221	46.61%	$7.07	$6,656	23.5
Totals					**$26,720**	**1,216**				
Ten-Year Notes										
2001	5	3	10	45	$6,594	249	51.41%	$26.48	$4,781	138.0
2002	5	3	10	45	($1,891)	250	46.80%	($7.56)	$10,000	NA

2003	5	3	10	45	($5,375)	249	47.39%	($21.59)	$8,672	NA
2004	5	3	10	45	($4,032)	249	47.39%	($16.19)	$9,813	NA
2005	5	3	10	45	$5,422	221	49.32%	$24.53	$2,125	255.0
Totals					**$718**	**1,218**				
5-Yr Notes										
2001	5	3	5	45	$1,250	249	46.59%	$5.02	$3,188	39.2
2002	5	3	5	45	$688	252	45.63%	$2.73	$5,234	13.1
2003	5	3	5	45	$4,531	250	51.60%	$18.13	$2,844	159.0
2004	5	3	5	45	($7,656)	249	46.59%	($30.75)	$8,234	NA
2005	5	3	5	45	$2,313	221	50.68%	$10.46	$2,453	94.3
Totals					**$1,126**	**1,221**				
Japanese Yen										
2001	40	2	5	45	($1,438)	250	47.60%	($5.75)	$9,175	NA
2002	40	2	5	45	$150	250	49.60%	$0.60	$10,100	1.5
2003	40	2	5	45	$5,725	248	49.60%	$23.08	$4,450	129.0
2004	40	2	5	45	$7,462	249	52.61%	$29.97	$4,288	174.0
2005	40	2	5	45	$3,075	221	51.58%	$13.91	$6,063	50.7
Totals					**$14,974**	**1,218**				
Euro Currency										
2001	*									
2002	*									
2003	*									
2004	5	2	5	50	$22,125	249	55.42%	$88.86	$8,875	249.0
2005	5	2	5	50	$6,925	221	55.20%	$31.33	$10,600	65.3
Totals					**$29,050**	**470**				
Swiss Franc										
2001	15	2	10	45	($1,500)	250	45.60%	($6.00)	$5,913	NA
2002	15	2	10	45	($11,613)	251	41.83%	($46.25)	$12,763	NA
2003	15	2	10	45	$2,288	249	49.40%	$9.19	$5,450	42.0
2004	15	2	10	45	($3,950)	249	48.19%	($15.86)	$6,838	NA
2005	15	2	10	45	$8,350	221	55.66%	$37.78	$5,563	150.0
Totals					**($6,425)**	**1,220**				

*Insufficient data—contract introduced in 1999.

TABLE 23.3 1989 Optimized S&P Numbers in 2001–2005

S&P	E	N	P	Q	Net	# Trades	% Profit	Profit/Trade	Max. DD	ROA
2001	5	4	5	25	$51,063	248	54.44%	$205.90	$36,800	139.1
2002	5	4	5	25	$21,625	252	50.40%	$85.81	$33,750	64.1
2003	5	4	5	25	($36,775)	252	48.02%	($145.93)	$59,575	NA
2004	5	4	5	25	$39,800	252	52.78%	$157.94	$11,025	361.0
2005	5	4	5	25	($5,700)	224	45.54%	($25.45)	$36,400	NA
Totals					$70,013	1,228				

but that's precisely the point. They give us serviceable results that we did not obtain by cheating.

Other parts of the optimization process are not as easy to demonstrate in such an objective fashion. Remember, when you're testing across several markets, you'll want to estimate which numbers would adequately serve the entire field. There is also some validity also to adjusting numbers according to sectors. We'll examine that in more depth later.

CHAPTER 24

"The Best System in the World"— (If Only!)

Popular software allows you to optimize for different factors. As noted, my preference is usually the "return on account (ROA)," which again is the net profit divided by the worst drawdown times 100. That's the function that's been behind our posted studies. The best performer, second best, and so forth are in ROA terms.

Sometimes the best ROA is also the best net profit, but not always. You see particular divergence when you're doing heavy filtering. As your total number of trades shrinks, so do the chances that the net profit will be huge. As a reminder, though, we'd rather see a system that makes $40,000 with an $8,000 worst drawdown than one that makes $100,000 and $80,000 respectively. You'd be both richer and safer trading three contracts on the former than one on the latter ($120,000 profit on $24,000 risk).

As you begin incorporating different objectives and trying to solve a bigger array of problems, you may find yourself testing for different criteria. Does your idea tend to occur infrequently enough that you're questioning its statistical validity? Your concern then is to make it less targeted and specific. At least some of your optimization studies might incorporate the "total number of trades" preference. Are you going to be changing your position size based on a given number of winners or losers in a row? You'll obviously find relevance in the number of times you get such unbroken strings. You might select the number of winning or losing trades or perhaps the average winning or losing trade function.

I've spent time pondering the implications of biases occurring over many, many intraday trades. (Sometimes hundreds of thousands of them!) Then I'm forced to move from theory to practice. You have to be able to make enough per trade to overcome slippage/commission. If you're doing limit orders, you have to adjust for the theoretical trades that won't be hit in reality, as we demonstrated earlier.

Still, if I see a big enough bias, I tend to want to find a way to tap into it. The overnight cups and cap strategy discussed earlier is one such example. The straight enter-on-close, exit-on-open version won't make enough money to overcome slippage commission. That aside, though, the formations demonstrate one of the most persistent and universal biases I've ever seen.

The difference between success and failure can come down to a couple ticks here and a couple there. I'm willing to ask all kinds of what-if questions. What if the slight barrier could be alleviated in the overnight session hours, say with the aid of limit orders that become market orders after a certain interval? Or maybe you can come out ahead by somehow mechanically skipping certain trades if you find there are enough ticks elsewhere to more than offset the difference.

What if we filter the condition a bit—the cup has to be low enough or high enough relative to a month's worth of prices for example. Maybe the actual shape of the cup could be differently defined—make the cup look more like a wine glass with a long Day 2 stem coming out the bottom. Any number of possibilities. I don't understand people who are so knee-jerk dismissive over this type of theorizing. It can't hurt to keep re-examining new outside-the-box what-ifs, particularly when they're screaming at you, "Yes, this is a *most* persistent bias!"

Maybe other analysts have so many good ideas they don't have to mess with anything unorthodox. Or maybe I'm just crazy. As for why I haven't just rolled up my shirtsleeves and done definitive studies myself— they're a bit beyond me, as much as I hate admitting that. There would have to be some manual walkthroughs supplementing the stuff I can program. That's not to say I won't get around to it.

Suppose one were to trade, not according to expectations about the market's next move—up or down—but rather, according to an idealized market blueprint? (I guess I'm getting precariously close here to veering off the 100 percent mechanical trading pathway despite being such a committed advocate. But don't panic, we're just brainstorming here.) It's not hard to generate such idealized blueprints. The challenge will be in converting them into a tradeable reality.

My latest Rubik's Cube (five out of six sides in alignment!) trades off one-minute bars in the emini S&Ps. Between 8:45 and 2:55 CDT, buy at the open of every bar minus the average five bar open-to-low. Sell short every bar at open plus the five bar average high-minus-open. Exit at 3:00. Use limit orders. Do it all day long. Knock yourself out.

You get many, many trades. Figure 24.1 shows the nonstop action.

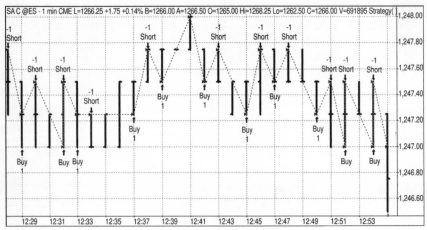

FIGURE 24.1 Many Theoretical Buys and Sells with Mega System: 1 Minute Emini S&Ps (*Source:* © TradeStation Technologies, Inc. 1991–2006. All rights reserved.)

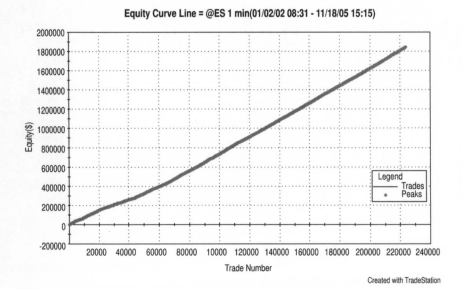

FIGURE 24.2 Mega System Equity Graph: Emini S&Ps (*Source:* © TradeStation Technologies, Inc. 1991–2006. All rights reserved.)

There are a lot of quick up and back movements—sometimes at advantageous levels, sometimes not. Overall, the cumulative buys appear to be lower than the sells. You can see very similar results no matter where you scroll throughout the field.

Figure 24.2 displays an equity graph—the progress of your account from Day 1. Not a hiccup anywhere. A solid upsloping 45 degree line. Perfect looking—like the monolith in *2001*.

Then we come to our magical performance summary. Table 24.1 shows the results from January 2002 through November 19, 2005. This time, we're including a $5 commission per trade, the TradeStation fee as of this writing. It would be pretty absurd to leave it out of this particular demonstration as it encompasses such a big percentage of each trade.

Even over and above that, we have a blueprint for theoretical perfec-

TABLE 24.1 Mega System—One-Minute Bars—$5 Commission per Trade. January 02 through 11-19-05

Total Net Profit	$1,840,357.50	Profit Factor	2.13
Gross Profit	$3,471,697.50	Gross Loss	($1,631,340.00)
Total Number of Trades	222,926	Percent Profitable	69.42%
Winning Trades	154,758	Losing Trades	68,168
Even Trades	0		
Avg. Trade Net Profit	$8.26	Ratio Avg. Win:Avg. Loss	0.94
Avg. Winning Trade	$22.43	Avg. Losing Trade	($23.93)
Largest Winning Trade	$507.50	Largest Losing Trade	($755.00)
Max. Consecutive Winning Trades	47	Max. Consecutive Losing Trades	20
Avg. Bars in Winning Trades	2.22	Avg. Bars in Losing Trades	3.46
Avg. Bars in Total Trades	2.60		
Max. Shares/Contracts Held	1	Account Size Required	$2,947.50
Return on Initial Capital	1,840.36%	Annual Rate of Return	76.48%
Return Retracement Ratio	1.30	RINA Index	478,469.64
Trading Period	3 Yrs, 10 Mths, 15 Dys, 5 Hrs, 53 Mins	Percent of Time in the Market	20.63%
Max. Equity Run-up	$1,840,520.00		
Max. Drawdown (Intraday Peak to Valley)		**Max. Drawdown (Trade Close to Trade Close)**	
Value	($3,022.50)	Value	($2,947.50)
Net Profit as % of Drawdown	60,888.59%	Net Profit as % of Drawdown	62,437.91%

Source: © TradeStation Technologies, Inc. 1991–2006. All rights reserved.

tion. The worst giveback throughout the history would have been $3023 on an intraday peak-to-valley basis. Sixty-nine percent of the trades would have been profitable. You'd average $8.26 profit-per-trade over nearly a quarter of a million of them. This is the kind of pain-free utopia that could make traders out of even the least risk-adverse among us.

But upon returning to the profit-per-trade line, we understand the crux of our dilemma. It's not that we're going to have skids—we're flipping positions all day long on limit orders. The problem lies with our recurring "touched-but-not-filled" issue. How many of these pristine trades are going to actually occur? What happens to the ones that don't materialize? How will we handle being positioned the wrong way when a "theoretical flip" is not actualized? How and for how long? How and when do we cry "uncle"? (Maybe we should ask Dr. Discretionary.)

Table 24.1 contains clues as to how much "give" we'd have. You can compute how many trades you could expect per day and how much profit you'd average on each. You'd have idealized objectives. Real-world trading would fall short, but could you use various tricks to stay in the ballpark?

How much could we be helped by keeping orders alive for up to 10 minutes after the prices are touched but not penetrated? Let's say we leave them up even after later opposite orders are filled (thereby making us periodically long or short more than one unit). We can get away with coming back and "picking up our spares" for awhile, as Figure 24.3 demonstrates. All buys that were potentially but not necessarily filled on the first bar low would definitely have been executed within 10 bars down the line because there was always a subsequent bar that traded lower than the theoretical buy entry level. Similarly, within 10 bars of the sell entry, there was always at least one bar that took out the one minute short signal bar high. Again, it doesn't matter if we're sometimes filled out of sequence as long as we get our price penetration sometime within ten minutes. In the Figure 24.3 timeframe, therefore, our actual profit would exactly match our projected one.

Does this get us closer to "home free"? Not if the Figure 24.4 time frame is the more dominant reality. We now see the dark side of attempting to pick up spares. We tend to be the most wrong when the market is at its most relentless. It's racking up ever more theoretical shorts at successively lower levels, and in actual trade, we're undoubtedly missing some if not all of them.

Meanwhile, we have no problem executing the countertrending long orders as the market continues to march lower. We may have missed as many as seven shorts and finally been forced to offset seven corresponding actual longs near the low of the move.

Again, though, if there were some way to capture 20 or 10 or even 5

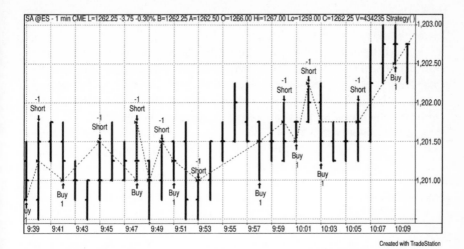

FIGURE 24.3 Mega System Emini S&Ps: All Buys and Sells Penetrated within 10 Bars (*Source:* © TradeStation Technologies, Inc. 1991–2006. All rights reserved.)

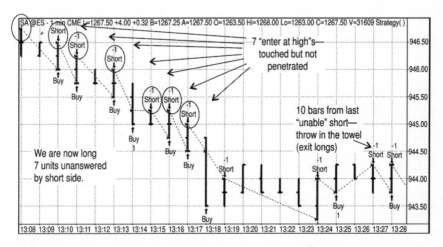

FIGURE 24.4 Mega System: Seven Sell Orders Touched But Not Penetrated (*Source:* © TradeStation Technologies, Inc. 1991–2006. All rights reserved.)

percent of the historic summary profits with, say, 10 times the drawdown, would you sign up? (Count me in, coach!) If there is such a route, it obviously lies in some sort of hybrid methodology. You allow yourself to get somewhat lopsided the wrong way, but you also have a rote way of chasing an escaped trade or skipping it under some circumstances or applying some sort of switch that identifies trending versus trading environments enabling two alternating approaches or trading some sort of matrix that lags behind the one you're seeing or . . .

It's a little much for me. Maybe "little" is the operative word, maybe not. It feels like it shouldn't be absolutely insurmountable but as we've observed, there is often a deceptiveness to "feel." Maybe my fellow technicians are right that there are better ways to spend our time. Still, if there is some genius out there who can make the necessary outside-the-box mental quantum leap—I'd like to hear from you. (Don't hesitate to call collect.)

CHAPTER 25

Targeting Sectors

The more inclusive and all-encompassing our testing is, the more faith we can have in the results. That means that one variable applying to all markets is more reliable than a group of variables each fitted to an individual one. The latter methodology will almost inevitably be doomed to failure.

Sector analysis falls in between the two scenarios as far as fortification. By choosing one variable for the currencies, another for the bonds, and a third for the indexes, we are increasing the chances that our results will be more a function of random chance than something portending consistent profit potential. There is no getting around that. The issue becomes, can we boost our profits enough so that in our weighting and balancing process, we can justify the decrease in reliability?

Obviously, we should first ask ourselves whether there is any justification at all to targeting sectors, or are we merely fooling ourselves in an attempt to ramp up numbers. There is controversy among the experts I've interviewed. Some of the **Beaters** remain consistently committed to the universality of their model. They have the wheel, the wheel rolls the same across all surfaces. Whatever else you can argue, you can't take away the fact that they are the least likely people to be fudging figures.

Others point to the different characteristics of, if not individual markets, at least market groups. One of the most widespread contentions I've encountered is that indexes—stock-market-related futures—are different from the entire remaining class of commodities. Commodities are more supply-demand driven. This makes intuitive sense when you consider a seasonal trek in the grains, for example—how all the agricultural participants tend to respond to typical evolving seasons. Indexes, by contrast, are more psychologically driven. That's also pretty hard to refute given the incendiary nature of Wall Street and the financial and political world arena in general. The other oft-heard appraisal is that commodities trend, and indexes countertrend. "Trend" can be an ambiguous concept here, but I'll add my two cents that it is easier to design breakout systems around the old traditional futures.

There are more individual characteristics that can be pinpointed than the mere difference between hard commodities and indexes. Nothing trends like the currencies. If you want to do well in that sector, you really ought to consider being very long-term in your approach. You can get good results with a very simple, widely used methodology—the opening price expansion. We'll resort to perhaps the most basic version of that most basic of methodologies—a perpetual system, always long or short—applied to a weekly bar chart:

Buy at Monday's opening price plus the previous week's range on a stop.

Sell short at Monday's opening price minus the previous week's range on a stop.

The big rub to achieving the Table 25.1 results is, again, we're trading it within weekly bars. That's a pretty wide range to be using without stops, but on the other hand, how much risk has been historically involved? In 23 years of yen trade, your worst single loss would have been $7,125. Your worst drawdown would have been under $18,000 compared to a $160,000 net profit. Granted we're leaving out slippage-commission in order to keep this comparable to our other posted skinnier biased-charts. Do the math, though—$100 per trade knocks a mere $21,000 off your total. You'd still be averaging $670 a trade on a contract whose minimum tick is worth $12.50.

When you're going with pure unadorned momentum, your risk eventually self-corrects. It would be a very cut-and-dried risk limit with N Day. Since the market could only go so far down before taking out the N Day low, endless bleeding is impossible. With our current range expansion, significant hemorrhaging isn't theoretically impossible (because you could still have the market go against you day after day in small increments that fall short of the reverse-range thresholds), but for all practical purposes, our risk is suitably limited. Probably sooner rather than later, the indicator will reverse in a relentlessly creeping or deteriorating market. This may seem self-evident, but it is not an automatic function that applies to all strategies. A big part of some of the systems my partner and I are using involves fading daily averages. For such methodologies, the worse a trade

TABLE 25.1 One Range Expansion: Weekly Yen—Contract Inception through 11-19-05

Total Net Profit	$160,287.50	Profit Factor	1.76
Gross Profit	$370,637.50	Gross Loss	($210,350.00)
Total Number of Trades	208	Percent Profitable	48.08%
Winning Trades	100	Losing Trades	108
Even Trades	0		
Avg. Trade Net Profit	$770.61	Ratio Avg. Win:Avg. Loss	1.90
Avg. Winning Trade	$3,706.38	Avg. Losing Trade	($1,947.69)
Largest Winning Trade	$20,775.00	Largest Losing Trade	($7,125.00)
Max. Consecutive Winning Trades	5	Max. Consecutive Losing Trades	6
Avg. Bars in Winning Trades	9.10	Avg. Bars in Losing Trades	4.74
Avg. Bars in Total Trades	6.84		
Max. Shares/Contracts Held	1	Account Size Required	$17,987.50
Return on Initial Capital	160.29%	Annual Rate of Return	4.07%
Return Retracement Ratio	0.08	RINA Index	101.66
Trading Period	23 Yrs, 5 Mths, 28 Dys	Percent of Time in the Market	99.92%
Max. Equity Run-up	n/a		
Max. Drawdown (Intraday Peak to Valley)		**Max. Drawdown (Trade Close to Trade Close)**	
Value	($20,825.00)	Value	($17,987.50)

Source: © TradeStation Technologies, Inc. 1991–2006. All rights reserved.

gets, the more the original entry signal *persists*. We're left with risk-related decisions that tend to be more arbitrary and therefore less satisfying.

Note that in Figure 25.1, there are some runs against you, but they don't approach the profit that would have resulted from the long entry at the beginning of August. It would be very hard for you to be trapped in a corresponding short without some successive day rallying enough to get you positioned the right way.

Figure 25.2 reveals a near-consistent 45-degree upslope from the contract's inception to the present.

For still more fortification, check out the yearly breakdown (Table 25.2).

Again, this idea is targeted to a perceived driver—namely that once a currency move starts, it will persist in a way that no other market does. If the results blew up in noncurrencies, we'd still have arguable results to consider. Surprisingly, we actually get do corroboration pretty much across the financial board as Table 25.3 reveals. True, our return on accounts might make risk prohibitive outside the currencies but we're not

FIGURE 25.1 Range Expansion: Yen Weekly Bar Chart (*Source:* © TradeStation Technologies, Inc. 1991–2006. All rights reserved.)

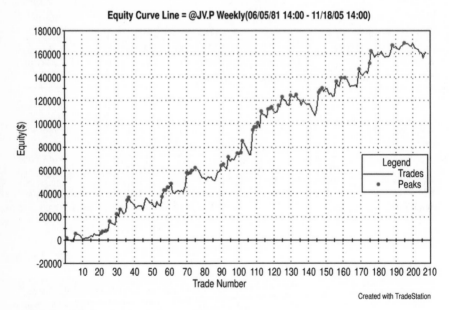

FIGURE 25.2 Range Expansion. Weekly Yen Equity Graph (*Source:* © TradeStation Technologies, Inc. 1991–2006. All rights reserved.)

TABLE 25.2 Range Expansion—Yen—Yearly Breakdown

	Net Profit	% Gain	Profit Factor	# Trades	% Profit
1982	$6,413	6.41%	2.76	6	66.67%
1983	($4,463)	-4.19%	0.21	9	22.22%
1984	$2,600	2.55%	2.02	8	62.50%
1985	$10,713	10.25%	6.99	7	51.14%
1986	$538	8.27%	2.17	10	40.00%
1987	$8,663	6.94%	1.65	11	45.45%
1988	$6,238	4.68%	1.49	12	50.00%
1989	$2,050	1.47%	1.2	11	63.64%
1990	$19,025	13.42%	6.6	7	71.43%
1991	($8,925)	-5.55%	0.4	14	35.71%
1992	$11,888	7.83%	6.17	7	71.43%
1993	$13,400	8.18%	2.69	10	50.00%
1994	($3,375)	-1.91%	0.75	8	37.50%
1995	$33,550	19.31%	4.42	10	60.00%
1996	$10,063	4.85%	2.66	9	66.67%
1997	$1,775	82.00%	1.09	14	28.57%
1998	$10,563	4.82%	1.8	12	50.00%
1999	$2,900	1.26%	1.21	10	50.00%
2000	$5,538	2.38%	1.5	12	41.67%
2001	$12,188	5.12%	2.67	7	57.14%
2002	$11,738	4.69%	3.15	8	75.00%
2003	$4,538	1.73%	1.67	9	55.56%
2004	($3,050)	-1.14%	0.74	15	33.33%
2005	$4,850	1.84%	1.59	6	33.33%

TABLE 25.3 One Week Expansion—Contract Inceptions—11-19-05

	Net Profit	# Trades	% Profit	Profit/Trade	Max. DD	ROA
S&P (Full)	($199,925)	189	57.81%	($1,058.00)	$333,500	NA
NASD (Full)	$46,000	64	42.19%	$718.75	$141,150	32.6
Russell (Full)	$163,700	94	44.68%	$1,741.49	$104,000	157.4
30-Yr. Bonds	$85,406	211	47.87%	$404.77	$20,031	426.4
10-Yr. Notes	$62,625	179	43.58%	$349.86	$16,594	377.4
5-Yr. Notes	$25,625	136	43.38%	$188.42	$10,234	250.4
Euro Currency	$82,425	42	54.76%	$1,962.50	$7,100	1,160.9
Swiss Franc	$120,925	266	45.86%	$454.61	$29,700	407.2

necessarily looking to trade the system elsewhere. We merely appreciate the additional affirmation. As always, it's better when other markets agree rather than refute.

The various bond contracts are actually hanging pretty close to the currency levels. The profits-per-trade are well past the $100 threshold, and the net profits are solid. The return on accounts aren't bad either, unless you're considering the fact that they culminated over 15, 20 years, or more. (Still better than a bank return.)

Bonds, in contrast to currencies, are among the most volatile and liquid of contracts. There are many big players behind them, including world governments. Unlike some markets, though—S&Ps for instance—you won't see bonds increasing in multiples of its current level. They won't, for example, quadruple in value because interest rates limit that upside possibility as surely as the downside potential doesn't go lower than zero. Bonds rise as interest rates drop, and obviously, rates have a finite downside. No one has convincingly argued where that is or where the corresponding upside futures boundaries are, but as all traders know, they're theoretically out there.

Since they are less trend-oriented than currencies, (as is everything else), we might expect to find practical bond ideas within daily bars—that is, we're scaling back our time horizon. We can probably apply momentum, but on a more limited basis. The system has to stop us out or reverse more often than the yen system. The following provided some amazingly good results over entire contract histories:

If the close is greater than the 25-day average close, then buy the next bar at the open plus one and a half times the previous range on a stop. Sell (but don't reverse) any time the market goes one and a half times the range under the open.

If the close is less than the 25-day average close, get short at the open minus one and a half times the range. The stop is the same one and a half range size above the open.

We're buying and selling off momentum, but a qualifier rather quickly ends that condition. (We've moved one and a half ranges from some successive opening.) This is an acknowledgment that the market trends without running away. The scaling back from weekly to daily similarly says

TABLE 25.4 1.5 Times 1 Day Expansion—Bonds—Contract Inception through 11-19-05

	Net Profit	# Trades	% Profit	Profit/Trade	Max. DD	ROA
30-Yr. Bonds	$125,250	304	50.00%	$412.01	$8,625	1,452.0
10-Yr. Notes	$72,344	265	49.43%	$273.00	$13,688	528.5
5-Yr. Notes	$39,687	229	49.78%	$173.31	$3,609	1,100.0

TABLE 25.5 1.5 Expansion—Other Markets—Contract Inception through 11-19-05

	Net Profit	# Trades	% Profit	Profit/Trade	Max. DD	ROA
S&P (Full)	$54,500	229	36.24%	$237.99	$139,975	39.0
NASD (Full)	$61,000	58	39.66%	$1,051.72	$111,800	54.6
Russell (Full)	$209,925	178	40.45%	$1,179.35	$71,800	292.4
Japanese Yen	$77,200	270	44.07%	$285.93	$30,313	254.7
Euro Currency	$22,463	70	47.14%	$320.89	$20,900	107.5
Swiss Franc	$93,800	367	41.96%	$255.59	$21,650	433.3

that we expect profit potential to exist in smaller timeframes than what we've seen in the currencies. Table 25.4 contains the results.

Table 25.5 shows us again receiving corroboration in the other markets. Were it not for the superior bond ROA column, one might mistake the indexes or currencies for having been the original model for the system.

We assuredly won't see such universal accommodation in our next chapter that targets the indexes for reasons that will quickly become apparent. In many ways, those markets are truly a world unto themselves.

CHAPTER 26

Index Biases
Part One—
Days of the Week

To reiterate, the more corroboration you have for any given idea, the better. A system should hold up over a variety of markets, particularly those that are closely related. Some of the experts I've encountered give more weight to recent time frames than distant ones. Even those people, however, would be happier if their super-performance in the last five years was complemented by moderately positive results in ancient data as opposed to earlier-time meltdown.

All else being equal, more time-tested is always better than less. More markets are better than less. More sectors that comply are better than less. Universality will fortify you better than systems that are more targeted or market specific. It's a better way of ensuring that you're uncovering actual biases rather than random anomalies.

The fourth rule of prudent optimization—understanding your drivers—does justify more narrow-casting, however. The majority of my work is focused on the stock indexes. Among the several systems I trade, most have some degree of persistence in other financials, particularly bonds. There tend to be reasons behind general nonconformance of other markets, however, which are easily acceptable from the onset.

Let's consider the world of stock trading for a moment. More than any other financial arena, it is psychologically driven. The entire world participates, and all sectors within it are directly affected. Whether you're talking the high powered program traders who move giant blocks of orders around in a nanosecond or the peasant in China wondering what he's going to get for his wares, there is a butterfly effect that permeates everything. Wall Street (and all the other rapidly emerging world centers) both reflect and influence the totality of our lives.

One of the interesting things about the various indexes—the S&Ps versus the Dow or the NASDAQ, for example, is how much independence they display relative to one another. Granted, in a 300-point Dow crash, all of them are certain to be underwater. Many days, however, will see the Dow up a few points while some of the other markets are down rather significantly. You can get decent corroboration of an S&P idea by running it in the other indexes, and you won't be merely reduplicating your results.

But why focus on indexes? As we've been implying, they're where the action is. The biggest cotton move imaginable isn't likely to make a front-page headline. The bonds command some world interest and perhaps crop failure would be big news in the Midwest, but nothing matches the all-encompassing presence of the stock market.

Aside from such definable distinctiveness, the indexes are perhaps the only current trading vehicles that are both sufficiently volatile and liquid enough for consistent day trading. They have wide intraday trading arcs. In the electronic markets, you get filled right at your intended stop price more often than not. In our displayed performance tables, you'll notice several S&P, NASDAQ and Russell average profit-per-trades significantly vaulting past the $100 slippage/commission barrier ($20 if you're talking minis). You don't have that kind of power in the other markets, which is why it is so hard to develop day trading methodologies within them.

Let's return to being market theoreticians for a moment. Given that stock holdings are a vast aggregate of both strong and weak hands, could we imagine potential psychological trigger points that would cause lopsided buying or selling? We're being really general here, but consider this example. Once upon a time, Mondays were such good performance days that they encompassed somewhere around 100 percent of the total historic net profits. The rest of the week was more of a flatline affair, largely the result of Friday being the week's only net loser. I used to actually trade off that. I'd sell the open on Friday and buy it back on the close. On Monday, I'd be long for the day.

Ah, the heartbreak of market drift. The idea isn't worth much anymore, particularly the "sell Friday" side. We can apply driver theory here as well I suppose—maybe today's large fund holdings are taking fear of impending long weekends out of the equation.

There are some nice contemporary biases surrounding days of the week, however. Let's start with Monday. If Friday had a higher close, then you want to be long on Monday and vice versa if Friday's close was lower. Table 26.1 shows the results of entering the S&P on Monday in the direction of Friday's net change (close to close) and exiting on the close. The profit-per-trade figure arguably says that we've already inched our way

TABLE 26.1   Monday Rule—Full Daily S&Ps—01-02-01 through 11-19-05

Total Net Profit	$29,400.00	Profit Factor	1.12
Gross Profit	$280,500.00	Gross Loss	($251,100.00)
Total Number of Trades	244	Percent Profitable	46.72%
Winning Trades	114	Losing Trades	129
Even Trades	1		
Avg. Trade Net Profit	$120.49	Ratio Avg. Win:Avg. Loss	1.26
Avg. Winning Trade	$2,460.53	Avg. Losing Trade	($1,946.51)
Largest Winning Trade	$10,125.00	Largest Losing Trade	($6,800.00)
Max. Consecutive Winning Trades	8	Max. Consecutive Losing Trades	9
Avg. Bars in Winning Trades	1.00	Avg. Bars in Losing Trades	1.00
Avg. Bars in Total Trades	1.00		
Max. Shares/Contracts Held	1	Account Size Required	$22,750.00
Return on Initial Capital	29.40%	Annual Rate of Return	5.27%
Return Retracement Ratio	0.19	RINA Index	0.00
Trading Period	4 Yrs, 10 Mths, 19 Dys	Percent of Time in the Market	0.00%
Max. Equity Run-up	$52,500.00		
Max. Drawdown (Intraday Peak to Valley)		**Max. Drawdown (Trade Close to Trade Close)**	
Value	($27,050.00)	Value	($22,750.00)
Net Profit as % of Drawdown	108.69%	Net Profit as % of Drawdown	129.23%
Max. Trade Drawdown	($7,375.00)		

Source: © TradeStation Technologies, Inc. 1991–2006. All rights reserved.

into full-blown system territory. Interestingly, the idea fails more often than not (46.72 percent profit), but obviously, its aggregate winners are sufficient to net out impressive results.

Table 26.2 shows how the idea played out in the other three main indexes. Note the really strong profit-per-trade figure in the NASDAQ. This is not incorporating the bubble, and in fact, the profits are consistent over

TABLE 26.2   Monday Rule—Remaining Markets—1-2-01 through 11-19-05

Full Contracts	Net Profit	# Trades	% Profit	Profit/Trade	Max. DD	ROA
NASD	$91,450	242	52.48%	$377.89	$24,150	378.7
Russell	$59,725	245	51.02%	$243.78	$26,850	222.4
Dow	$11,700	243	50.21%	$48.15	$8,260	141.6

TABLE 26.3 Turnaround Tuesday—Fade Monday's Direction—1-2-01 through 11-19-05

Full Contracts	Net Profit	# Trades	% Profit	Profit/Trade	Max. DD	ROA
S&P	$21,550	229	50.66%	$94.10	$18,850	114.3
NASD	$92,300	229	55.02%	$403.06	$23,800	387.8
Russell	$32,100	232	52.16%	$138.06	$34,275	93.7
Dow	$16,940	229	51.53%	$73.97	$6,770	250.2

an annual basis. There is not a losing year in the last five. The Russell is roughly in the same ballpark. The return on accounts are impressive considering you can only be in the market 20 percent of the time.

Next, let's consider an old axiom known as "Turnaround Tuesday." The idea here is, Tuesday will produce a direction opposite Monday's. We're market scientists, trained to be skeptical of old saws. Of course, they can't all be wrong—can they?—or we'd have the ultimate trading system—fade all axioms.

Well surprise, in at least the stock index futures, Turnaround Tuesday proves to be correct. Table 26.3 shows convincing results in all four indexes.

Tuesday suggests a countertrending mentality and as it turns out, so does the rest of the week. In a nutshell, after Tuesday, the largest open-to-close move since Monday becomes the focus. It is a fade indicator. On Wednesday, you go opposite the biggest open-to-close of the last two days. On Thursday, you do the same with the previous three, and on Friday, you're looking at the previous four. Table 26.4 shows results of the last three days of the week and Table 26.5 combines all five days of the week into a single system.

In short, Monday is the only go-with indicator. The rest of the week has a bias toward "too much one way, let's take it the other." Obviously, we're talking rough tendencies, otherwise trending markets wouldn't be possible. As far as preliminary clues regarding what to expect in the indexes, however, the day of the week indicator can be an effective tool in your arsenal.

TABLE 26.4 Wed.–Fri.—Fade Biggest Open-Close—1-2-01 through 11-19-05

Full Contracts	Net Profit	# Trades	% Profit	Profit/Trade	Max. DD	ROA
S&P	$196,938	749	54.34%	$262.93	$31,525	624.7
NASD	$97,000	737	49.93%	$131.61	$67,750	143.2
Russell	$46,400	740	49.86%	$62.70	$73,800	62.9
Dow	$68,750	744	53.36%	$92.41	$17,030	403.7

TABLE 26.5 Complete Day of Week System—1-2-01 through 11-19-05

Full Contracts	Net Profit	# Trades	% Profit	Profit/Trade	Max. DD	ROA
S&P	$247,888	1,222	52.13%	$202.85	$56,925	435.5
NASD	$280,750	1,208	51.41%	$232.41	$57,000	492.5
Russell	$138,225	1,217	50.53%	$113.58	$71,050	194.5
Dow	$97,390	1,216	52.38%	$80.09	$18,470	527.3

Index Biases Part Two— Days of the Month

(Or How to Beat the Stuffings out of the Bellwether S&P Indicator)

Being the consummate ham, I present the following riddle at my lectures: How could you have made money in the entire 20-some year history of the S&P futures contract being nothing but short? I then remind everyone of the near-relentless up-sloping of the market (millennial bubble-burst aside). Even considering that our current level is discounted roughly 20 percent off the all-time high, the contract's gain, from inception to now, is roughly tenfold.

I'll make it even more interesting. You'd be short the market for roughly 50 percent of its entire history. Figure 27.1 shows a multiyear daily bar chart with the trigger in place. All the way up that steep mountain and others like it, the signal continues to rack up net profits in the direction completely opposite the major trend. How could that possibly be?

Table 27.1 in the S&Ps and Table 27.2 in the remaining indexes confirm it. On top of that, there is a buy-side counterpart that we're keeping nonactivated for the moment, which, as you'd expect, produces many times the short-side returns. What could all this possibly entail?

It involves a very pronounced tendency for the market to rise during certain times of a given month and fall during the remainder. The ascending times are in and around the end of a month, and the retreating times are in the middle.

There is a very obvious driver behind this phenomenon. It has to do with monthly window-dressing. A fund manager can advertise his company's holdings with no further elaboration about when the stocks were

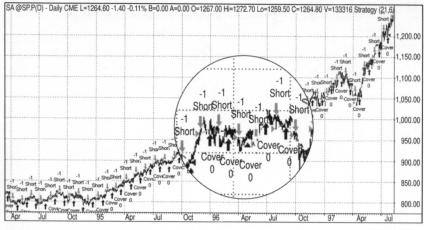

FIGURE 27.1 Methodically Racking Up Profits in the Relentlessly Upward Slop-ing S&P Market . . . Using Nothing But Short Sales! (*Source:* © TradeStation Technologies, Inc. 1991–2006. All rights reserved.)

owned, how his clients did during the holding period, and so forth. All the official need do is state that the hot stock, XYZ, was in his portfolio at the month's end. Because of this loophole, which amounts to little more than a promotional scam, there is a tendency for portfolio managers to bid up hot stocks during monthly (and especially quarterly) rollovers. They want the world to believe they were participating in the hot hands. (Again, not necessarily the case.)

If there is a skewed overperforming time frame, it stands to reason there would be a corresponding cooling-off period. You might think we'd be talking a time of lesser gains, but we're actually seeing net losses over certain dates. I set up some ground rules in my testing. Although I had fig-ured you'd get the best results allowing the long time frame to last longer than the short, I ruled against that outcome. I wanted both time frames to be equal, thereby reducing the risk of flukey results coming from dates be-ing too narrow and targeted.

I did the study being ever cognizant of the probable window-dressing driver—in other words, I expected to be working around an end of month long-biased window. Validation of that is evident right away. You can see it in tests stipulating longs right at the rollover, or x number of days before and after. From there, it was a matter of finding the optimal boundaries

TABLE 27.1 Perennially Short S&Ps—Contract Inception through 11-19-05

Total Net Profit	$80,675.00	Profit Factor	1.15
Gross Profit	$623,375.00	Gross Loss	($542,700.00)
Total Number of Trades	280	Percent Profitable	48.21%
Winning Trades	135	Losing Trades	143
Even Trades	2		
Avg. Trade Net Profit	$288.13	Ratio Avg. Win:Avg. Loss	1.22
Avg. Winning Trade	$4,617.59	Avg. Losing Trade	($3,795.10)
Largest Winning Trade	$38,250.00	Largest Losing Trade	($23,575.00)
Max. Consecutive Winning Trades	6	Max. Consecutive Losing Trades	7
Avg. Bars in Winning Trades	11.53	Avg. Bars in Losing Trades	11.56
Avg. Bars in Total Trades	11.55		
Max. Shares/Contracts Held	1	Account Size Required	$119,762.50
Return on Initial Capital	80.68%	Annual Rate of Return	2.53%
Return Retracement Ratio	0.04	RINA Index	(28.34)
Trading Period 23 Yrs, 4 Mths, 17 Dys		Percent of Time in the Market	49.33%
Max. Equity Run-up	$208,375.00		
Max. Drawdown (Intra-day Peak to Valley)		**Max. Drawdown (Trade Close to Trade Close)**	
Value	($128,162.50)	Value	($119,762.50)
Net Profit as % of Drawdown	62.95%	Net Profit as % of Drawdown	67.36%
Max. Trade Drawdown	($31,300.00)		

Source: © TradeStation Technologies, Inc. 1991–2006. All rights reserved.

for long dates, and then corresponding short ones. Testing uncovered the following:

If today's date is the 21st (or as close thereafter as you can get considering weekends and holidays), then buy tomorrow on the opening. Hold the long through the month's end, up through and including the following 6th.

If today is the 6th, (or again, as close thereafter as possible), then reverse and sell short on the next opening. Hold the short through the following 21st.

Table 27.3 shows some impressive S&P profits, confirmed in the other markets. The Russell return on account is a notable, albeit probably

TABLE 27.2 Short Remaining Indexes—Contract Inceptions through 11-19-05

Full Contracts	Net Profit	# Trades	% Profit	Profit/Trade	Max. DD	ROA
NASD	$56,470	112	50.89%	$504.20	$188,165	30.0
Russell	$136,775	150	51.33%	$911.83	$62,150	220.1
Dow	$30,520	94	56.38%	$56.38	$23,210	131.5

TABLE 27.3 Index Day of the Month Indicator—Perpetual—01-02-01 through 11-19-05

Full Contracts	Net Profit	# Trades	% Profit	Profit/Trade	Max. DD	ROA
S&P	$181,625	116	60.34%	$1,565.73	$64,150	283.1
NASD	$66,100	116	54.31%	$569.83	$69,200	95.5
Russell	$244,325	116	58.62%	$2,106.25	$34,200	714.4
Dow	$60,070	116	56.03%	$517.84	$20,080	299.2

over-optimistic standout. If it managed to rack up half its projections, though, we'd be happy.

We're seeing some hefty profits-per-trade as well. These numbers will normally tend to be bigger than the day systems on which we've been focusing, but even for interday systems, they're pretty formidable. We'd be further fortified by our percentage of times correct—60 percent of the time in the S&P and over 50 percent in all the remaining.

Again, this is not a day system, but rather one where'd we'd be perpetually long or short, roughly 15 calendar days per side. Admittedly, that would be a logistically difficult trade to hang onto without some stop adjustment, but for now, let's just concentrate on the biases.

There is also some persistence in the day trade version of the monthly indicators. Table 27.4 shows the results of entering longs every day from the 22d through the following 6th and exiting each day on the close. The corresponding shorts are obviously placed from the 7th through the 21st.

TABLE 27.4 Index Day of Month As Day Trade—01-02-01 through 11-19-05

Full Contracts	Net Profit	# Trades	% Profit	Profit/Trade	Max. DD	ROA
S&P	$123,963	1,228	50.90%	$100.95	$89,925	137.9
NASD	$57,550	1,226	50.08%	$46.94	$85,850	67.0
Russell	$201,850	1,226	51.63%	$164.64	$42,800	471.6
Dow	$45,510	1,228	49.84%	$37.06	$31,390	145.0

TABLE 27.5 Day of Month—Buy after Lower Closes, Sell after Higher—01-02-01 through 11-19-05

Full Contracts	Net Profit	# Trades	% Profit	Profit/Trade	Max. DD	ROA
S&P	$103,938	583	52.14%	$178.28	$46,675	222.7
NASD	$11,500	598	50.33%	$19.23	$65,200	17.6
Russell	$137,150	564	52.48%	$243.17	$36,300	377.8
Dow	$46,850	601	51.75%	$77.95	$10,180	460.2

The fact that the bias doesn't depend on overnight action will prove helpful in developing more combination day systems.

By adding a simple filter, we can get slightly better overall return on accounts as Table 27.5 affirms. Take longs only after lower closes and shorts following higher ones.

CHAPTER 28

Index Biases
Part Three—Month
of the Year Indicator

H ere's another index market tendency, constructed in the same way as the days of the month. The idea was again to break the total data field into two equal parts. If we could be long and short roughly the same amount of time over the same dates each year, and the results produced profit on both ends, that's probably something worth knowing. Testing produces the following: be long from November 2 (or as close to it thereafter as possible) through May 1st and short from May 2 through November 1. Table 28.1 shows results in our targeted indexes.

Considering the length of each trade, we have to look at as much data as we can. We're covering the entire life of each contract, which takes us as far back as 1982 in the S&Ps and as nearby as 1998 in the Dow. Despite our extended data field, we're only able to generate a handful of trades in

TABLE 28.1 Index Month of the Year Indicator—Life of Contracts through 11-19-05

Full Contracts	Net Profit	# Trades	% Profit	Profit/Trade	Max. DD	ROA
S&P	$202,713	46	54.35%	$4,407.00	$49,325	411.0
NASD	$55,365	18	44.44%	$3,076.00	$143,100	38.7
Russell	$123,600	25	64.00%	$4,944.00	$99,800	123.8
Dow	$61,960	15	66.67%	$4,131.00	$16,040	386.3

each market. We'll have to temper our enthusiasm here, although there are a couple things we should note.

1. The parameters are in line with what we know to be true. September–October is the well-known bugaboo period—the time of most of the harrowing market crashes. There is also a frequent malaise in the summer months. Our shorts reflect this. Conversely, we're long through the traditional Santa Claus rally and yearly rollover. Sometimes common knowledge does work out.

2. All four markets conform. There is not only consistent net profit across the board, but even an annual periodic breakdown suggests that the profit periods more or less emanate from the entire field (Table 28.2).

This is another bias which in and of itself isn't going to be too effective. (The risk is off the page, for one thing.) As always, though, we can

TABLE 28.2 Index Month of Year—Year By Year Breakdown

Full Contracts	S&P Net Profit	NASD Net Profit	Russell Net Profit	Dow Net Profit	Total Net Profit
1982	$875				$875
1983	$4,900				$4,900
1984	($2,913)				($2,913)
1985	$4,350				$4,350
1986	$2,038				$2,038
1987	$19,888				$19,888
1988	$25				$25
1989	$3,763				$3,763
1990	$6,425				$6,425
1991	$17,713				$17,713
1992	$300				$300
1993	($5,738)	($19,075)			($24,813)
1994	($9,513)	($2,975)			($12,488)
1995	$2,825	($25)			$2,800
1996	$3,025	$5,625	$32,300		$40,950
1997	($8,300)	($13,695)	($56,500)		($78,495)
1998	$77,975	$50,045	$89,275	$10,270	$227,565
1999	$55,950	$87,935	$42,825	$29,660	$216,370
2000	($22,600)	($37,745)	$5,150	($10,230)	($65,425)
2001	$50,700	$30,200	$55,200	$24,850	$160,950
2002	$19,225	($16,450)	$69,300	$12,670	$84,745
2003	($14,125)	($16,350)	($51,800)	($7,280)	($89,555)
2004	$17,975	($100)	$22,100	$8,550	$48,525
2005	($10,200)	($23,600)	($47,825)	($2,760)	($84,385)

TABLE 28.3 Combining the Month of Year and Day of Month Indicators—Life of
Contracts through 11-19-05

Full Contracts	Net Profit	# Trades	% Profit	Profit/Trade	Max. DD	ROA
S&P	$273,050	300	56.67%	$910.17	$40,375	676.3
NASD	$97,045	118	50.00%	$822.42	$95,275	101.9
Russell	$271,825	163	57.67%	$1,667.64	$41,700	651.9
Dow	$66,920	98	63.27%	$682.86	$20,130	332.4

start thinking in terms of how we can apply it in combination with other
elements. Table 28.3 shows what happens if we combine the day of month
and month of year signals as follows.

*If it's the between November 1 and April 30 (inclusive) and between
the 21st of the month and the following 5th, then buy the next day at the
market.*

*If it's between May 1 and October 31 and also the date falls between
the 6th and the 20th, then sell short next day at market.*

*For both buy and sell, exit on the next opening if either condition
changes.*

We can actually make a very good day system out of combining the
day of month and month of year signals. Besides exiting on every close,
the only additional qualifier is that the opening must be lower than the
previous close and vice versa for sells. Table 28.4 shows five-year results
that are actually in the ballpark of the interday approach—something you
don't see very often. Note the drawdown and return on account figures.
We now have something that most people would consider manageable
(particularly if applied to mini contracts).

Let's go back to the interday approach for a moment. How would we
do entering if all three of our calendar indicators were in agreement? If
the day of the week indicator is signaling a long between November 2 and
May 1, and it's also between the 21st of the month and the following 5th
then we're buyers and if everything is the opposite, we're sellers. If on any
close, the three signals are no longer giving unanimous support, exit on

TABLE 28.4 Combining the Month of Year and Day of Month Indicators—
Day Trade 01-02-01 through 11-19-05

Full Contracts	Net Profit	# Trades	% Profit	Profit/Trade	Max. DD	ROA
S&P	$94,725	263	54.75%	$360.17	$16,375	578.5
NASD	$77,450	260	52.31%	$297.88	$13,700	565.3
Russell	$69,575	251	52.19%	$277.19	$24,050	289.3
Dow	$15,300	267	57.30%	$57.30	$15,060	101.6

TABLE 28.5 First 2 Calendars Agree versus All Three Agree—Interday—
01-02-01 through 11-19-05

Full Contracts	Net Profit	# Trades	% Profit	Profit/Trade	Max. DD	ROA
S&P						
2 Agree	$105,350	59	62.71%	$1,785.59	$40,375	260.9
3 Agree	$82,525	120	60.83%	$687.71	$27,575	299.3
NASD						
2 Agree	$47,900	59	52.54%	$811.86	$39,100	122.5
3 Agree	$31,300	113	56.64%	$276.99	$28,950	108.1
Russell						
2 Agree	$128,425	59	64.41%	$2,176.69	$41,700	308.0
3 Agree	$127,250	120	60.83%	$1,060.42	$40,950	310.7
Dow						
2 Agree	$36,680	59	55.93%	$621.69	$20,130	182.2
3 Agree	$41,820	110	60.91%	$380.18	$14,600	286.4

TABLE 28.6 Two Out of Three Calendars with Fade Open—Day System—
01-02-01 through 11-19-05

Full Contracts	Net Profit	# Trades	% Profit	Profit/Trade	Max. DD	ROA
S&P	$163,250	547	53.02%	$298.45	$27,850	586.2
NASD	$183,550	566	51.77%	$324.29	$41,100	446.6
Russell	$90,850	548	48.72%	$165.78	$40,575	223.9
Dow	$45,630	575	52.17%	$79.36	$14,770	308.9

the next opening. For comparison purposes, we'll include a five year study of the previous interday dual calendar signals (see Table 28.5).

A day system variation (Table 28.6) has us entering each day in the direction of the majority of the three indicators using the same opening qualifier from before. (It must be lower for buys, higher for sells.) Exit on the close.

CHAPTER 29

Index Biases Part Four—Combining Day of Week, Monthly, and Previous Eight Indicators

L et's try a different mix and match combo. By assigning a plus+/–1 value to the monthly date, a second such value to the day of the week, and a third to the majority direction of our previous eight indicator system, can we again get a "whole" that exceeds the sum of its parts? Table 29.1 shows such a system in the S&Ps. We enter on openings in the direction of at least two out of three indicators. Once in the trade, we either stay in the position or flip when the majority reverses direction. We're perpetually long or short. The results are so good that we can almost forget about the fact that we don't have tight risk control. (I did say "almost.")

Table 29.2 shows the results of each individual component compared to the combined total.

Across the board, the net profits are best in the combined row. Half the return on accounts combos surpass the individual ones. No individual component dominates anywhere, so again, your two logical choices would be to trade three contracts on each individually or one on the combined signals. You would make $320,500 with a $55,500 drawdown in the combined NASDAQ. That compares to a $556,800 profit with triple the exposure. Again, by combining our basic building blocks we've been able to significantly improve our system.

TABLE 29.1 Monthly Date, Day of Week, Eight Indicator Combo—S&P—
01-02-01 through 11-19-05

Total Net Profit	$400,950.00	Profit Factor	1.77
Gross Profit	$918,900.00	Gross Loss	($517,950.00)
Total Number of Trades	376	Percent Profitable	58.51%
Winning Trades	220	Losing Trades	156
Even Trades	0		
Avg. Trade Net Profit	$1,066.36	Ratio Avg. Win:Avg. Loss	1.26
Avg. Winning Trade	$4,176.82	Avg. Losing Trade	($3,320.19)
Largest Winning Trade	$38,250.00	Largest Losing Trade	($22,500.00)
Max. Consecutive Winning Trades	9	Max. Consecutive Losing Trades	5
Avg. Bars in Winning Trades	4.45	Avg. Bars in Losing Trades	4.01
Avg. Bars in Total Trades	4.26		
Max. Shares/Contracts Held	1	Account Size Required	$55,200.00
Return on Initial Capital	400.95%	Annual Rate of Return	32.97%
Return Retracement Ratio	0.57	RINA Index	102.70
Trading Period	4 Yrs, 10 Mths, 19 Dys	Percent of Time in the Market	99.78%
Max. Equity Run-up	$455,900.00		
Max. Drawdown (Intra-day Peak to Valley)		**Max. Drawdown (Trade Close to Trade Close)**	
Value	($59,275.00)	Value	($55,200.00)
Net Profit as % of Drawdown	676.42%	Net Profit as % of Drawdown	726.36%

Source: © TradeStation Technologies, Inc. 1991–2006. All rights reserved.

TABLE 29.2 Monthly Date, Day of Week, Eight Indicators—Separate versus
Combined—01-02-01 through 11-19-06

Full Contracts	Net Profit	# Trades	% Profit	Profit/Trade	Max. DD	ROA
S&P						
Day of Week	$247,888	1,222	52.13%	$202.85	$56,925	435.5
Day of Month	$181,625	116	60.34%	$1,565.73	$64,150	283.1
8 Indicator Majority	$290,138	910	56.37%	$318.83	$38,675	750.2
Combined	**$400,950**	**376**	**58.51%**	**$1,066.36**	**$55,200**	**726.4**
NASDAQ						
Day of Week	$280,750	1,208	51.41%	$232.41	$57,000	492.5
Day of Month	$66,100	116	54.31%	$569.83	$69,200	95.5
8 Indicator Majority	$209,950	903	51.05%	$232.50	$90,950	230.8
Combined	**$320,500**	**359**	**60.72%**	**$892.76**	**$55,500**	**577.5**
Russell Day of Week	$138,225	1,217	50.53%	$113.58	$71,050	194.5
Day of Month	$244,325	116	58.62%	$2,106.25	$34,200	714.4
8 Indicator Majority	$217,500	868	53.11%	$250.58	$36,500	595.9
Combined	**$239,100**	**361**	**54.02%**	**$662.33**	**$57,600**	**455.0**
Dow						
Day of Week	$97,390	1,216	52.38%	$80.09	$18,470	527.3
Day of Month	$60,070	116	56.03%	$517.84	$20,080	299.2
8 Indicator Majority	$41,810	911	51.48%	$54.68	$14,600	286.4
Combined	**$100,980**	**370**	**54.86%**	**$272.92**	**$18,060**	**559.1**

CHAPTER 30

The Dow-Spoo Spread— "Told You So!"

The latter part of the above heading is something of a private joke directed at my trading associates. I became an adherent, and then a major touter of the idea years before I could test it, which earned me skepticism and good-natured needling. I'm not sure the Dow-Spoo indicator is "the world's best signal" as I used to claim, but it is a pretty good one as we'll see. Even my scoffing associates were finally forced to admit it.

Another necessary aside here—spoo means S&P. It is shorthand that sort of evolved from the fact that when you write out S&P 500, it kind of resembles "spoo."

Back to the methodology—the S&Ps lead the Dow. I can't take credit for the discovery—it has been a floor axiom for years. To eyeball it on an apples-to-apples basis, you have to convert the two respective markets into like units. One full S&P point (or 10 ticks on the full contract, 4 on the mini) is equivalent to roughly 8 Dow points. Once you have that, it's easy to ascertain whether a given rally is S&P or Dow led. If the former is up five full points and the latter is up 16, the spoos are definitely stronger. If the former is up 2 points and the latter is up 24 points, it's Dow dominated.

Similarly, a downward charge could be led by one side or the other. The leading indicator concept means that if the S&Ps are in fact stronger on an up move or weaker on a down one, you can have more faith than if the Dow is stepping out more. If the Dow is going faster, up or down, traders would regard the move with suspicion, and perhaps even expect an imminent change in direction.

For years, I took note of the market's relationship, and it became apparent that my existing S&Ps systems were adhering to the principle.

If I was long and the spoos were leading, I'd expect even more profit by the end of the day. If it were Dow led, I'd get anxious—frequently with justification.

I finally left the floor for the convenience of online testing-order execution. By then, the eight point gauging had become superfluous—what I really wanted to know was the daily net change of each market on a percentage basis (computed by dividing the net change by the previous close). The resulting plus or minus fraction in each market could be compared without the need for manual calculations. The automated live systems constantly monitored and updated.

I soon developed several techniques that all reached the same conclusion—trust the S&P strength/weakness relative to the Dow. Table 30.1 is the first of several five-minute bar charts incorporating the emini S&Ps

TABLE 30.1 Dow-Spoo Perpetual: Emini S&Ps with Mini Dow Inserted—Five Minute Bars 04-05-02 through 11-19-05

Total Net Profit	$52,962.50	Profit Factor	1.22
Gross Profit	$297,550.00	Gross Loss	($244,587.50)
Total Number of Trades	4,644	Percent Profitable	41.67%
Winning Trades	1,935	Losing Trades	2,326
Even Trades	383		
Avg. Trade Net Profit	$11.40	Ratio Avg. Win:Avg. Loss	1.46
Avg. Winning Trade	$153.77	Avg. Losing Trade	($105.15)
Largest Winning Trade	$3,250.00	Largest Losing Trade	($2,025.00)
Max. Consecutive Winning Trades	9	Max. Consecutive Losing Trades	16
Avg. Bars in Winning Trades	22.51	Avg. Bars in Losing Trades	14.18
Avg. Bars in Total Trades	16.87		
Max. Shares/Contracts Held	1	Account Size Required	$7,275.00
Return on Initial Capital	52.96%	Annual Rate of Return	8.36%
Return Retracement Ratio	0.45	RINA Index	(74.76)
Trading Period	5 Yrs, 30 Dys, 2 Hrs, 30 Mins	Percent of Time in the Market	71.24%
Max. Equity Run-up	$58,275.00		
Max. Drawdown (Intraday Peak to Valley)		**Max. Drawdown (Trade Close to Trade Close)**	
Value	($7,712.50)	Value	($7,275.00)
Net Profit as % of Drawn	686.71%	Net Profit as % of Drawn	728.01%
Max. Trade Drawdown	($2,725.00)		

Source: © TradeStation Technologies, Inc. 1991–2006. All rights reserved.

with the mini Dow as an insert. This one confirms the concept at its most basic level. You're perpetually committed—long if the spoos are stronger than the Dow, short if they're weaker.

With all the following intraday charts, remember to size them so they reflect regular hours only—in this case, 8:30 A.M.–3:15 P.M. CST.

Since we're always referencing net changes relative to the previous day's close, however, the Dow-Spoo indicator makes more sense as a day trading methodology. Table 30.2 shows that variation at its most elemental level. Enter in the Dow Spoo direction any time between 8:45 and 2:45—exit at 3:00. The start-end times are pretty arbitrary. They're set wide because the concept persists so well—why not take all the trades you can get?

This is one of those rare instances in which you actually improve a system by converting it to day trade. The net profit, percentage profitable, profit per trade, worst drawdown and resulting return on account are all superior in Table 30.2. Clearly this driver has a day trading nature.

TABLE 30.2   Dow Spoo Basic Day Trade Version—04-05-02 through 11-19-05

Total Net Profit	$59,437.50	Profit Factor	1.25
Gross Profit	$292,700.00	Gross Loss	($233,262.50)
Total Number of Trades	4,556	Percent Profitable	42.65%
Winning Trades	1,943	Losing Trades	2,240
Even Trades	373		
Avg. Trade Net Profit	$13.05	Ratio Avg. Win:Avg. Loss	1.45
Avg. Winning Trade	$150.64	Avg. Losing Trade	($104.14)
Largest Winning Trade	$1,750.00	Largest Losing Trade	($3,412.50)
Max. Consecutive Winning Trades	9	Max. Consecutive Losing Trades	13
Avg. Bars in Winning Trades	20.65	Avg. Bars in Losing Trades	13.60
Avg. Bars in Total Trades	15.99		
Max. Shares/Contracts Held	1	Account Size Required	$5,062.50
Return on Initial Capital	59.44%	Annual Rate of Return	9.17%
Return Retracement Ratio	0.45	RINA Index	664.75
Trading Period	5 Yrs, 30 Dys, 2 Hrs, 30 Mins	Percent of Time in the Market	14.68%
Max. Equity Run-up	$63,812.50		
Max. Drawdown (Intra-day Peak to Valley)		**Max. Drawdown (Trade Close to Trade Close)**	
Value	($5,687.50)	Value	($5,062.50)
Net Profit as % of Drawn	1,045.05%	Net Profit as % of Drawn	1,174.07%

Source: © TradeStation Technologies, Inc. 1991–2006. All rights reserved.

Created with TradeStation

FIGURE 30.1 Dow-Spoo in Choppy Time Frame (*Source:* © TradeStation Technologies, Inc. 1991–2006. All rights reserved.)

We see a huge total number of trades in the performance summary. Figure 30.1 shows how we arrive there—there are instances in which the signal flips back and forth many times.

Other times, the tone of the day is set early on and persists throughout the day. Figure 30.2 shows one profitable long trade, initiated just after 8:45, the earliest allowable entry time, and exited at 3:00.

Created with TradeStation

FIGURE 30.2 Dow-Spoo in Trend Mode (*Source:* © TradeStation Technologies, Inc. 1991–2006. All rights reserved.)

Dow-Spoo also works in the NASDAQ and Russell (see Table 30.3). (Again, we're using minis here.) Table 30.3 shows the perpetual system on the top lines and the day adjustment on the bottom.

As a further aside, the overall systems in this section will be referred to as Dow-Spoo even when we're referencing markets other than the S&P. We have to have some sort of shorthand after all.

The only thing you need to keep constant is the Dow as the comparison market. The Dow is slower and less reactive than the others. Why is that? What is the driver we're witnessing? Apparently, aggregate owners of a broader basket of stocks are quicker to sense a changing market vibe than those limited to the narrow Dow 30 stocks. Or to look at it another way, perhaps the holders of staid 30 blue chips are less sensitive to market noise and therefore less inclined to budge from their positions. This makes sense. The biggest likelihood of a market crash, for example, is when you have widespread participation. Minor tremors will automatically affect some number of weak hands which will then unnerve slightly stronger hands and so on until you get a ripple effect. A panic that drives everyone to exit all at once is obviously going to be more catastrophic if the room is jammed with people—that is, more participants with a wider basket of stocks.

Whatever the ultimate truth, Dow-Spoo is a robust concept. We're about to see it hold up under a wide array of alterations. For starters, it doesn't matter what time frame you use. Table 30.4 shows the day system applied to different bar increments ranging from a minute to an hour. It holds up in all fields across our three targeted markets.

Justifiably fortified, we might next begin altering our entry requirements. At given levels, the market is apt to waffle back and forth between buy and sell signals. Why not require that they persist for a given number of bars before we follow them? That would certainly figure to alleviate some of the whipsaw.

Table 30.5 shows an optimization of the number of bars in a row that

---

TABLE 30.3 Dow-Spoo also Works in NASDAQ and Russell—Perpetual and Day 1-02-01 through 11-19-05

Mini Contracts	Net Profit	# Trades	% Profit	Profit/Trade	Max. DD	ROA
NASDAQ						
Perpetual	$16,770	3,255	30.51%	$5.15	$8,390	199.9
Day	$33,630	3,250	33.66%	$10.35	$4,380	767.8
Russell						
Perpetual	$58,910	3,776	37.10%	$15.60	$11,020	534.6
Day	$67,770	3,683	39.56%	$18.40	$7,610	890.5

TABLE 30.4 Dow-Spoo Day—Different Time Frames—04-05-02 through 11-19-05

Mini Contracts	Net Profit	# Trades	% Profit	Profit/Trade	Max. DD	ROA
S&P						
1 Min.	$42,700	14,922	36.26%	$2.86	$7,300	584.9
5 Min.	$59,438	4,556	42.65%	$13.05	$5,063	1,174.0
10 Min.	$63,887	2,977	46.52%	$21.46	$4,925	1,297.2
15 Min.	$69,688	2,518	48.33%	$27.69	$4,975	1,400.8
30 Min.	$56,463	1,809	50.03%	$31.21	$4,963	1,137.7
NASDAQ						
1 Min.	$24,780	7,810	25.86%	$3.17	$7,920	312.9
5 Min.	$33,630	3,250	33.66%	$10.35	$4,380	767.8
10 Min.	$33,370	2,406	37.53%	$14.02	$3,210	1,039.6
15 Min.	$35,390	2,162	39.82%	$16.37	$3,650	969.6
30 Min.	$29,100	1,643	44.37%	$17.71	$3,360	866.1
Russell						
1 Min.	$50,890	7,932	35.05%	$6.42	$10,010	508.4
5 Min.	$67,770	3,683	39.56%	$18.40	$7,610	890.5
10 Min.	$69,450	2,676	42.53%	$25.95	$7,020	989.3
15 Min.	$72,290	2,373	43.53%	$30.46	$9,150	790.1
30 Min.	$64,830	1,791	47.01%	$36.20	$8,790	737.5

must agree regarding the Dow-Spoo direction. The only other adjustment is that the initiation time has been moved up to 9:30. That way, when we optimize from one bar to 12, we are only accessing current day Dow-Spoo signals.

As usual, we're testing for best return on account, and for this study, we see that 3 is the top variable. The average profit-per-trade issue looms

TABLE 30.5 Dow-Spoo Optimized for Number of Five Min Bars that Must Agree—Day 04-05-02 through 11-19-05

U	Net Profit	# Trades	% Profit	Profit/Trade	Max. DD	ROA
1	$36,325	3,812	42%	$9.53	$5,100	712.3
2	$46,200	1,900	48%	$24.32	$4,763	970.0
3	$49,075	1,508	51%	$32.54	$4,338	1,131.0
4	$45,038	1,378	51%	$32.68	$4,738	950.6
5	$41,575	1,290	52%	$32.23	$4,900	848.5
6	$40,113	1,244	52%	$32.16	$5,113	784.5
7	$41,400	1,186	52%	$34.91	$5,050	819.8
8	$40,413	1,145	51%	$35.29	$6,125	659.8
9	$40,988	1,109	52%	$36.96	$6,338	646.7
10	$36,103	1,089	53%	$33.07	$7,063	511.2
11	$35,963	1,076	53%	$33.42	$6,700	536.8
12	$38,375	1,058	53%	$36.27	$6,525	588.1

especially large here—many trades each averaging skinny profits, and we haven't factored in slippage/commission. Still, in the overwhelming majority of trials, we're past the $20 per trade that is conventionally applied to minis.

The NASDAQ optimization (Table 30.6) shows similar results, although the average profit per trades are probably not strong enough to allow actual involvement. As always, though, we're grateful for the theoretical corroboration. The Russell (Table 30.7) returns us to practical trade levels. Again, notable results seem to cluster around the 3–5 area with 3 being a reasonable across-the-board choice.

Let's return to the interday analysis for a moment. Here is a strategy that produces, among other things, some huge average profits per trade. It's again set up in the five-minute charts. Between 9:00 and 2:45 CST, if the close is above the average 50 bar close for the first time in a row, and Dow-Spoo is bullish, buy the next bar. If the close is under the 50 average (the previous wasn't) and Dow-Spoo points south, sell short. That's it. Table 30.8 shows that even without stops, your worst loss is only $2,438, and the worst drawdown is $7,563, resulting in a healthy 621 percent return on account. Again, not bad at all considering the unadorned nature of the strategy.

Table 30.9 shows confirmation in the Russell and at least positive numbers in the NASDAQ. My partner and I have debated jettisoning or deemphasing the NASDAQ in our portfolio. It certainly has been dogging it lately, but then my partner raised the question, "Do we want to say that tech stocks are finished forever?" I guess that adds perspective to a difficult question.

Here's another day trade application. Between 9:00 and 2:30 CDT, if

TABLE 30.6 Dow-NASDAQ Optimized—04-05-02 through 11-19-05

U	Net Profit	# Trades	% Profit	Profit/Trade	Max. DD	ROA
1	$14,890	2,639	35%	$5.64	$4,700	316.8
2	$20,100	1,721	40%	$11.68	$4,990	402.8
3	$21,000	1,454	43%	$14.44	$4,240	495.3
4	$15,840	1,350	45%	$11.73	$4,330	365.8
5	$17,640	1,281	46%	$13.77	$4,470	394.6
6	$14,650	1,226	46%	$11.95	$5,560	263.5
7	$14,630	1,193	48%	$12.26	$5,560	263.1
8	$12,040	1,152	47%	$10.45	$5,870	205.1
9	$11,640	1,133	48%	$10.27	$5,710	203.9
10	$12,020	1,111	48%	$10.82	$5,320	225.9
11	$9,980	1,101	49%	$9.06	$4,870	204.9
12	$12,480	1,090	49%	$11.45	$4,220	295.7

TABLE 30.7 Dow-Russell Optimized—04-05-02 through 11-19-05

U	Net Profit	# Trades	% Profit	Profit/Trade	Max. DD	ROA
1	$53,170	3,034	41%	$17.52	$6,740	788.9
2	$55,720	1,907	44%	$29.22	$5,910	942.8
3	$52,030	1,567	46%	$33.20	$7,430	700.3
4	$48,990	1,433	46%	$34.19	$7,210	679.5
5	$50,170	1,357	49%	$36.97	$6,830	734.6
6	$49,350	1,298	49%	$38.02	$6,920	713.2
7	$43,970	1,248	48%	$35.23	$7,190	611.5
8	$42,200	1,215	49%	$34.73	$7,280	579.7
9	$36,880	1,199	48%	$30.76	$7,440	495.7
10	$31,170	1,178	48%	$26.46	$7,290	427.6
11	$31,500	1,147	48%	$27.46	$7,370	427.4
12	$32,340	1,132	49%	$28.57	$7,200	449.2

TABLE 30.8 Dow-Spoo with 50-Day Average—Perpetual—04-05-02 through 11-19-05

Total Net Profit	$46,962.50	Profit Factor	1.50
Gross Profit	$140,450.00	Gross Loss	($93,487.50)
Total Number of Trades	614	Percent Profitable	42.35%
Winning Trades	260	Losing Trades	338
Even Trades	16		
Avg. Trade Net Profit	$76.59	Ratio Avg. Win:Avg. Loss	1.95
Avg. Winning Trade	$540.19	Avg. Losing Trade	($276.59)
Largest Winning Trade	$4,062.50	Largest Losing Trade	($2,437.50)
Max. Consecutive Winning Trades	6	Max. Consecutive Losing Trades	11
Avg. Bars in Winning Trades	161.25	Avg. Bars in Losing Trades	93.25
Avg. Bars in Total Trades	120.95		
Max. Shares/Contracts Held	1	Account Size Required	$7,562.50
Return on Initial Capital	46.96%	Annual Rate of Return	7.57%
Return Retracement Ratio	0.41	RINA Index	130.64
Trading Period	5 Yrs, 30 Dys, 2 Hrs. 30 Mins	Percent of Time in the Market	71.24%
Max. Equity Run-up	$48,712.50		
Max. Drawdown (Intraday Peak to Valley)		**Max. Drawdown (Trade Close to Trade Close)**	
Value	($8,075.00)	Value	($7,562.50)
Net Profit as % of Drawn	581.58%	Net Profit as % of Drawn	620.99%
Max. Trade Drawdown	($2,737.50)		

TABLE 30.9 Dow NASDAQ and Dow Russell with 50-Day Averages—
04-05-02 through 11-19-05

Mini Contracts	Net Profit	# Trades	% Profit	Profit/Trade	Max. DD	ROA
NASDAQ	$5,010	625	35.20%	$8.02	$13,200	38.0
Russell	$44,880	556	41.73%	$80.72	$12,140	369.7

six bars in a row confirm the Dow-Spoo direction then buy at that six bar high on a stop. Vice versa for shorts. Exit at 3 P.M.

We know the validity of buying/selling the nth highest/lowest bars on stops. (It's one of the most renowned and yet simple mechanical systems out there. Back in the 1970s commodities markets heyday, it was allegedly the main engine behind systems that made several traders rich.) Obviously, we're also becoming evermore convinced about the effectiveness of the "Spoo leads the Dow" principle. In short, our components are basic and trustworthy. Table 30.10 shows they're also profitable.

A limit order variation says after the first 15 minutes into the day session, if the close exceeds the average of the previous six highs and Dow-Spoo points up, then buy at the close minus half that range. If the close is less than the average of the last six lows, then sell short at the close plus half the range. We're still in five minute bars, so with the first three trades some of the highs/lows we'd be accessing would be from the previous day. Exit at 3:00 P.M. (See Table 30.11.)

It's interesting that, at first glance anyway, this seems to be an improvement over the stop entries. It's not what we'd expect from ideas that are largely momentum-oriented. On the other hand, don't lose sight of our earlier limit order pitfall discussion. When you force the markets to conform to our extra ticks/extra penalty requirement, the ever-lagging NASDAQ does go under water. This makes it harder to categorically state which system is superior.

The next Dow-Spoo system accesses information from only the current day on more of a dynamic basis. In other words, if the trade is initiated early, we'd only be referencing a few bars so as not to incorporate

TABLE 30.10 Dow-Spoo—Six Bar High/Low Stop—Day System—
04-05-02 through 11-19-05

Mini Contracts	Net Profit	# Trades	% Profit	Profit/Trade	Max. DD	ROA
S&P	$34,950	1,126	51.07%	$31.04	$6,963	501.9
NASDAQ	$10,690	1,092	48.63%	$9.79	$5,280	202.5
Russell	$50,090	1,134	50.00%	$44.17	$7,440	673.3

TABLE 30.11   Dow-Spoo—Six Bar High/Low Limit—Day—04-05-02
through 11-19-05

Mini Contracts	Net Profit	# Trades	% Profit	Profit/Trade	Max. DD	ROA
S&P	$63,825	1,723	49.10%	$37.04	$4,675	1365.0
NASDAQ	$34,250	1,868	41.54%	$18.34	$4,150	825.3
Russell	$67,740	1,869	44.52%	$36.24	$5,990	1131.0

previous day data. As the day goes on, the number of bars referenced increases. It's not an exact bars-since-entry formula, but it closely mimics it.

Between 9:30 and 9:55 A.M., the previous 12 bars must confirm the Dow-Spoo direction for a long or short to be entered. Successive time frames determine the following number of bars to be referenced.

10:00–10:25—18

10:30–10:55—24

11:00–11:25—30

11:30–11:55—36

12:00–12:25—42

12:30–12:55—48

See Table 30.12.

You enter at market in the net direction of Dow-Spoo according to the number of bars accessed at the given time. Exit at 3:00 P.M.

This is one of those organic disclose-as-I-develop-and-refine scenarios and, admittedly, it's not quite what I'd hoped for. Still, it does give us some diversity on the basic Dow-Spoo idea, not just in terms of flexible bar reference but also because of the enter-at-market order entries. We can get similarly good results whether we're entering in that fashion, or on stops

TABLE 30.12   Dynamic Dow-Spoo—Day—04-05-02 through 11-19-05

Mini Contracts	Net Profit	# Trades	% Profit	Profit/Trade	Max. DD	ROA
S&P	$39,887	1,168	52.57%	$34.15	$7,963	500.9
NASDAQ	$13,340	1,190	47.65%	$11.21	$4,680	285.0
Russell	$26,980	1,182	48.65%	$22.83	$9,430	286.1

or limits. We're again looking at many trials. We're getting confirmation from several sources.

Think of Dow-Spoo as being a kind of spice or flavoring—it enhances old tried and true ideas such as N Day or range expansion breakouts. Whatever old index system you've got laying around, Dow-Spoo could well make it better. But even as a stand-alone approach, Dow-Spoo delivers.

CHAPTER 31

Intraday Day Trading Part One: The Most Significant Price in Your Arsenal

*R*eminder: *We use day session only hours for all our intraday studies, so you must adjust your windows accordingly under TradeStation's "use custom session" option. For the indexes, input 8:30 A.M.—3:15 P.M. CST for start-end times. For all other financials, use 7:20 A.M.–2:00 P.M.*

Obviously, biases that relate to probable daily direction are only a small part of mechanical trading possibilities. Professional traders respond to ongoing market action. It doesn't matter whether we're talking mechanical traders, pit traders, or otherwise. The markets are dynamic and constantly changing. They're also largely, as we've stated, random noise, but that doesn't mean there aren't diamonds to be found in the overall rough.

Let's start with an indicator that is ridiculously simple, surprisingly effective, and pretty-much-overlooked. There is a price in every trading session that can be used as an ultimate demarcation line. If you're on one side of it, you should be inclined to buy, reluctant to sell—if on the other, just the opposite. What price would that be?

The daily opening price. If the market is higher than where it opened, then it is exhibiting upward pressure. This doesn't mean you should not be following whatever system is disagreeing with that. It just means that all else being equal, you should be more buy-friendly. North of the line, you should be looking for long entry excuses as well as reasons to exit shorts. Conversely, if the market has been languishing below the opening, you should be more partial to the sell side.

TABLE 31.1 Entering in Direction Relative to Daily Opening—Emini S&Ps—30-Min. Bars 10-24-00 through 11-19-05

X	Net Profit	# Trades	% Profit	Profit/Trade	Max. DD	ROA
9:00	$14,788	1,213	51.53%	$12.19	$19,325	76.5
9:30	$15,763	1,235	51.98%	$12.76	$12,413	127.0
10:00	$88	1,244	50.40%	$0.07	$10,600	0.8
10:30	$31,088	1,244	53.14%	$24.29	$6,825	455.5
11:00	($5,338)	1,244	51.85%	($4.29)	$19,613	NA
11:30	($1,988)	1,242	51.29%	($1.60)	$16,800	NA
12:00	$24,825	1,243	53.26%	$19.97	$12,538	198.0
12:30	$15,088	1,232	53.08%	$12.25	$17,250	87.5
1:00	$23,825	1,238	54.36%	$19.24	$8,963	265.8
1:30	$29,638	1,236	54.29%	$23.98	$5,000	592.8
2:00	$23,988	1,243	52.29%	$19.30	$4,300	557.9
2:30	$8,525	1,247	50.36%	$6.84	$5,988	142.4

Why do I say this? Imagine a series of trades keying off 30-minute bars in the emini S&Ps, regular day session. The first one enters at 9:00 CDT. If the close is above the daily opening (8:30) then buy, if it's lower, sell. The next one is a 9:30 entry, then a 10:00 entry and so forth, all the way through 2:30. Every trade exits on the close (3:15 CDT). Each entry time has a series of trades that can be observed and tabulated. Table 31.1 shows the results.

We then do the same run-through in the other indexes. (I trust you'll accept a cutback to hourly increments as sufficient evidence of the phenomenon.) From there, we test the remaining financials, which necessitate a daily open-close time adjustment, but it's the same principle.

Table 31.2 shows the results in our remaining markets. Except for a few nonconforming outcomes in the currencies, the concept is sound—*be long if you're above the daily opening, short if below.*

Let's apply the principle to another system, this time using 60-minute bar charts. The "Two-Bar in Row versus Open" system has the following rules:

Beginning at least two hours into the trading day, if both hourly closes were above the daily open and the last close was also greater than the one before it, then enter at market on the next bar. Initiate through two hours before the beginning of the last hour (1:30 in the indexes and 12:20 in the remaining financials), and exit one hour later (2:30 indexes, 1:20 others). Table 31.3 reveals a concept that holds up over thousands of trials across an especially wide market array. Note the absence of negative results.

Another variation, the "Final Third System" works as follows. Divide

TABLE 31.2 Entering Re Daily Opening—30 Min Bars—10-24-00—11-19-05
Indexes—05-24-01—11-19-05 Remaining

X	Net Profit	# Trades	% Profit	Profit/Trade	Max. DD	ROA
NASD (mini)						
9:30	$35,080	1,235	52.23%	$28.40	$14,370	244.1
10:30	($9,730)	1,247	49.48%	($7.80)	$16,350	NA
11:30	$12,200	1,247	51.08%	$9.78	$17,680	69.1
12:30	$8,950	1,249	51.32%	$7.17	$14,650	61.1
1:30	$8,850	1,245	52.21%	$7.11	$12,750	69.4
2:30	$640	1,242	48.47%	$0.52	$10,170	6.3
Russell (Mini.)						
9:30	$8,190	995	51.96%	$8.23	$10,660	76.8
10:30	$14,120	983	52.80%	$14.36	$9,590	147.2
11:30	$31,330	990	54.95%	$31.65	$8,390	373.4
12:30	$55,580	993	57.30%	$55.97	$5,630	987.2
1:30	$50,100	987	58.97%	$50.76	$3,050	1643.0
2:30	$24,020	995	53.97%	$24.14	$4,270	562.5
Thirty Year Bonds						
8:20	($16,563)	1,026	50.68%	($16.14)	$24,125	NA
9:20	$26,000	1,047	53.01%	$24.83	$14,188	183.3
10:20	$34,125	1,052	54.09%	$32.44	$7,813	436.8
11:20	$19,188	1,059	50.33%	$18.12	$10,781	178.0
12:20	$28,281	1,060	51.70%	$26.68	$6,938	407.6
13:20	$34,656	1,171	50.90%	$29.60	$5,031	688.8
Ten-Year Notes						
8:20	($18,959)	1,049	47.76%	($17.98)	$22,453	
−84.4						
9:20	$19,563	1,060	53.14%	$24.29	$6,825	286.6
10:20	$26,000	1,047	53.01%	$24.83	$14,188	183.3
11:20	$26,000	1,047	53.01%	$24.83	$14,188	183.3
12:20	$26,000	1,047	53.01%	$24.83	$14,188	183.3
13:20	$26,000	1,047	53.01%	$24.83	$14,188	183.3
Five-Year Notes						
8:20	($18,959)	1,049	47.76%	($17.98)	$22,453	NA
9:20	$19,563	1,060	53.14%	$24.29	$6,825	286.6
10:20	$31,109	1,060	55.94%	$29.35	$4,563	681.8
11:20	$17,015	1,059	51.46%	$16.07	$6,156	276.4
12:20	$20,671	1,061	52.31%	$19.48	$4,922	420.0
13:20	$7,828	1,050	49.24%	$7.46	$3,531	221.7
Japanese Yen						
8:20	($5,050)	1,080	44.17%	($4.68)	$9,250	NA
9:20	($575)	1,087	49.22%	($0.53)	$13,000	NA
10:20	($2,238)	1,106	42.68%	($2.02)	$10,850	NA
11:20	($9,038)	1,108	42.24%	($8.16)	$13,613	NA
12:20	($11,063)	1,101	42.33%	($10.05)	$15,663	NA
13:20	($5,050)	1,080	44.17%	($4.48)	$9,250	NA

TABLE 31.2 *(Continued)*

X	Net Profit	# Trades	% Profit	Profit/Trade	Max. DD	ROA
Euro Currency						
8:20	($10,788)	1,093	41.17%	($9.87)	$13,363	NA
9:20	$26,588	1,102	50.18%	$24.13	$9,825	270.6
10:20	$9,888	1,107	48.51%	$8.93	$10,388	95.2
11:20	($17,263)	1,104	46.47%	($15.64)	$22,000	NA
12:20	$2,813	1,105	46.61%	$2.55	$9,963	28.2
13:20	($10,788)	1,093	41.17%	($9.87)	$13,363	NA
Swiss Franc						
8:20	$21,913	1,065	50.14%	$20.58	$9,950	220.2
9:20	$16,738	1,082	50.18%	$15.47	$6,125	273.3
10:20	$7,750	1,085	47.83%	$7.14	$9,488	81.7
11:20	($12,488)	1,087	43.51%	($11.49)	$16,950	NA
12:20	($13,100)	1,084	43.36%	($12.08)	$18,413	NA
13:20	($7,013)	1,072	40.58%	($6.54)	$11,975	NA

your trading day into as close to three equal parts as possible. The indexes have 405-minute sessions, which would produce exactly 135 bars. The other financials trade from 7:20 A.M. to 2 P.M. CDT—410 minutes. That coincidently also conveniently rounds to 135-minute segments. For indexes, your intraday 135-minute bars end at 10:45 and 1:00 respectively—for the remaining financials, it's 9:35 and 11:50. If the time is 1:00 indexes, 11:50 others—that is, the beginning of the last third of the trading day—and both previous bars closed above the daily open, then buy at the market. If both bars closed lower than the open, sell short. Exit at the end of the day. Results are in Table 31.4.

TABLE 31.3 Two Bar in Row versus Open—60 Minute Bars—10-24-00 through 11-19-05 Indexes—05-24-01 through 11-19-05 Remaining

	Net Profit	# Trades	% Profit	Profit/Trade	Max. DD	ROA
S&P (mini)	$12,138	1,186	51.94%	$10.23	$7,588	160.0
NASD (mini)	$9,280	1,200	50.75%	$7.73	$9,720	95.4
Russell (mini)	$22,470	963	51.82%	$11.91	$5,670	396.3
30-Yr. Bonds	$22,250	1,045	51.58%	$21.29	$6,031	368.9
10-Yr. Notes	$22,000	1,033	53.34%	$21.30	$5,625	391.1
5-Yr. Notes	$10,218	967	51.09%	$10.57	$4,000	255.5
Japanese Yen	$4,075	1,076	46.10%	$3.79	$7,263	56.1
Euro Currency	$27,413	1,088	49.08%	$25.20	$6,900	397.3
Swiss Franc	$17,800	1,075	48.28%	$16.56	$8,088	220.1

TABLE 31.4   Entering on Final Third of Day 1-2-01 through 11-19-05
(Indexes)—6-7-01 through 11-19-05 (All Others)

	Net Profit	# Trades	% Profit	Profit/Trade	Max. DD	ROA
S&P (mini)	$23,213	951	55.84%	$24.41	$6,175	375.9
NASD (mini)	$11,260	970	53.51%	$11.61	$12,030	93.6
Russell (mini)	$43,280	796	60.05%	$54.37	$3,970	1,090.0
30-Yr. Bonds	$2,437	852	50.35%	$2.86	$10,844	22.5
10-Yr. Notes	$9,828	849	50.65%	$11.58	$6,031	163.0
5-Yr. Notes	$5,390	823	49.70%	$6.55	$3,125	172.5
Japanese Yen	($16,713)	867	39.45%	($19.28)	$17,413	NA
Euro Currency	($13,825)	888	46.85%	($15.57)	$16,213	NA
Swiss Franc	($6,138)	877	45.15%	($7.00)	$9,788	NA

Currencies aside, this is another validation of trading only in the direction relative to the opening. Why fight it? The opening price is like the wind at your back.

CHAPTER 32

Intraday
Part Two—
The Switch

*(Can Promising Trading
Environments Be Anticipated?)*

One of the downsides of mechanical systems is their tendency to thrive in some market environments and blow up in others. This is one of the main reasons so many traders are reluctant to go down the mechanical trading road in the first place. During my floor trader days, I was the poster child for dogmatic stay-the-course trading. I'd admit aloud that I didn't like some position I was holding and the other traders concurred—the system was wrong this time so why put myself through that?

And I'd tell them I'm a system player, and I'd hold fast and often wind up booking a rather painful loss. Once in awhile, I'd listen to them and violate the system and then it would turn around and rack up huge paper profits without me aboard. Murphy's Law. The point is, system trading isn't always the prettiest thing for an outsider to witness. Most people cling to the idea that there are logical ways to eject or massage bad trades in progress. They don't want any part of the apparent masochism. The second major reason they tend to dismiss mechanical trading is it involves hard work. Adherents realize there's no way around that.

As a mechanical trader views his personal history, he may perceive having lived dual realities. There are periods where trading seems like the falling-off-a-log simplest thing imaginable. During other broad time frames, everything seems futile to the point where the trader may begin wondering if any other endeavor in the world wouldn't make more sense.

Are there tangible differences between the two environments? It often feels like that's the case. When you're successfully trading momentum, you may recall big strings of up days following up days and vice versa.

More days when highs and lows are taken out, both inter and intraday. You may remember a forgiving day trade environment in which you get a second or third chance to fill an order you missed earlier. But once the move really starts, it keeps going. Less false moves, perhaps bigger overall ranges.

If only you knew ahead of time which environments to sidestep. Like a hibernating bear, you could take some weeks or months off, keep your powder dry and return with renewed firepower and vigor.

This concept of the trading "switch" is controversial among mechanical advocates. Some maintain that if you could design something to anticipate changing environments, you could rule the world; the implication being that's not likely to happen. Others regard the idea as not so all-encompassing, but rather, more of a glorified filter. Filters are an everyday part of mechanical systems. "Don't take a given long if the RSI index is too high." "Don't initiate trades if volume is lower than the lowest of the previous five-day volume." The switch is referring to something that would toggle back and forth between complete trading environments.

For an example, let's view a market outside our radar so far—soybeans. Just being an agricultural, it tends to have characteristics different from what we've seen. Even among ags, though, the soybean market has a schizophrenia that puts it in a class by itself.

For years, soybeans will trade like one of the industry's more docile and range-bound markets. Then, some major fundamental change occurs, usually weather-related. You then see market activity rivaling coffee region freezes, oil shortages, and stock market crashes in terms of volatility (and opportunity).

What generalizations can you make about the hyper environment? It tends to be short-lived. On bar charts, a weather market looks like a spike with the down leg being just as violent as the up. It's almost certainly going to be a bull market, meaning relatively high prices. Bear markets in the grains are steady grinders. There are none of the near-instantaneous price spikes we're talking about here. Last week's low, for example, might have been $4.65, and this week it got down to $4.57—water torture for the bulls. (You can, on the other hand, get harrowing plummets after the market has already rallied sharply.)

Almost by definition, a frenzied market will have trading ranges significantly larger than normal. Such markets need a lot of room to swing around. This may seem like a contradiction of our earlier coiling observations, but our horizons are different. Tight ranges suggest sharp imminent moves, but bigger ones define broader-based market volatility. (I can imagine a successful system acting off immediate tight ranges that have occurred within a broader field of huge ones, but now I'm digressing). The point is, it's hard to envision really good trading opportunities without attendant huge price moves.

So the bottom line is, we have definable threshold levels. A switch could toggle on and off between them. Your programming code could contain something like "if the average three-day range is greater to or equal to two times the average 200 day range" for an entry qualifier. It could be something even more static like "if the close is greater than or equal to $7.00 . . ." Seven dollar-plus beans have historically behaved in a distinct manner, but it's better to trust systems more if they key off something dynamic—expanding and contracting ranges, for example.

The following system shows a way of activating entry rules according to theoretically promising trading time frames. Both previously discussed filters are incorporated—the idea of prices tending to be higher rather than lower, and/or recent ranges being relatively large.

Two conditions—identical for buys and sells—(not vice versa).

1. The highest high of the last 20 days minus the close equals 10 percent or less of the entire 20-day range.

2. The average five-day range is at least twice the size of the prior average 20-day range. (The 20-day average spans from 25 days ago up through 6 days ago—concluding just before the recent five-day average inception.)

If either or both are met, buy at the open plus the previous range on a stop. Sell short at the open minus the same distance. However many days into a long you are, the profit target is the next opening plus 50 percent of the 20-day range, (which granted, doesn't always result in a profitable trade if successive days are moving lower.) The stop loss is the open minus 40 percent of that range. (Not necessarily a loss.) Vice versa for sells.

Figure 32.1 shows how the system tends to play out. The first cluster of signals is scaling a steep incline that corresponded to the spring drought of 1988. The exit arrow that occurs just to the right of the high represents the last action we get for nearly two months. From there, when a trade hits, it's likely to be a lengthy one as the market starts moving under thresholds that would trigger exits. The last exit occurs on 2-17-89. The picture doesn't fully reveal it, but the next signal—a sell—doesn't hit until 7-6-89. In other words, the party has ended, so our system elects to pull in its horns.

These kinds of activity flourishes surrounded by no action at all are pretty typical of the whole 20-year field. Table 32.1 shows the performance

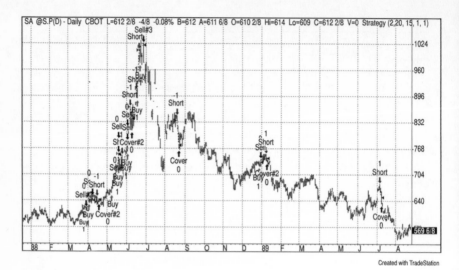

FIGURE 32.1 Soybean Switch Causes Trades to Cluster in Certain Time Frames (*Source:* © TradeStation Technologies, Inc. 1991–2006. All rights reserved.)

results. We see a respectable bottom line, the sum of some huge profit-per-trade figures. It's shown that we're committed to the market only 54 percent of the time. Our total trades (110) may be less than we normally like to see, but on the other hand, this is another case of knowing ahead of time what we're searching for. As we've said, you tend to need less confirmation when you're testing in support of known drivers.

This is perhaps a more specialized, less universal idea than we've been presenting, but there is some persistence in other markets. Two close bean cousins, wheat and corn, also show net profits. Gold, silver, and several of the exotics also comply. Meats don't work, but maybe that's not so surprising considering how chronically stuck in range-bound trade they tend to be. Some of our normal targeted financials hold up. I've included currencies as they seem to be the markets least cooperative to our more financially-oriented ideas, and yet we haven't seen a yen performance to match this one. It's not a perfect world, but we do see persistence. See Table 32.2.

TABLE 32.1 Soybean Switch—1986 through 11-19-05

Total Net Profit	$70,043.75	Profit Factor	2.59
Gross Profit	$114,081.25	Gross Loss	($44,037.50)
Total Number of Trades	110	Percent Profitable	54.55%
Winning Trades	60	Losing Trades	48
Even Trades	2		
Avg. Trade Net Profit	$636.76	Ratio Avg. Win:Avg. Loss	2.07
Avg. Winning Trade	$1,901.35	Avg. Losing Trade	($917.45)
Largest Winning Trade	$11,950.00	Largest Losing Trade	($3,187.50)
Max. Consecutive Winning Trades	5	Max. Consecutive Losing Trades	4
Avg. Bars in Winning Trades	30.27	Avg. Bars in Losing Trades	21.02
Avg. Bars in Total Trades	25.70		
Max. Shares/Contracts Held	1	Account Size Required	$5,000.00
Return on Initial Capital	70.04%	Annual Rate of Return	2.67%
Return Retracement Ratio	0.11	RINA Index	142.26
Trading Period	19 Yrs, 10 Mths, 17 Dys	Percent of Time in the Market	54.31%
Max. Equity Run-up	$75,750.00		

Max. Drawdown (Intraday Peak to Valley)		**Max. Drawdown (Trade Close to Trade Close)**	
Value	($7,875.00)	Value	($5,000.00)
Net Profit as % of Drawn	889.44%	Net Profit as % of Drawn	1,400.88%
Max. Trade Drawdown	($5,787.50)		

Source: © TradeStation Technologies, Inc. 1991–2006. All rights reserved.

TABLE 32.2 Bean Switch Applied to Other Markets—01-02-86 through 11-19-05

	Net Profit	# Trades	% Profit	Profit/Trade	Max. DD	ROA
Wheat	$17,250	124	42.74%	$139.11	$5,413	318.7
Corn	$7,725	123	34.96%	$62.80	$5,325	145.1
Coffee	$62,670	129	45.74%	$485.81	$64,808	96.7
Cocoa	$19,270	174	34.48%	$110.75	$9,280	207.7
Orange Juice	$3,552	177	35.59%	$20.07	$11,378	31.2
Gold	$8,342	106	40.57%	$78.70	$14,384	58.0
Silver	$32,285	95	41.05%	$339.84	$12,100	266.8
Japan Yen	$57,013	164	44.51%	$347.64	$18,275	312.0
Euro Currency	$7,388	59	42.37%	$125.21	$16,150	45.8
Swiss Franc	($15,863)	155	39.35%	($102.34)	$32,525	NA

CHAPTER 33

Intraday Part Three— An Effective Index Switch

In a trending time frame, you should see more up days followed by up days and down days followed by down days. When moves are less defined, up moves will be more often followed by down moves and vice versa.

Let's start with a basic filterless idea that works decently in the stock indexes. Every day, look to buy at the opening price plus 50 percent of the previous three-day average range and sell short the same distance under the open. You're perpetually long or short, and you do get flipped a lot.

For a second modified version, we'll add a filter constructed as follows. We'll assign the variable x a +1 value whenever two closes in a row are in the same direction, up or down. If it's an up followed by a down or vice versa, then $x = 0$. If over a given number of days, x is greater than or equal to a given threshold, we'll activate our basic breakout entries.

A robust threshold number turns out to be 0.6. If the last 20 x's average out to 0.6 or better, we place both buy and sell entries for the next day. Once we're in a trade, we can exit at any 0.5 stop in the direction opposite our position, regardless of whether we're at the filter threshold. The qualifier affects the entry only, not the exit. Table 33.1 compares the breakout with and without the qualifier. This time, 10 years' worth of data gets us a reasonable sample size.

The qualifier has isolated 14 percent of the total Dow trades and consequently, turned a $58,000 loser into an $8,200 profit. As we've filtered out 80 percent of the trades across the four markets, our resulting overall net profits understandably decrease, but again, we always view them in relative terms. Would you rather sit through a $125,400 drawdown to make $344,300

TABLE 33.1	Range Expansion with and without "Two Same-way" Filter—Daily Bars 01-02-96 through 11-19-05, S&P—From Contract Inception through 11-19-05, Other Markets					

Full Contracts	Net Profit	# Trades	% Profit	Profit/Trade	Max. DD	ROA
S&P						
without filter	$153,575	1,155	40.43%	$132.97	$181,800	84.5
with filter	$60,425	216	40.28%	$279.75	$33,325	181.3
NASD						
without filter	$344,300	1,069	44.15%	$322.08	$125,400	274.6
with filter	$201,250	246	49.59%	$818.09	$31,000	649.2
Russell						
without filter	$715,975	1,120	45.89%	$639.26	$84,225	850.1
with filter	$259,475	280	46.79%	$926.70	$29,425	881.8
Dow						
without filter	($58,000)	938	36.14%	($61.83)	$99,030	NA
with filter	$8,200	134	41.79%	$61.19	$22,670	36.2

in the NASDAQ, or a $31,000 drawdown before earning $201,250? The return account has more than doubled here and not in any of our markets did it decrease. The average profit per trade has also seen a unanimous improvement. It costs significantly less to bankroll the filtered side. Figure 33.1 gives further visual affirmation in the Dow of the system's periodic shifts between action and dormancy—the definition of our driver. Clearly the switch is doing its job.

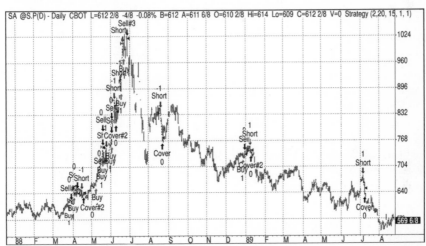

Created with TradeStation

FIGURE 33.1 Index Switch: Daily Full-Sized Dow (*Source:* © TradeStation Technologies, Inc. 1991–2006. All rights reserved.)

Where else might we find similar demarcation lines? In a trending market, we're more likely to be trading near the multiday highs or lows than in a middle ground. Our daily bars may look the same way—more closes within x percent of the high or low in trending markets. Volume may provide a clue, or perhaps the frequency that highs or lows are taken out within a given time frame. We could key off weekly signals for our daily bar entries. We could compare total up and down closes rather than noting the number of two-day like closes. There could be some sort of angle application giving us information about the speed of a move.

Again, your potential thresholds are limited only by your imagination.

CHAPTER 34

Intraday
Part Four—
A Financial Switch

As previously noted, we can not advocate gut trading for anyone except the rarified small ranks of the blessed. (That's not you if you're still having doubts after all this time.) But to further reiterate, trading reflections have a valid place in the system construction time frame. They're a pathway to understanding market drivers for one thing. Sometimes, you'll be wrong about what you believe about market tendencies, but testing results will expose such fallacies before you commit money. The good ideas will be validated.

Here's one in line with the switch concept. If you have been trading long enough, you certainly remember relatively painless, effortless days where your profit is steadily increasing. As the session progresses, you're gaining conviction that you'll have more money by the end of the day. These aren't paranormal premonitions or hocus pocus—they are thoughts that are keyed into some aspects of the market dynamic. As usual, it would help us to be able to quantify that sort of thing in order to be able to respond to it.

In such scenarios, the market is moving evermore in your direction. If you're long, you're getting continuous new daily highs. The pullbacks are shallow. They don't last very long. There's an overall consistency to the trend. Again, you may only need some sort of rough filter to help you capture a significant number of such days. The "12:30 Entry

TABLE 34.1 12:30 Entry—Five Min. Bars—1-2-01 through 11-19-05 (Indexes)— 5-15-01 through 11-19-05 (All Others)

	Net Profit	# Trades	% Profit	Profit/Trade	Max. DD	ROA
S&P (mini)	$4,075	216	57.87%	$18.87	$7,275	56.01
NASD (mini)	$5,340	205	56.10%	$26.05	$4,440	120.30
Russell (mini)	$10,900	113	67.26%	$96.46	$1,640	664.60
30-Yr. Bonds	$2,625	168	47.02%	$15.63	$2,313	113.50
10-Yr. Notes	$4,875	180	51.67%	$27.08	$1,156	421.70
5-Yr. Notes	$1,640	145	46.21%	$11.31	$1,406	116.60
Japanese Yen	$1,863	94	55.32%	$19.81	$1,738	107.20
Euro Currency	$675	128	44.53%	$5.27	$1,850	36.49
Swiss Franc	$1,300	101	45.54%	$12.87	$1,863	69.78

System" says that at 12:30, three conditions must be met for you to be a buyer.

1. The daily open must be within the lowest 25 percent of the total range.
2. The high must be higher than it was at 11:30.
3. The 11:30 high must be higher than the 9:30 high.

As always, opposite conditions make you a seller. The same formula applies to all nine of our markets with the only obvious difference centering on closing times. Exit all trades at 10 minutes before the close, (3:05 P.M. indexes, 1:50 all others). The open-to-target times represent a different percentage of the whole days' duration when you're talking indexes versus the other markets. That does skew our symmetry a bit, although maybe it's the shared times that hold the most significance. We're reconciled to results that hold up significantly better than if the entry times were more dynamic relative to percentages of the whole day's duration. But hold up they do, as Table 34.1 reveals. This is conceptually close to the "final third" system outlined earlier only now we're referencing a bit more than the relationship to the daily open.

CHAPTER 35

Intraday Part Five—
Four Combined
Entry Signals
in the Indexes

What about identifying and combining some basic intraday biases? We'd probably want to target the indexes—again, the current best bet for day trading. As we've done before, we might ask ourselves what market tendencies would probably lend themselves to successful longs or shorts. We know that Dow-Spoo is a powerful indicator. We've seen the wisdom of being long if we're on the north side of the daily open.

Here's another theory. An intraday long-friendly environment would probably see a majority of recent bars have higher open-to-closes and vice versa for shorts. We'll assign variable $x + 1$ value for every higher open-to-close and -1 for every lower one. We optimize for number of days we're considering for a simple majority indicator. In a five-minute bar chart, nine pops out as a fairly robust number. Start trading at 9:15 so that you're never accessing more than the current day's data. From there through 2:45, you're long or short according to whether the nine bar "x" average is plus or minus. Exit at 3 P.M.

Slight aside: all of the testing in this section was done with mini Dow contracts inserted. Some of the components involved Spoo-Dow relationships, and I wanted to keep everything apples-to-apples. That did, however, decrease the number of days TradeStation could access—ergo the unorthodox start times.

Table 35.1 shows the results in the mini S&P, NASDAQ, and Russell. However slight, we have uncovered another biased building block.

Here is a second component. Use the same five-minute bars and 9:15–2:45 trading time frame for the following variation on the opening

TABLE 35.1 Going with Majority Direction of Nine Open-Closes—Five-Min. Bars—
04-05-02 through 11-19-05

Mini Contracts	Net Profit	# Trades	% Profit	Profit/Trade	Max. DD	ROA
S&P	$9,338	7,724	34.36%	$1.21	$14,500	64.4
NASD	$5,410	7,614	34.21%	$0.71	$4,990	108.4
Russell	$73,700	7,438	37.17%	$9.91	$8,550	862.0

price technique. Throughout that time frame, be long when your last close is in the higher half of the daily range, be short when it's in the lower. Simple and frill-free, just the way we like it. Table 35.2 shows our targeted index results.

The percent profit hovers in the 20–25 percent range, which is pretty low. That is consistent with the purest momentum ideas, however, and if you're always moving toward the direction of the closest high/low extreme, that's definitely momentum-oriented. Overall, it serves as another building block. The average profit per trade is acceptable, considering it's just a partial indicator and we're talking mini contracts. The net totals are also impressive. The ROA in the Russell is so good that it's unlikely we'll surpass it with any combination system. We have to consider it in conjunction with all the markets' profit per trade, however. That figure could (and should) be improved if we're going to be trading past the $20 per trade mini contract threshold level.

At any rate, we now have a few intraday ingredients we can apply to our index stew. Let's see if we can come up with results comparable to our previous day indicators. Our four intraday either-or components are (for longs):

1. The last Dow-Spoo closing bar points up.
2. The close is higher than the daily open.
3. A majority of the last nine open-to-closes were positive.
4. The close is in the higher half of the total daily range.

TABLE 35.2 Midpoint of Daily Range As Demarcation Line—04-05-02
through 11-19-05

Mini Contracts	Net Profit	# Trades	% Profit	Profit/Trade	Max. DD	ROA
S&P	$25,513	4,881	21.53%	$5.23	$12,588	202.7
NASD	$21,960	4,587	22.30%	$4.79	$4,040	543.6
Russell	$88,910	4,007	25.43%	$22.19	$3,640	2,443.0

TABLE 35.3 Four Indicators: 5-Min. Emini S&P—Mini Dow Insert—04-05-02
through 11-19-05

Total Net Profit	$35,237.50	Profit Factor	1.27
Gross Profit	$166,187.50	Gross Loss	($130,950.00)
Total Number of Trades	1,130	Percent Profitable	48.05%
Winning Trades	543	Losing Trades	573
Even Trades	14		
Avg. Trade Net Profit	$31.18	Ratio Avg. Win:Avg. Loss	1.34
Avg. Winning Trade	$306.05	Avg. Losing Trade	($228.53)
Largest Winning Trade	$1,712.50	Largest Losing Trade	($1,712.50)
Max. Consecutive	8	Max. Consecutive	9
Winning Trades		Losing Trades	
Avg. Bars in Winning Trades	56.98	Avg. Bars in Losing Trades	39.61
Avg. Bars in Total Trades	48.10		
Max. Shares/Contracts Held	1	Account Size Required	$8,887.50
Return on Initial Capital	35.24%	Annual Rate of Return	5.91%
Return Retracement Ratio	0.44	RINA Index	922.79
Trading Period	5 Yrs, 1 Mth,	Percent of Time in the Market	11.65%
	8 Dys, 2 Hrs,		
	30 Mins		
Max. Equity Run-up	$37,475.00		

Max. Drawdown (Intra-		**Max. Drawdown (Trade**	
day Peak to Valley)		**Close to Trade Close)**	
Value	($8,950.00)	Value	($8,887.50)
Net Profit as % of Drawn	393.72%	Net Profit as % of Drawn	396.48%

Source: © TradeStation Technologies, Inc. 1991–2006. All rights reserved.

Each long condition assigns our x variable a +1 value, each opposite condition a −1. Enter when all four agree (plus or minus 4). Tables 35.3–35.5 show some pretty healthy numbers. We get ROAs of 396 percent, 259 percent, and 881 percent in the S&P, NASDAQ, and Russell respectively.

Once again, improved results spring from minor tinkering, in this case, the addition of an exit trigger. If we're long and the last two x variables in a row are less than zero or short and the two are both positive, then exit at the market. Table 35.6 compares the combined signals with and without the qualifier.

On balance, the added exit slightly decreases the average profit per

TABLE 35.4   Four Indicators: 5-Min. Emini NASD—Mini Dow Insert—04-05-02 through 11-19-05

Total Net Profit	$17,800.00	Profit Factor	1.16
Gross Profit	$127,640.00	Gross Loss	($109,840.00)
Total Number of Trades	1,261	Percent Profitable	46.71%
Winning Trades	589	Losing Trades	645
Even Trades	27		
Avg. Trade Net Profit	$14.12	Ratio Avg. Win:Avg. Loss	1.27
Avg. Winning Trade	$216.71	Avg. Losing Trade	($170.29)
Largest Winning Trade	$1,100.00	Largest Losing Trade	($860.00)
Max. Consecutive Winning Trades	9	Max. Consecutive Losing Trades	14
Avg. Bars in Winning Trades	58.01	Avg. Bars in Losing Trades	37.76
Avg. Bars in Total Trades	47.40		
Max. Shares/Contracts Held	1	Account Size Required	$6,860.00
Return on Initial Capital	17.80%	Annual Rate of Return	3.21%
Return Retracement Ratio	0.37	RINA Index	548.01
Trading Period	5 Yrs, 1 Mth, 8 Dys, 2 Hrs, 30 Mins	Percent of Time in the Market	12.53%
Max. Equity Run-up	$21,240.00		
Max. Drawdown (Intra-day Peak to Valley)		**Max. Drawdown (Trade Close to Trade Close)**	
Value	($7,110.00)	Value	**($6,860.00)**
Net Profit as % of Drawdown	**250.35%**	**Net Profit as % of Drawdown**	**259.48%**

Source: © TradeStation Technologies, Inc. 1991–2006. All rights reserved.

trades. This is consistent with the fact that we have more easily triggered exits and therefore more total trades. The ROA jump, however, is significant. Overall, we appear to have an undeniable system in the Russell and a marginal one in the S&Ps. The NASDAQ is at least corroborating the principle. Someday, when it finally breaks out of its malaise, it too may be a good vehicle for this and similar ideas.

TABLE 35.5 Four Indicators: 5-Min. Emini Russell—Mini Dow Insert—04-05-02 through 11-19-05

Total Net Profit	$56,650.00	Profit Factor	1.34
Gross Profit	$221,500.00	Gross Loss	($164,850.00)
Total Number of Trades	1,191	Percent Profitable	48.78%
Winning Trades	581	Losing Trades	600
Even Trades	10		
Avg. Trade Net Profit	$47.57	Ratio Avg. Win:Avg. Loss	1.39
Avg. Winning Trade	$381.24	Avg. Losing Trade	($274.75)
Largest Winning Trade	$1,610.00	Largest Losing Trade	($1,140.00)
Max. Consecutive Winning Trades	9	Max. Consecutive Losing Trades	10
Avg. Bars in Winning Trades	57.91	Avg. Bars in Losing Trades	38.35
Avg. Bars in Total Trades	48.01		
Max. Shares/Contracts Held	1	Account Size Required	$6,430.00
Return on Initial Capital	56.65%	Annual Rate of Return	11.05%
Return Retracement Ratio	0.45	RINA Index	1,255.18
Trading Period	4 Yrs, 23 Dys, 6 Hrs, 5 Min	Percent of Time in the Market	15.19%
Max. Equity Run-up	$59,140.00		

Max. Drawdown (Intraday Peak to Valley)		**Max. Drawdown (Trade Close to Trade Close)**	
Value	($6,670.00)	Value	($6,430.00)
Net Profit as % of Drawn	849.33%	Net Profit as % of Drawn	881.03%

Source: © TradeStation Technologies, Inc. 1991–2006. All rights reserved.

TABLE 35.6 Four Combined Intraday Index with Added Exit Rule—04-05-02 through 11-19-05

Mini Contracts	Net Profit	# Trades	% Profit	Profit/Trade	Max. DD	ROA
S&P						
Without exit	$35,238	1,130	48.05%	$31.18	$8,888	396.5
With exit	$34,500	1,416	38.35%	$24.36	$6,350	543.3
NASD						
Without exit	$17,800	1,261	46.71%	$14.12	$6,860	259.5
With exit	$17,620	1,553	37.80%	$11.35	$4,430	397.7
Russell						
Without exit	$56,650	1,191	48.78%	$47.57	$6,430	881.0
With exit	$64,130	1,383	42.44%	$46.37	$4,280	1,498.0

When It Gets Extreme—What to Do after Five Closes in the Same Direction

The vast majority of mechanical systems incorporate some form of momentum. Not only is trend following one of the most successful trading techniques, it is possibly the most conspicuous and universally exploitable market phenomenon. True, markets tend to be nondirectional more often than not, but the 60-some percent choppy time frames rarely offer much to the market scientist. For robust, reliable performance, one almost inevitably looks to breakouts.

Momentum is the cornerstone behind the world's most successful systems, including those of billionaire trader/Red Sox owner John Henry and Richard Dennis and the Turtles. Some of the interviewees in *Market Beaters* allege that any technique incorporates momentum; that it's all down to the duration of the trend, however long or short. We may be talking semantics here. Just being in a winning trade involves capitalizing on a positive line of price movement after all.

A bar chart or open-high-low-close column is like a blank canvass. There are so many ideas you can impose before you start grinding out numbers. One of the first things I tend to notice on an average chart is that give and take is almost everywhere. Even pronounced bull markets usually provide some good selling opportunity and vice versa.

Maybe it's all random walk as some people believe. Maybe there are subtle rules. It almost doesn't matter. A natural serial correlation of numbers probably means opportunity regardless of the ultimate nature.

It could be my (perhaps unfortunate) gambling inclination that causes me to wonder when something is overdone. Granted it means nothing if a red turns up 20 times in a row on the roulette wheel—the odds of the next spin being black are no different than ever—18 out of 38 or 47.37 percent. You lose some such cut-and-dryness, though, when you've seen similar extremes in markets. Remember, human psychology is the fuel behind a good percentage of short-term activity. Trials are therefore not as independent as they are in your average casino game. There figures to be a point where people unload their overdone longs or shorts, thereby "normalizing" the prices.

Here are some of the best tendencies I've found along those lines. It's not something quite as simple as "fade x number of up (down) closes in a row"—you need an additional setup mechanism.

If the market closes down five days in a row *and then up on the sixth day*, buy the next day and vice versa. That first contrary close is apparently telling the world, "about time!" and there tends to be one more day of confirmation. Table 36.1 shows 10-year results.

Even going back 10 years, we don't have a lot of trials. As we might expect, markets don't usually trade the same direction for five days in a row. Even pronounced bull markets usually contain short-term pullbacks and freefalls have their dead cat bounces. Still, there has to be an "overdone" marker somewhere—the trick is in ascertaining its statistical significance. Ideas like this could be especially market-drift prone. Although turnaround points have to materialize somewhere, that doesn't mean that this era's significant "five" won't be the next one's "three" or "six." On the other hand, five—a week's worth—is not exactly left field. Still, it would be prudent to consider periodic reoptimization if you're going to be fading extremes.

For now, we have confirmation in six out of nine markets. The index profit-per-trades are huge—the Russell notwithstanding. The driver is intuitively valid—again, every market backs and fills somewhere. It's probably also fair to assume that—very roughly speaking—when a string is

TABLE 36.1 Going with First Contrary Close after Five Same Directional in Row Daily—1-2-96 through 11-19-05

	Net Profit	# Trades	% Profit	Profit/Trade	Max. DD	ROA
S&P (Full)	$32,588	59	54.24%	$552.33	$15,525	209.9
NASD (Full)	$19,925	61	45.90%	$326.64	$35,580	56.0
Russell (Full)	($13,475)	64	46.88%	($210.55)	$27,875	NA
30-Yr. Bonds	($1,594)	69	40.58%	($23.10)	$4,406	NA
10-Yr. Notes	$1,688	67	46.27%	$25.19	$2,063	81.8
5-Yr. Notes	$4,219	62	54.84%	$68.04	$938	449.8
Japanese Yen	$1,488	58	48.28%	$25.65	$5,450	27.3
Euro Currency	$63	51	45.10%	$1.23	$2,675	2.4
Swiss Franc	($25)	61	54.10%	($0.41)	($3,075)	NA

broken, there would likely be a short-term piling-on effect as countertrending traders get their first sign of a new direction. Again, there's a pronounced psychological component to short-term moves.

A broader question we might ask, though, is once such an extreme formation ends, does it signal a longer-term end of the move—a more significant bottom or top? (The five-day aberration proves to be the overdone climax, in other words.) Or would we find that the opposite is true—a unidirectional five-close anomaly is the insistent move and the one day flip is just a temporary letup?

It turns out the latter is true—our new direction is the countermove, and we can't exploit it any further than the single day we've outlined. The reversal is actually a bias within a bigger bias that says "heed the five down closes—this market remains weak." Table 36.2 shows the result of going long after five up days in a row followed by a down, and short when you get the exact opposite. This time, you don't exit at the end of the day, but rather, perpetually hold your position until you get a reverse signal.

In short, we're now making money on the exact same entry signals as before assuming the opposite position. It's just a matter of holding on longer—not exiting on the first day.

If a day trade makes money by buying a first up day after five down days in a row, but a longer-term trade mandates a sell under the exact same circumstances, we're actually saying the following: *skip a day* after five down closes in a row followed by a higher one and then go short. That should give us an automatic improvement over Table 36.2's perpetual system because, as we've seen, there is an opposite side bias to the first day in the trade (Table 36.1). It should also provide a viable day technique as well: use the original five-day fade system, only we initiate the trade one

TABLE 36.2 Going with Five Same-way Closes In Row—Long-Term Perpetual
1-2-96 through 11-19-05

	Net Profit	# Trades	% Profit	Profit/Trade	Max. DD	ROA
S&P (Full)	$270,863	24	58.33%	$11,286.00	$54,375	498.1
NASD (Full)	$27,770	27	48.15%	$1,029.00	$183,925	15.1
Russell (Full)	$68,100	26	42.31%	$2,619.00	$75,425	90.3
30-Yr. Bonds	$26,594	35	54.29%	$759.82	$17,156	155.0
10-Yr. Notes	$24,844	29	44.83%	$856.68	$10,938	227.1
5-Yr. Notes	$9,500	29	41.38%	$327.59	$11,984	79.3
Japanese Yen	$56,626	26	53.85%	$2,175.00	$17,313	327.1
Euro Currency	$19,938	22	63.64%	$906.25	$41,825	47.7
Swiss Franc	($950)	32	37.50%	($29.69)	$33,863	NA

day later and in the opposite direction. This is getting more convoluted than the basic approaches we've been favoring, but we've already demonstrated the validity of fading the two-day move. We did it in relation to two open-to-closes in a row and as part of the two-day five-day indicator (two-day is the fade average, five-day the go-with). So again, we're not coming into this clear out of left field.

Perhaps there's a conceptually better way to simplify the concept.

An unbroken five-day directional close points the direction of a longer-term market bias. It takes about two days for the normal countertrend reaction to play out. Get in the dominant direction then.

Table 36.3 shows the five closes in one direction, then an opposite

TABLE 36.3 Five One-way Closes, One Opposite, One Irrelevant—Day and Perpetual—1-2-96 through 11-19-05

	Net Profit	# Trades	% Profit	Profit/Trade	Max. DD	ROA
S&P (Full)						
Day	$44,875	59	64.41%	$760.59	$14,175	316.6
Perpetual	$320,438	24	66.67%	$13,351.56	$24,725	1,296.0
NASD (Full)						
Day	$66,730	61	55.74%	$1,093.93	$20,300	328.7
Perpetual	$59,855	27	51.85%	$2,217.00	$169,450	35.3
Russell (Full)						
Day	$46,600	65	61.54%	$716.92	$13,550	343.9
Perpetual	$44,350	26	34.62%	$1,706.00	$79,025	56.1
30-Yr. Bonds						
Day	$1,875	69	53.62%	$27.17	$7,094	26.4
Perpetual	$18,906	35	45.71%	$540.18	$19,406	97.4
10-Yr. Notes						
Day	$7,453	67	56.72%	$111.24	$1,219	611.4
Perpetual	$21,788	29	48.28%	$747.84	$10,813	201.5
5-Yr. Notes						
Day	$2,281	62	53.23%	$36.79	$1,578	144.6
Perpetual	$10,781	29	44.83%	$371.77	$9,328	115.6
Japanese Yen						
Day	$5,675	57	56.14%	$99.56	$2,600	218.3
Perpetual	$53,000	26	53.85%	$2,038.00	$17,225	307.7
Euro Currency						
Day	($1,375)	51	50.98%	($26.96)	($3,575)	NA
Perpetual	$22,300	22	63.64%	$1,013.63	$41,238	54.1
Swiss Franc						
Day	$1,988	61	54.10%	$32.58	$2,963	67.1
Perpetual	$8,575	32	37.50%	$267.97	$29,763	28.8

direction, then a day where the direction doesn't matter. The resulting signal is in the majority or prevailing direction. The top lines are day trades and the second have us perpetually committed. Those second lines are an improvement over the day earlier entry results of Table 36.2—again, they'd have to be, given all the facets we've uncovered. Also note the improvement of this day's version over the original day system.

CHAPTER 37

Some Additional Fade Ideas

Fade systems won't likely to be your biggest money makers, but they do have a very desirable function. Since most systems are momentum driven, anything considerably different can serve as a diversification tool. Complementing your main drivers with something performing in a roughly opposite fashion is one way huge portfolio managers smooth out their equity performances.

The "third day fade" is, as usual, simplicity personified.

If the close is less than the previous day's low for two days in a row, then buy today at the open minus 50 percent of the average three-day range on a limit order. Hold the trade overnight. Tomorrow, take profit at today's high, or place your stoploss one tick below yesterday's low. If neither side is hit then exit on close. Vice versa for sells.

Again, in its dopey-simplicity, what is it actually saying? Once again, something that our gut is probably telling us—that any trend, however big or small, has an overdone point somewhere. All we've done is half measure, half jerry-rig one. After seeing two successive closes lower than the previous daily ranges, we're forcing the market to go down some more a third time. In our broad numbers game, a snapback occurs often and/or forcefully enough for us to sail well past slippage/commission in two out of three of the indexes. Again, we have to be mindful of the limit order compensation we've outlined earlier but in the spoos and NASDAQ at least, we've moved far beyond it. See Table 37.1.

A similar variation follows. This time, we decide in off market hours

TABLE 37.1   Third Day Fade—1-2-96 through 11-19-05

	Net Profit	# Trades	% Profit	Profit/Trade	Max. DD	ROA
S&P (Full)	$106,188	219	51.14%	$487.87	$23,625	449.5
NASD (Full)	$181,860	224	44.20%	$811.88	$48,520	374.8
Russell (Full)	($21,125)	279	43.73%	($75.72)	$64,600	NA
30-Yr. Bonds	$1,031	193	48.19%	$5.34	($13,750)	NA
10-Yr. Notes	$12,813	204	52.94%	$62.81	$3,094	414.1
5-Yr. Notes	$4,891	201	50.25%	$24.33	$3,844	127.2
Japanese Yen	$7,188	241	46.06%	$29.82	$8,638	83.2
Euro Currency	$2,363	132	44.70%	$17.90	$8,325	28.4
Swiss Franc	($1,175)	184	45.11%	($6.39)	$8,925	NA

TABLE 37.2   Closes beyond 5-Day Low/High Averages—1-2-96 through 11-19-05

	Net Profit	# Trades	% Profit	Profit/Trade	Max. DD	ROA
S&P (Full)	$181,313	187	55.98%	$969.69	$36,700	494.0
NASD (Full)	$306,750	192	51.56%	$1,597.66	$36,125	849.1
Russell (Full)	$89,525	232	52.59%	$385.88	$39,175	228.5
30-Yr. Bonds	$29,125	197	52.28%	$147.84	$7,969	365.5
10-Yr. Notes	$16,359	203	56.16%	$80.59	$3,750	436.2
5-Yr. Notes	$7,594	188	49.47%	$40.39	$4,391	172.9
Japanese Yen	$11,263	220	51.82%	$51.19	$13,363	84.3
Euro Currency	($8,850)	145	51.72%	($61.03)	$20,738	NA
Swiss Franc	($6,913)	177	53.67%	($39.05)	$13,450	NA

whether we've met a too high/too low threshold condition, which will
then trigger a market order entry on the next open. For buys:

*If the close is less than the previous close for two days in a row and
the close is less than the five-day average low for three days in a row
then buy the next day on the opening. Stay in the position over two
nights. On the third day, the previous day's high is the profit target, and
the stop loss is that day's low minus one tick. Failure to hit either
means exit on the close. Vice versa for sells.*

See Table 37.2.

CHAPTER 38

Another Look at N Day and an Alternative Stop Approach

N Day is one of the world's most familiar trading systems. It's the ultimate in momentum following—stop enter a long position at the highest N Day high, sell short at the lowest N Day low. At its most elemental stripped-down level, there are no exit stops; only reversals. You're perpetually long or short.

"N" is whatever you choose it to be. Twenty is a fairly celebrated variation, largely stemming from the legend of Richard Dennis and his hand-picked traders, the Turtles. There were reportedly a few millionaires who emerged from that whole "can people be taught to trade or is the instinct inborn?" experiment. The underlying methodology, fine points aside, reputedly involved a 20-day incarnation.

The system is now available on the Internet under the "Turtle System" moniker, much to Dennis' annoyance. He doesn't like the implication that he is endorsing it, considering he moved onto to other more esoteric methodologies years ago. He also maintains that the markets have changed since the 1970s–1980s heyday and that almost all the old reliable bellwethers are now ineffective.

I reexamined the system for reasons aside from Dennis. This is partially an organic, live-as-it-happens exercise, remember. My deadline is less than two months away, I've got most of the core skeleton done and now I'm concentrating on backing, filling, and adding more material as I discover it. From here, the research comes first, the writing follows. (Although "here" may not translate chronologically for you. Sorry. Just indulge me for a minute.)

Through the discover-and-disclose process, I came up with an alternate idea for stop losses. Most of the time, a system will stipulate an exit based on a bad place the market is going—something negative the market is doing. It's too low—get out of your longs. What about if you turned the concept on its head? A winning trade in progress should have a positive x characteristic—anything short of that and you should exit. Not surprisingly, there is at least one simple way to encompass that. Before we examine the specifics, let's find an existing system we can tack it onto. (Like N Day.)

Dennis is probably right that N Day is no longer viable, but whether it has completely blown up and lost its bias is another issue. For N Day to be a control, we have to monitor what it's been doing in recent history, unadorned with nothing new added. Table 38.1 shows a yearly breakdown of our nine markets.

There is obvious confirmation that the indexes have been out of synch with the concept for a few years now, but even within the sector, look at the divergences. The NASDAQ was actually positive in the overall last two dismal stock years. Its one bad year was nearly offset by one of the better ones in the Russell. Once again, we're seeing a surprising lack of lock-step correlation between the indexes.

The other markets cover the gamut regarding where their drawdowns hit. The 30-year bonds are nearly a mirror image of the equities with best years occurring in 2004 and 2005, and it's weakest in 2001. There was not one year in which all three currencies were unanimously plus or minus. As for overall performance, the yen was the only market that booked a net five-year loss.

Table 38.2 shows how the profits and losses would have lined up on a yearly rather than individual market basis. To address the issue of how N Day is faring beyond the mere theoretical, we'll dock $100 slippage commission penalty from each trade.

We don't have a lot of total trials to consider. (It doesn't make much sense to dwell on ancient history, when we know N Day was working.) We're not witnessing awesome profits. There is admittedly a net loss over the last three years although systems in general have underperformed in that timeframe. Still, only 2005 booked a significant loss, and that was also the only year where more markets booked losers than winners.

Apparently, the most elemental momentum system of all isn't quite dead. But the fact is, we probably should have been more surprised if it had blown up. It is, after all, the most basic distillation of momentum, a concept we've been validating throughout the book.

TABLE 38.1	Twenty-Day N Day System—Yearly Performance Summary

S&P (Full)

	Net Profit	% Gain	Profit Factor	# Trades	% Profit
2001	$74,000	74.00%	5.12	6	66.67%
2002	$15,225	8.75%	1.37	9	33.33%
2003	($18,125)	−9.58%	0.73	10	30.00%
2004	($7,125)	-4.16%	0.78	9	33.33%
2005	($24,200)	−14.76%	0.34	11	27.27%
Total	**$39,775**				

NASD (Full)

	Net Profit	% Gain	Profit Factor	# Trades	% Profit
2001	$32,650	32.65%	1.39	6	50.00%
2002	$27,850	21.00%	1.94	8	50.00%
2003	($31,250)	−19.47%	0.42	10	30.00%
2004	$15,600	12.07%	2.25	7	42.86%
2005	$5,900	4.07%	1.29	9	44.44%
Total	**$50,750**				

Russell (Full)

	Net Profit	% Gain	Profit Factor	# Trades	% Profit
2001	$69,600	69.60%	8.73	5	80.00%
2002	$13,950	8.23%	1.32	10	40.00%
2003	$26,200	14.27%	1.56	8	50.00%
2004	($19,800)	−9.44%	0.75	9	33.33%
2005	($17,125)	−9.02%	0.69	9	33.33%
Total	**$72,825**				

30-Year Bonds

	Net Profit	% Gain	Profit Factor	# Trades	% Profit
2001	($8,906)	-8.91%	0.41	10	30.00%
2002	$2,938	3.22%	1.26	8	37.50%
2003	$2,500	2.66%	1.19	9	33.33%
2004	$5,094	5.28%	1.51	7	42.86%
2005	$5,938	5.84%	4.96	6	66.67%
Total	**$7,564**				

10-Yr Notes

	Net Profit	% Gain	Profit Factor	# Trades	% Profit
2001	$516	52.00%	1.08	8	50.00%
2002	$10,969	10.91%	5.78	6	33.33%
2003	$3,391	3.04%	1.85	7	42.86%
2004	$4,016	3.50%	1.66	7	42.86%
2005	$1,047	88.00%	1.30	8	50.00%
Total	**$19,939**				

(continues)

TABLE 38.1 *(Continued)*

5 Yr Notes

	Net Profit	% Gain	Profit Factor	# Trades	% Profit
2001	$4,063	4.06%	3.06	6	66.67%
2002	$10,116	9.62%	9.43	6	66.67%
2003	$1,844	1.62%	1.65	7	42.86%
2004	$2,813	2.43%	1.75	7	42.86%
2005	$1,859	1.57%	2.10	8	50.00%
Total	**$20,695**				

Japan Yen

	Net Profit	% Gain	Profit Factor	# Trades	% Profit
2001	$3,363	3.36%	1.39	9	55.56%
2002	($475)	46.00%	0.95	8	50.00%
2003	($9,838)	−9.56%	0.40	11	18.18%
2004	($2,150)	−2.31%	0.77	9	22.22%
2005	$100	11.00%	1.01	8	37.50%
Total	**($9,000)**				

Euro Currency

	Net Profit	% Gain	Profit Factor	# Trades	% Profit
2001	($2,738)	−2.74%	0.77	8	25.00%
2002	($3,513)	−3.61%	0.85	10	20.00%
2003	$21,363	22.79%	3.97	7	71.43%
2004	$9,788	8.50%	2.36	5	40.00%
2005	($2,738)	−1.91%	0.82	8	25.00%
Total	**$22,162**				

Swiss Franc

	Net Profit	% Gain	Profit Factor	# Trades	% Profit
2001	$4,100	4.10%	1.74	6	33.33%
2002	$538	52.00%	1.04	8	37.50%
2003	$2,988	2.86%	1.33	9	55.56%
2004	$1,988	1.85%	1.24	7	42.86%
2005	($1,788)	−1.63%	0.82	8	37.50%
Total	**$7,826**				

TABLE 38.2   N Day Year by Year—100/Trade Slippage/Commission

	2001	2002	2003	2004	2005
S&P (Full)	$73,450	$14,425	($19,025)	($8,925)	($25,200)
NASD (Full)	$32,100	$27,150	($32,150)	$15,000	$5,100
Russell (Full)	$69,150	$13,050	$25,500	($20,600)	($17,925)
30 Yr Bonds	($9,856)	$2,238	$1,700	$4,494	$5,438
10 Yr Notes	($234)	$10,469	$2,791	$3,416	$347
5 Yr Notes	$3,512	$9,516	$1,244	$2,213	$1,159
Japanese Yen	$2,513	($1,175)	($10,838)	($2,950)	($600)
Euro Currency	($3,488)	($4,413)	$20,763	$9,388	($3,088)
Swiss Franc	$3,550	($163)	$2,188	$1,388	($2,488)
TOTAL	**$170,697**	**$71,097**	**($7,827)**	**$3,424**	**($37,257)**

Let's move on—here's the new stop idea.

If you've been in a long trade at least 10 days and you have failed to make both a highest high and a highest close relative to 11 days back, then exit the next day on the opening. Vice versa for shorts.

This has a reasonable symmetry when we apply it to N Day. The trade is entered off 20-day highs and lows; we begin monitoring failure at half that distance. The warning source is that new favorable extremes haven't been made in a while—the trade may be running out of steam. Table 38.3 displays N Day with and without the new qualifier.

TABLE 38.3 N Day with and without 10-Day Stops—01-02-01 through 11-19-05

	Net Profit	# Trades	% Profit	Profit/Trade	Max. DD	ROA
S&P (Full)						
Original	$31,725	40	32.50%	$793.17	$73,875	42.9
New Stop	$74,800	52	40.38%	$1,438.46	$77,725	96.2
NASD (Full)						
Original	$43,100	35	40.00%	$1,231.43	$82,200	52.4
New Stop	$36,300	48	43.75%	$756.25	$63,700	57.0
Russell (Full)						
Original	$67,975	36	44.44%	$1,888.19	$80,875	84.1
New Stop	$109,500	50	50.00%	$2,190.00	$91,075	120.2
30-Yr. Bonds						
Original	$4,813	35	37.14%	$137.50	$18,969	25.4
New Stop	$18,156	44	45.45%	$412.64	$13,375	135.7
10-Yr. Notes						
Original	$18,359	31	45.16%	$592.24	$9,125	201.2
New Stop	$20,969	42	47.62%	$499.26	$8,969	233.8
5-Yr. Notes						
Original	$19,375	29	55.17%	$668.10	$5,266	367.9
New Stop	$16,047	41	46.34%	$391.39	$4,750	337.8
Japanese Yen						
Original	($17,013)	40	30.00%	($425.31)	$25,400	NA
New Stop	($9,588)	54	37.04%	($177.55)	$18,800	NA
Euro Currency						
Original	$17,400	33	33.33%	$527.27	$15,663	111.1
New Stop	$4,113	51	35.29%	$80.64	$19,613	21.0
Swiss Franc						
Original	$4,513	33	42.42%	$136.74	$14,550	31.0
New Stop	$2,513	49	42.86%	$51.28	$14,300	17.6

CHAPTER 39

Taking On the Axioms Part One— The RSI Indicator

There is a partial black box component to my understanding of the RSI indicator. Unlike just about everything else I utilize, I can't completely reconstruct the tool from scratch. I have to rely on the TradeStation presets, which, I realize, is a bit lame. The RSI is not all that complex. (Okay, I'll confess, I haven't been all that interested in tearing into it, although maybe the pending demonstration will prove to be an incentive to do so.)

As most of us know, the RSI is generally regarded as an overbought-oversold oscillator. I'll reprint TradeStation's steps for calculating it verbatim so nothing gets lost in the translation. It is assuming 14 days for the number of total days referenced whereas our upcoming 5-minute bar version will use 9.

1. *Calculate the sum of the UP closes for the previous 14 days and divide this sum by 14. This is the average UP close.*
2. *Calculate the sum of the DOWN closes for the previous 14 days and divide 14. This is the average DOWN close.*
3. *Divide the average UP close by the average DOWN close. This is the Relative Strength (RS).*
4. *Add 1 to the RS.*
5. *Divide the result obtained in Step 4 into 100.*
6. *Subtract the result obtained in Step 5 from 100. This is the first RSI.**

---

*Welles Wilder Jr., *New Concepts in Technical Trading Systems* (McLeansville, NC: Trend Research).

From there, the user guide goes on to describe how to do a daily update, which won't be necessary for anyone automating the strategy using the "RSI" preset. But hopefully at this point, we have a pretty good understanding of what the indicator is supposed to be measuring.

A conventional approach has it that when the reading gets over 80, the market is overbought and when under 20, it's oversold. Any number of additional tools can be used in conjunction, such as acting off moving average crossovers during extreme readings. Because of the variety of added techniques as well as the different variables you can input into the lengths and overbought/oversold readings, I would not feel comfortable categorically debunking the contrarian nature of the oscillator. I can, however, reveal a setup in which it behaves as anything but.

If you are 45 minutes or more into the session and the RSI is 85 or more, then buy on the opening of the next bar. You can initiate up until a half hour before the close.

If you are 45 minutes or more into the session and RSI is 15 or less, then sell short on the opening of the next bar. All other rules are the same.

Exit all trades at 5 minutes before the close.

This is another idea in which you get reversals that solely unfold out of the technique—no arbitrary stops. Perhaps further tweaking would be necessary to make this viable. Still, look at the consistent results of going with the overextended readings rather than fading them in the manner they were intended (Table 39.1).

RSI Go-with underscores an axiom that seasoned traders understand well. Nothing is ever too high to buy nor too low to sell. I lost a small fortune years ago trying to bottom-pick sugar after it went under three cents

TABLE 39.1 RSI Go-With System—5 Min. Bars—1-2-01 through 11-19-05 (Indexes)—5-15-01 through 11-19-05 (All Others)

	Net Profit	# Trades	% Profit	Profit/Trade	Max. DD	ROA
S&P (Mini)	$8,813	218	58.72%	$40.42	$2,575	342.3
NASD (Mini)	$14,920	248	57.26%	$60.16	$2,410	619.0
Russell (Mini)	$4,140	323	57.28%	$12.82	$5,580	74.2
30-Yr. Bonds	$8,688	276	51.45%	$31.48	$4,531	191.7
10-Yr. Notes	$9,234	235	56.17%	$39.30	$2,672	345.6
5-Yr. Notes	$1,250	277	49.82%	$4.51	$4,891	25.6
Japanese Yen	$2,050	191	45.03%	$10.73	$2,663	77.0
Euro Currency	$22,138	189	59.26%	$117.13	$2,150	1,029.7
Swiss Franc	$7,838	214	52.80%	$36.62	$2,750	285.0

a pound. I vowed I would let it go to zero before taking a loss. Then I realized I could lose significantly more than the three cents when monthly rollovers were accounted for. D'oh! The upshot was, what I confidently bought at around three, I humbly dumped at around two. The market continued to languish in rounding bottom fashion for months before it finally moved off the mat.

It gets back to momentum. You just can't seem to get too far afield of it.

CHAPTER 40

Taking On the Axioms Part Two— The Reversal Day Indicator

B ack in simpler times, when widespread technical awareness wasn't permeating every corner of the investment field from do-it-your-selfer individuals to complex program trading funds, the following depicted popular reversal signals at their most basic:

It was *bullish* if the low was less than the previous low and the close was greater than the previous close.

It was *bearish* if the high was greater than the previous high and the close was lower than the previous low.

They were quaint ways of sizing up a move in progress (we're higher than yesterday's high) and the subsequent resolution (but we couldn't hold it—we closed lower).

People still routinely use them to affirm or challenge a position. Plenty of them appear in textbook fashion at the very tops or bottoms of moves. The reason they're not automatically profitable, of course, is because they also occur so often more in the middle. Your eyes are not as likely to lock onto those signals as the ones bracketing the ultimate extremes.

Is there anything to them anymore (or for that matter, was there ever)? Again, there are many ways reversals can be filtered and qualified. (One of the most common is to stipulate that for a buy reversal, yesterday's low had to be lower than x number of preceding days in a row, not just the day before). Because of all the potential permutations, I again won't claim to be puncturing any cherished balloons. I'll only once again demonstrate a setup that works contrary to expectations. This is an interday system.

TABLE 40.1 Fading Reversals—Daily—01-01-01 through 11-19-05

	Net Profit	# Trades	% Profit	Profit/Trade	Max. DD	ROA
S&P (Full)	$62,550	325	58.15%	$192.46	$76,525	81.7
NASD (Full)	$86,500	317	63.72%	$272.87	$40,100	215.7
Russell (Full)	$16,675	304	60.86%	$54.85	$104,700	15.9
30-Yr. Bonds	$6,219	287	64.46%	$21.67	$19,844	31.3
10-Yr. Notes	$7,281	300	64.33%	$24.27	$10,172	71.6
5-Yr. Notes	$11,421	265	63.77%	$43.10	$4,859	235.0
Japanese Yen	($8,063)	161	63.98%	($50.08)	$13,263	NA
Euro Currency	($2,763)	218	61.47%	($12.67)	$14,950	NA
Swiss Franc	($6,350)	202	60.40%	($31.44)	$13,838	NA

If yesterday's high was greater than the day before and the close was less than the previous close, then buy next bar at market.

If yesterday's low was less than the day before and the close was greater, then sell short.

Don't misconstrue what you're seeing. Both buy and sell indicators are the opposite of what they traditionally are.

Once in the trade, we'll return to our previous technique of using the entry day's high/low extremes as the respective profit target-stop loss. For buys, the first day's high is the target and the low minus one tick is the stop level. For this system, those numbers stay constant for however many days hence it takes to fill one of them. Don't put up the exit orders if the new day is signaling in the same direction as your position. Table 40.1 shows the results.

CHAPTER 41

Potpourri—Systems as I Discover and/or Rediscover Them—In No Particular Order

200 PERCENT RANGE EXPANSION—FOUR DAYS IN TRADE

Here's another system firmly aligned with our simplicity/universality sensibilities.

Buy at tomorrow's opening plus 200 percent of the average three day range. Sell short at the opening minus the same distance.

So far, so good. It's a simple range breakout idea that dovetails a bit with the switch concept. Momentum trades will have an especial chance of success in relatively volatile environments. We've rigged the game accordingly: any market that travels twice its normal range is likely to be active. The profit targets and stop losses are similarly ground we've covered before.

Look to exit three days after the entry (fourth day in the trade). If long, take profit on the previous day's high. Set stop loss at the previous day's low. If neither is hit, exit on the close. Vice versa if you're short.

We're again forced to look at a long history (20 years), considering the infrequent signaling. (Which is kind of switch-like—relative long periods of no activity.) Table 41.1 features results in our nine financials.

Granted, the results may be responding to some jerry-rigging on our part. The over-the-top NASDAQ performance is again tech-bubble-related ($71,600 profit just in 2000, more than 100 percent of the total). The yen posted a $13,063 gain in 1998—the year of the Pacific Rim currency crisis.

On the other hand, "Four Day Range Expansion" in effect plays to the anomaly. That's kind of intrinsic to the setup.

176

TABLE 41.1   Four-Day Range Expansion—1-2-86 through 11-19-05

	Net Profit	# Trades	% Profit	Profit/Trade	Max. DD	ROA
S&P (Full)	$5,388	153	49.02%	$35.21	$67,225	8.0
NASD (Full)	$54,610	32	59.38%	$1,707.00	$50,700	107.7
Russell (Full)	$34,750	144	54.86%	$241.32	$42,075	82.6
30-Yr. Bonds	$25,813	214	56.07%	$120.62	$9,406	274.4
10-Yr. Notes	$12,484	244	58.61%	$51.17	$6,188	201.7
5-Yr. Notes	($1,172)	281	53.74%	($4.17)	$10,141	NA
Japanese Yen	$15,750	270	45.19%	$58.33	$15,713	100.2
Euro Currency	$9,813	67	50.75%	$146.46	$6,875	142.7
Swiss Franc	$14,100	214	53.34%	$65.89	$16,288	86.6

TABLE 41.2   Four-Day Range Expansion Other Markets—1-8-86 through 11-19-05

	Net Profit	# Trades	% Profit	Profit/Trade	Max. DD	ROA
Soybeans	$4,794	177	51.98%	$27.08	$7,688	62.4
Corn	$3,963	224	48.21%	$17.69	$3,450	114.9
Wheat	($7,406)	148	47.97%	($50.04)	$10,531	NA
Live Cattle	$9,778	175	58.86%	$55.87	$4,231	231.1
						196.0
Live Hogs	($2,973)	125	45.60%	($23.79)	$5,614	NA
Pork Bellies	$13,605	126	54.76%	$107.97	$6,183	220.0
Gold	$8,788	278	52.52%	$31.61	$6,176	142.3
Silver	$10,155	260	45.38%	$39.06	$13,130	77.3
Coffee	($13,868)	225	49.78%	($61.63)	($73,035)	NA
Cocoa	$7,090	298	45.64%	$23.79	$7,730	91.7
Orange Juice	$29,124	329	55.62%	$88.52	$4,083	713.3

The concept shows unusual persistence across an additional sector array as Table 41.2 reveals. It seems to do the best in the thinnest markets (pork bellies, orange juice).

THE CONTINUOUS 66 PERCENT MOMENTUM SYSTEM

The next system is a barnburner in the indexes, and a borderline indicator in several of the remaining financials. It's a longer-term methodology triggered off daily charts. It's simple and non-arbitrary. All the entries, exits, and reversals stem from one principle: buy on momentum a certain distance off a daily opening, but only if the previous close is closer to an x day low than an x day high. Vice versa for sells. The x day range becomes a working part of the system, as do two segments that comprise it: the *x* day high minus the last close, and the close minus the *x* day low. There are no tacked-on stops—they flow out of the methodology itself. I like this a lot because it is pure momentum coupled with the idea that you'll be trying to exploit a move earlier rather than later.

Set a value for 9 day high minus close: XH

Set a value for close minus 9 day low: XL

Set a value for the bigger of the two: XX

If XH > XL, then buy the next day at the open plus 66 percent of XL on a stop. The stoploss is the entry price −1.32 (twice 0.66) times XX

If XH < XL then sell short on the next open minus 66 percent of XH stop. Buy to cover at the entry price +1.32 times XX

You can't find much fault in the Table 41.3 results. Apart from the huge net profit and high profit-per-trade figure, note how accurate the system is.

TABLE 41.3 Nine-Day 66 Percent Momentum System—Full sized S&Ps— 01-02-01 through 11-19-05

Total Net Profit	$179,125.00	Profit Factor	1.46
Gross Profit	$566,775.00	Gross Loss	($387,650.00)
Total Number of Trades	188	Percent Profitable	62.77%
Winning Trades	118	Losing Trades	70
Even Trades	0		
Avg. Trade Net Profit	$952.79	Ratio Avg. Win:Avg. Loss	0.87
Avg. Winning Trade	$4,803.18	Avg. Losing Trade	($5,537.86)
Largest Winning Trade	$23,250.00	Largest Losing Trade	($28,500.00)
Max. Consecutive Winning Trades	10	Max. Consecutive Losing Trades	4
Avg. Bars in Winning Trades	6.19	Avg. Bars in Losing Trades	9.16
Avg. Bars in Total Trades	7.30		
Max. Shares/Contracts Held	1	Account Size Required	$30,775.00
Return on Initial Capital	179.13%	Annual Rate of Return	21.00%
Return Retracement Ratio	0.43	RINA Index	36.05
Trading Period	4 Yrs, 10 Mths, 19 Dys	Percent of Time in the Market	96.08%
Max. Equity Run-up	$193,225.00		
Max. Drawdown (Intraday Peak to Valley)		**Max. Drawdown (Trade Close to Trade Close)**	
Value	($51,325.00)	Value	($30,775.00)

Source: © TradeStation Technologies, Inc. 1991–2006. All rights reserved.

TABLE 41.4 Nine-Day 66% Momentum System—Yearly Performance— Full Sized S&Ps

	Net Profit	% Gain	Profit Factor	# Trades	% Profitable
2001	$82,925	82.92%	1.71	37	70.27%
2002	$38,025	20.79%	1.34	43	58.14%
2003	$19,375	8.77%	1.29	37	62.16%
2004	$23,025	9.58%	1.43	38	57.89%
2005	$15,500	5.89%	1.36	38	57.89%

TABLE 41.5 Nine-Day 66% Momentum—Continuous—01-02-01 through 11-19-05

	Net Profit	# Trades	% Profit	Profit/Trade	Max. DD	ROA
NASD (Full)	$83,550	180	56.11%	$464.17	$119,400	70.0
Russell (Full)	$186,950	202	64.36%	$925.50	$45,300	412.7
30-Yr. Bonds	$22,375	175	59.43%	$127.86	$26,719	83.7
10-Yr. Notes	$5,172	166	60.24%	$31.16	$15,609	33.1
5-Yr. Notes	($6,953)	166	53.61%	($41.89)	$16,359	NA
Japanese Yen	$8,338	167	59.88%	$49.93	$13,725	60.8
Euro Currency	($7,625)	180	54.44%	($42.36)	$36,188	NA
Swiss Franc	$13,213	174	59.77%	$75.93	$24,863	53.1

You're right 66 percent of the time in this sample. Table 41.4 shows how evenly your results are distributed—not a losing year. Similar ballpark results appear in the other indexes and further confirmation occurs most of the remaining financials (Table 41.5).

CONTRACTING RANGES—BUYING OFF LOWER CLOSES—SELLING OFF HIGHER ONES

If the close is less than both the previous close and the average 5-day close, and the average 10-day range is less than the average 25-day range, then buy tomorrow at the opening plus 20 percent of the previous range on a stop.

Straight stoploss: entry price minus the 25-day average range.

Conditional stoploss: if the close is greater than both the previous close and the previous five-day average close, exit at next open minus 20 percent of the previous range on a stop.

If the close is greater than both the previous close and the average five day close, and the average 10-day range is less than the average 25-day range, then sell short tomorrow at the opening minus

20 percent of the previous range on a stop.

Straight stoploss: entry price plus the 25-day average range.

Conditional stop loss: if the close is less than both the previous close and the previous five-day average close, exit at next open plus 20 percent of the previous range on a stop.

This may seem more involved than what we've been advocating, but despite the verbiage, the underlying concepts are pretty simple. You want your setup to involve tight daily ranges—we've seen validity to the "coiling" concept. We're allowing longs when we're closer to the bottom of a given channel, and sells when we're relatively higher up. Despite using a condition that could be classified as "fade," we're still entering on stops, that is, momentum. The "conditional" long-side stop is merely the short selling order without the range size qualifier. It's just saying that the contrarian part of our buy qualifier no longer applies—we're now above the ranges—look to exit on the 20 percent move. The straight stop is in place in the event the other doesn't set up. It's simple and yet dynamic, that is, keyed to range sizes. Each component has been previously demonstrated, and you can't dismiss the Table 41.6 results.

TABLE 41.6 Contracting Range—Fade Close on Momentum—Daily— 01-02-01 through 11-19-05

	Net Profit	# Trades	% Profit	Profit/Trade	Max. DD	ROA
S&P (Full)	$138,875	257	46.69%	$540.37	$38,800	357.9
NASD (Full)	$66,150	287	44.25%	$230.49	$43,750	151.2
Russell (Full)	$113,475	272	50.00%	$417.19	$49,900	227.4
30-Yr. Bonds	$37,969	271	46.13%	$140.11	$5,469	694.3
10-Yr. Notes	$24,141	267	45.69%	$90.41	$3,078	784.3
5-Yr. Notes	$6,479	254	39.76%	$25.47	$4,079	158.8
Japanese Yen	$17,213	284	36.97%	$60.61	$13,238	130.0
Euro Currency	$27,575	267	38.95%	$103.28	$17,987	153.3
Swiss Franc	($950)	247	38.46%	$38.46	$17,188	NA

TABLE 41.7 5- versus 15-Day Closing Averages—01-02-01 through 11-19-05

	Net Profit	# Trades	% Profit	Profit/Trade	Max. DD	ROA
S&P (Full)	$49,500	76	40.79%	$651.97	$117,300	42.2
NASD (Full)	$22,900	78	30.77%	$293.59	$117,900	19.4
Russell (Full)	$134,975	68	42.65%	$1,984.93	$137,450	98.2
30-Yr. Bonds	$6,563	67	37.31%	$97.95	$15,625	42.0
10-Yr. Notes	$5,125	62	40.32%	$82.66	$13,984	36.7
5-Yr. Notes	$4,672	64	40.63%	$73.00	$8,688	53.8
Japanese Yen	($12,088)	79	43.04%	($153.01)	$32,163	NA
Euro Currency	$17,275	78	33.33%	$221.47	$13,813	125.1
Swiss Franc	($4,888)	78	35.90%	($62.66)	$15,163	NA

FIVE VERSUS 15-DAY CLOSING AVERAGES

Buy at the market when the 5-day average closes above the 15-day closing average for 3 days in a row. Vice versa for shorts. No stops.

Back to "simple" in description as well as makeup. Not much need be added. See Table 41.7.

A SOYBEAN PLAY THAT HAS WORKED 70 PERCENT OF THE TIME OVER THE LAST 40 YEARS

Aside from the fact that this is out of place in a financial futures book, it's not even the kind of research I normally endorse. The sample is small. There is not my omnipresent buy-sell symmetry—this is strictly a long entry play (although I'll offer a corresponding sell that also works, though not quite as consistently).

The biggest argument for caution (or even skepticism) is that such apparent biases can be found all over the market world, but a certain percentage of them are going to be the result of sheer randomness. Given enough markets and enough years, that's an inevitability. You'd see occasional extreme outcomes in known chance events, such as coin tossing. Given enough 20-toss trials, you'll get some that come up 70, 80, or 90 percent heads. There are vendors out there who have done well exploiting such a numbers game. What's the deal?—why am I throwing my support in this direction?

Because I'm applying something else I normally stay clear of—my perception of a fundamental truth about soybeans. Fundamental as in fundamentalist analysis—a normally futile pursuit in my experience. Perhaps this will prove an exception.

Soybeans may be the one old-line supply/demand-driven actual product market that has a large psychological component to it. I have been swept along by the floor hysteria—usually with dismal results. I have been one of the locals forever thinking that this summer—the one we're in—is going to be the blight of all blights. Monster drought, pestilence—something that is going to make the crop as valuable as gold and all of us rich as a result.

It almost never happens. Even when there is environmental pressure, the crop has incredible resilience. It prevails in a way that neither corn nor oats nor just about anything else can. As one trader ruefully observed, soybeans are a weed growing in a rain forest.

The moral—don't buy beans for a summer play. *However*—despite the failure of the crop-ravaged pipe dreams to ultimately pay off, there are moments where psychology and uncertainty make it look like they *might*. Year after year, there is almost an inevitable pop of 30, 40, 50 cents or more in a short time frame. (Usually presummer when the seeds aren't even in the ground.)

After enough years of slapping my forehead and saying, "Why am I trying to buy in the *summer?!*" I began piecing together market action leading up to it. In spring 1987, a full year before the last big drought, I bought 10 out-of-the-money bean option calls for $1000. It was strictly a seat-of-the-pants play, and I was pretty much a trading fool in those days. I was going for the super-home run—$50,000. I wasn't going to settle for a dime less.

People have trouble believing this today—I wish I could remember the exact strike, dates, etc.— but at one point, those options momentarily exploded to $30,000 in value. As options tend to go, though, the next day, I would have had to settle for something like half of that value, and by the next day, the party was all but over. I watched $30,000 plummet to zero.

During each subsequent passing year, I would remember that somewhere along the line I'd get "a thrill for my money" being long—almost always in the spring. Uncertainty and speculative bullishness would pop the beans and everybody would say, "This is it!" It wasn't, but again, there was a near-inevitability to that momentary ride.

I'm including this one narrow little seasonal trade because I'm convinced I understand the driver. The driver is Mack and Hat and Landis and Jack and me—and every other floor trader sensitive to potential crop damage. Some time during just about every season, something will happen to cast an element of doubt over the crop's general health and well being. It happens earlier than most traders bargain for. By July 1, it's all over but the shouting.

So here's how I quantified that experience. I optimized entry and exit dates. No matter how I shook up the numbers, the July inception was the marker for *not being long anymore*—completely dovetailing with my experience. The entry date figured to be sometime in the first few months of the year. The size of the pop was somewhat debatable, although I figured you would need to settle for less than half a dollar if you wanted your percentage of winners to be high. That kind of analytical targeting is further a reason to treat this offering with somewhat of a grain of salt—what does big percentage of winners in and of itself really mean, after all? I guess I can sometimes be as psychologically driven as the next guy. One of my market puzzle exercises is to decide trades that are likely to pay off *right now!*

Buy November beans the first trading day in March. Take a $2,000 profit (40 cents) or a $4,000 loss (80 cents). If neither side is hit, exit on the second trading day in July. See Table 41.8.

Table 41.9 shows a yearly summary since 1966. As you'll notice, the July 2 deadline determines losses more often than the 80 cent stop. You hit the –$4000 four times since 1966—the last being in 1991. Basically, it

TABLE 41.8 Soybean Seasonal: Buy in March—1965–2005

Total Net Profit	$31,725.00	Profit Factor	2.47
Gross Profit	$53,325.00	Gross Loss	($21,600.00)
Total Number of Trades	40	Percent Profitable	70.00%
Winning Trades	28	Losing Trades	12
Even Trades	0		
Avg. Trade Net Profit	$793.13	Ratio Avg. Win:Avg. Loss	1.06
Avg. Winning Trade	$1,904.46	Avg. Losing Trade	($1,800.00)
Largest Winning Trade	$2,450.00	Largest Losing Trade	($4,250.00)
Max. Consecutive Winning Trades	7	Max. Consecutive Losing Trades	3
Avg. Bars in Winning Trades	40.93	Avg. Bars in Losing Trades	69.25
Avg. Bars in Total Trades	49.42		
Max. Shares/Contracts Held	1	Account Size Required	$8,312.50
Return on Initial Capital	31.72%	Annual Rate of Return	0.69%
Return Retracement Ratio	0.08	RINA Index	138.03
Trading Period	39 Yrs, 9 Mths, 15 Dys	Percent of Time in the Market	19.10%
Max. Equity Run-up	$36,687.50		
Max. Drawdown (Intraday Peak to Valley)		**Max. Drawdown (Trade Close to Trade Close)**	
Value	($9,800.00)	Value	($8,312.50)

Source: © TradeStation Technologies, Inc. 1991–2006. All rights reserved.

TABLE 41.9 40-Year Soybean Long Side Seasonal

	Net Profit	% Gain	Profit Factor	# Trades	% Profitable
1966	$2,000	2.00%	100	1	100.00%
1967	($494)	−0.48%	0	1	0.00%
1968	($675)	−0.66%	0	1	0.00%
1969	($206)	−0.20%	0	1	0.00%
1970	$1,181	1.17%	100	1	100.00%
1971	$825	0.81%	100	1	100.00%
1972	$919	0.90%	100	1	100.00%
1973	($4,063)	−3.92%	0	1	0.00%
1974	($4,250)	−4.27%	0	1	0.00%
1975	$2,250	2.36%	100	1	100.00%
1976	$2,006	2.06%	100	1	100.00%
1977	$2,006	2.02%	100	1	100.00%
1978	$2,006	1.98%	100	1	100.00%
1979	$2,006	1.94%	100	1	100.00%
1980	($4,006)	−3.80%	0	1	0.00%
1981	$2,006	1.98%	100	1	100.00%
1982	($1,663)	−1.61%	0	1	0.00%
1983	$2,275	2.23%	100	1	100.00%
1984	$2,006	1.93%	100	1	100.00%
1985	$2,006	1.89%	100	1	100.00%
1986	($988)	−0.91%	0	1	0.00%
1987	$2,006	1.87%	100	1	100.00%
1988	$2,006	1.84%	100	1	100.00%
1989	($138)	−0.12%	0	1	0.00%
1990	$2,006	1.81%	100	1	100.00%
1991	($4,006)	−3.54%	0	1	0.00%
1992	$88	−0.08%	0	1	0.00%
1993	$2,006	1.84%	100	1	100.00%
1994	$2,006	1.81%	100	1	100.00%
1995	$2,000	1.77%	100	1	100.00%
1996	$2,000	1.74%	100	1	100.00%
1997	$2,000	1.71%	100	1	100.00%
1998	($1,025)	−0.86%	0	1	100.00%
1999	$2,050	1.74%	100	1	100.00%
2000	$2,000	1.67%	100	1	100.00%
2001	$1,300	1.07%	100	1	100.00%
2002	$2,000	1.62%	100	1	100.00%
2003	$2,000	1.60%	100	1	100.00%
2004	$2,000	1.57%	100	1	100.00%
2005	$2,450	1.90%	100	1	100.00%

was included as a mere acknowledgement that some "cry uncle" point is better than none.

It is January 2006 as I write this. A friend of mine has agreed that maybe this is a prudent position to put on, so we have a sort of pact to do so in 2006. If you recall hearing a scream from the general direction of Geneva, Illinois, sometime in mid-2006, you'll now know why. (There's just something really irritating about giving yet more money to the bean market.) This will be slightly before this book becomes available, so you'll have to wait until 2007 for your turn.

And now for that not-quite symmetrical short-side rejoinder I promised (You'll notice that both the profit and loss targets are larger.)

Sell short the first trading day of July. Take a $4,000 profit (80 cents) or a $5,000 loss. If neither side is hit, exit on the second trading day of November. See Table 41.10.

TABLE 41.10	Soybean Seasonal: Sell in July—1965–2005		
Total Net Profit	$31,675.00	Profit Factor	1.69
Gross Profit	$77,262.50	Gross Loss	($45,587.50)
Total Number of Trades	40	Percent Profitable	60.00%
Winning Trades	24	Losing Trades	16
Even Trades	0		
Avg. Trade Net Profit	$791.88	Ratio Avg. Win:Avg. Loss	1.13
Avg. Winning Trade	$3,219.27	Avg. Losing Trade	($2,849.22)
Largest Winning Trade	$6,000.00	Largest Losing Trade	($5,700.00)
Max. Consecutive Winning Trades	3	Max. Consecutive Losing Trades	3
Avg. Bars in Winning Trades	52.71	Avg. Bars in Losing Trades	59.50
Avg. Bars in Total Trades	55.42		
Max. Shares/Contracts Held	1	Account Size Required	$10,706.25
Return on Initial Capital	31.67%	Annual Rate of Return	0.69%
Return Retracement Ratio	0.07	RINA Index	67.21
Trading Period	39 Yrs, 9 Mths, 15 Dys	Percent of Time in the Market	21.52%
Max. Equity Run-up	$39,262.50		
Max. Drawdown (Intra-day Peak to Valley)		**Max. Drawdown (Trade Close to Trade Close)**	
Value	($13,406.25)	Value	($10,706.25)

Source: © TradeStation Technologies, Inc. 1991–2006. All rights reserved.

TABLE 41.11   Three-Day 30-Day Crossover—01-02-01 through 11-19-05

	Net Profit	# Trades	% Profit	Profit/Trade	Max. DD	ROA
S&P (Full)	$89,475	52	36.54%	$1,720.67	$39,150	228.5
NASD (Full)	$25,350	55	34.55%	$460.91	$43,900	57.7
Russell (Full)	$33,475	57	31.58%	$587.28	$94,250	35.5
30-Yr. Bonds	$18,125	53	35.85%	$341.98	$14,531	124.7
10-Yr. Notes	$14,890	54	38.89%	$275.75	$6,938	214.6
5-Yr. Notes	$13,828	50	46.00%	$276.56	$4,906	281.9
Japanese Yen	($13,588)	67	28.36%	($202.80)	$20,813	NA
Euro Currency	$26,063	64	40.63%	$407.23	$8,725	298.7
Swiss Franc	$5,075	66	37.88%	$76.89	$13,875	36.58

Just for further information, the $4,000 profit was hit in each of the last three years. However else you feel about this part of the seasonal picture, the results should drive the point home one more time: *stay the heck out of the long side of soybeans during the summer!*

YET ANOTHER MOVING AVERAGE CROSSOVER— THE 3-DAY 30-DAY SYSTEM

If the 3-day closing average is higher than the 30-day closing average for three days in a row, buy the next day on the open. Exit the day after the 3-day closes under the 30-day. Vice versa for sells. See Table 41.11.

THE 15–30 DAY CLOSE INDICATOR

Is there any momentum–related significance to being above or below individual closes x number of bars back? It would seem to make intuitive sense. After all, closing averages can serve as triggers—why not individual closes as well? Classic technical analysis pays attention to where a market is relative to a month or a year back, for example.

I've gotten good results stipulating that a market has to be above or below two distinct points. Granted, this could be a particularly vulnerable spot for overoptimization—given enough numerical pairs, we're likely to stumble over something after all. I attempt to mitigate this by stipulating that the distance between the two numbers be the same as how far back

TABLE 41.12   15–30 Day Close Indicator—01-02-01 through 11-19-05

	Net Profit	# Trades	% Profit	Profit/Trade	Max. DD	ROA
S&P (Full)	$45,225	114	44.74%	$396.71	$77,700	58.2
NASD (Full)	$73,250	109	44.95%	$672.02	$55,700	131.5
Russell (Full)	$153,125	100	38.00%	$1,531.25	$64,000	239.3
30-Yr. Bonds	$20,344	98	39.80%	$207.59	$10,094	201.5
10-Yr. Notes	$25,547	94	44.68%	$271.78	$5,891	433.7
5-Yr. Notes	$17,563	100	48.00%	$175.63	$4,672	375.9
Japanese Yen	($600)	109	44.95%	($5.50)	$21,175	NA
Euro Currency	$25,125	112	40.18%	$224.33	$12,150	206.8
Swiss Franc	$7,213	104	34.62%	$69.35	$9,825	73.4

the most recent of the two is from the market's last close. In other words, your close is above the closes both 10 and 20-days back, or 25 and 50. This suggests three equidistant points on a line, and we're in effect looking for a little more follow-through beyond.

Table 41.12 shows rather consistent results using the following methodology:

If the close is higher than both the close 15 days ago and the close 30 days ago, then buy the next day at market. Exit the trade any time the close settles below either marker. Vice versa for sells.

THE BONDS LEAD THE INDEXES

Let's return to the concept of one market keying off another. You can find a pronounced bias along the lines of "Spoo leads Dow" when you insert 30-day bonds into an intraday index chart. As floor traders well know, the bonds lead the indexes. I traded briefly in the now defunct Maxi pit at the Board of Trade. (The contract's makeup most closely approximated to-day's Dow future.) The locals would key off many things, several of which eluded me. The bond contract, though, was an obvious trigger. Each new bond tick seemed to precipitate renewed Maxi response.

What is the correlation? Actually, you can see 180 degree variations. Sometimes, the sectors move in same-directional lock step, as when the economy is thriving and expanding in an orderly fashion. When the environment becomes more uncertain and volatile, however, the two tend to move inversely. Either equities are seen as risky relative to the more predictable bond yields, or as the equities enjoy renewed favor, the bonds drop because people feel their yield is smaller than what they can get in stocks. Again, it's the bonds that normally tip their hands first.

This dichotomy makes straight-ahead ideas, such as buying on bond strength, difficult. Sometimes, the opposite approach is correct. Traders' day-to-day connection with world events and the immediate environment will tell them which paradigm they're in more readily than inflexible system rules. Even a system, however, can be made to recognize that if the bonds are trading in extreme fashion, the equites will be following suit. If the intraday bonds are near a daily high or low, it's good bet the indexes will similarly gravitate if they haven't done so. Again, a trader knows that bonds are climbing, and therefore the S&Ps will fall soon given the immediate environment. How do we similarly alert a system? How about this:

If x amount of time into a trading day, the S&Ps and bonds are both higher than their respective daily openings, and the bonds are within the top 25 percent of the daily range, that's bullish, figuring to produce a lock step scenario in the spoos. Buy at market, exit on the close.

Scenario 2 would also be bullish. It's the same time of day as above and again, the spoos are higher than the open. This time, though, the bonds are lower than the open and trading in the bottom quarter of the daily range. That's bullish suggesting inverse price movement. Again, buy at that time and hold through the rest of the trading day.

The key to both is that the intraday bond close is within 25 percent of the day's high or low. This is a rough and primitive way of suggesting that the bonds are trending somewhat and that the S&Ps will follow suit—but in their own direction relative to their opening.

Figure 41.1 shows two trades in 10 minute bar charts. Both are initiated at 2:00 and exited at 3:10 CST. In the first, the bond insert (lower bars) are signaling a buy via their strength (near the high of the day). The second buy is signaled in opposite fashion—at their 2:00 close, the bonds are near session lows at the same time the S&Ps have been showing strength.

Table 41.13 shows an optimization of the time of day you enter when the above conditions are met. The pit bond session trade is inserted in the regular hours session of the emini S&P, both using 10-minute bar charts. These are day trades, all exiting at five minutes before the close (3:10 CST).

The 10:00 entry provides the best return on account. It's near the top of the fields in the other indexes also, although most of the other variables also prove effective. (You could, for example, turn this into a late time of day system using a 2:00 entry.)

Table 41.14 shows the 10:00 entry, 3:10 exit results.

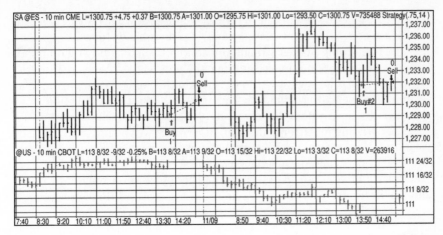

Created with TradeStation

FIGURE 41.1   Bonds Signaling Index Buys, in Tandem and Inverse (*Source:* © TradeStation Technologies, Inc. 1991–2006. All rights reserved.)

TABLE 41.13   Bond-Index Optimization—10 Minute emini S&Ps, 30 Year Bond Insert—05-15-01 through 11-19-05

B	Net Profit	# Trades	% Profit	Profit/Trade	Max. DD	ROA
9:00	$18,288	394	57	$46.41	$7,950	230.0
10:00	$13,563	348	55	$38.97	$4,288	316.3
11:00	$5,713	385	57	$14.84	$6,663	85.7
12:00	$8,163	416	55	$19.62	$5,713	142.9
1:00	$7,800	408	58	$19.12	$6,850	113.9
2:00	$9,063	439	56	$20.64	$3,550	255.3

TABLE 41.14   Bond-Index Indicator—10:00 Entry—10-Min. Bars—01-02-01 through 11-19-05

Mini Contracts	Net Profit	# Trades	% Profit	Profit/Trade	Max. DD	ROA
S&P	$13,563	348	55.46%	$38.97	$4,088	331.8
NASDAQ	$12,300	362	55.80%	$33.98	$4,630	265.7
Russell	$14,880	322	54.66%	$46.21	$3,620	411.0
Dow	$5,300	282	54.61%	$18.79	$4,100	129.3

A Final
Step-by-Step System
Construction—
The Six
Signal Indicator

A rather late refinement—extremely simple. It's the bellwether I'm currently tracking on a couple of web sites (Elite Trader and Tiger-sharktrading.com). It again incorporates the technique of entering on the open and exiting on the close. Just add one component to the original 5 either-or indicators, (page 39). The sixth signal, again, designed to flash daily save for the rare tie, involves fading the majority direction of the last three open-closes.

If at least two out of the last three open to closes were lower, that's a long signal (+1). A higher majority indicates sell (−1). Table 42.1 shows how that indicator pulls its weight. We might regard it as impressive given

TABLE 42.1 Fading Two out of Three Open-to-Closes—Daily—01-02-01 through 11-19-05

	Net Profit	# Trades	% Profit	Profit/Trade	Max. DD	ROA
S&P (Full)	$203,213	1,228	53.75%	$165.48	$47,400	428.7
NASD (Full)	$4,250	1,226	50.16%	$3.47	$92,950	4.6
Russell (Full)	$58,050	1,226	50.41%	$47.35	$88,325	65.7
30-Yr. Bonds	$18,813	1,220	49.43%	$15.42	$12,906	145.8
10-Yr. Notes	$9,531	1,221	50.20%	$7.81	$10,094	94.4
5-Yr. Notes	$16,656	1,223	50.78%	$13.62	$5,578	298.6
Japanese Yen	$863	1,222	48.20%	$0.71	$10,075	8.6
Euro Currency	$23,988	1,220	52.38%	$19.66	$25,463	94.2
Swiss Franc	$913	1,222	50.16%	$0.75	$20,638	4.4

TABLE 42.2 Six Indicator (Simple Majority)—Daily—01-02-01 through 11-19-05

	Net Profit	# Trades	% Profit	Profit/Trade	Max. DD	ROA
S&P (Full)	$259,238	666	57.81%	$389.25	$23,275	1,114.0
NASD (Full)	$98,550	669	51.72%	$147.31	$74,050	133.1
Russell (Full)	$106,625	632	51.27%	$168.71	$50,775	210.0
30-Yr. Bonds	$56,063	685	54.60%	$81.84	$6,906	811.8
10-Yr. Notes	$34,688	665	53.23%	$52.16	$5,063	685.1
5-Yr. Notes	$27,641	675	55.26%	$40.95	$3,359	822.9
Japanese Yen	($500)	712	50.14%	($0.70)	$9,513	NA
Euro Currency	$14,700	701	52.07%	$20.97	$18,025	81.6
Swiss Franc	$10,050	703	51.64%	$14.30	$14,950	67.2

its simplicity, although hopefully by now, we're getting used to the idea that "simple" works just fine.

Add the new indicator to the original five and you'll get daily totals between –6 (bearish) and +6 (bullish) including 0 (neutral). The Results of Table 42.2 show that you get improvements over the eight indicator system (Table 17.2 in Chapter 17) in some areas, and diminished results in other. The important return on account increases in five out of the nine markets with the new methodology.

I'm partial to the idea that all the elements are among the constantly flashing variety. As we move through this section, we'll see how they're positively impacted by what the non–either-or indicators are saying.

Interestingly, I found no threshold number that performs better overall than a simple majority. In other words, unlike the eight signal system, waiting until you get +/–3 is counterproductive. The system says be long if

TABLE 42.3 Six Indicator with 66% Stoploss—01-02-01 through 11-19-05

	Net Profit	# Trades	% Profit	Profit/Trade	Max. DD	ROA
S&P (Full)	$242,263	666	57.81%	$363.76	$27,450	882.6
NASD (Full)	$141,800	669	48.88%	$211.96	$43,550	325.6
Russell (Full)	$130,500	632	48.73%	$206.49	$44,200	295.2
30-Yr. Bonds	$51,656	685	51.68%	$75.41	$5,000	1,033.0
10-Yr. Notes	$30,516	665	50.08%	$45.89	$4,484	680.5
5-Yr. Notes	$24,172	675	52.15%	$35.81	$2,906	831.8
Japanese Yen	$13	712	47.33%	$0.02	$9,013	0.1
Euro Currency	$13,263	701	48.93%	$18.92	$12,963	102.3
Swiss Franc	$15,400	703	49.22%	$21.91	$8,263	214.8

you're above zero, short if below, and it offers no special weighting significance beyond that.

On the other hand, there is improvement when you apply our previous 66 percent of the last three day average range stops. As you'll recall, that distance was subtracted from our entry for the buy stop, and added to it for the sell stop. If we're not hit, we exit on the close as usual. See Table 42.3.

CHAPTER 43

Combining the Non–Either-Or Indictors

Here is a recap of five non–either-or daily indicators we have previously applied to our nine targeted financial futures. For buys:

1. Five down closes in a row are followed by an up close (all close to close).
2. Five up closes in a row were followed by a down close—all one day back. The direction of the most recent (seventh) close is irrelevant.
3. Cups and caps (Table 15.1 in Chapter 15).
4. Three Day 20 percent support-resistance (Table 16.1 in Chapter 16).
5. Fade 2 same directional open-to-closes in a row.

Let's give each a +1/–1 value, combine them and go with the simple majority. Table 43.1 shows the results.

TABLE 43.1 Five Combined Non–Either-Or Indicators—01-02-01 through 11-19-05

	Net Profit	# Trades	% Profit	Profit/Trade	Max. DD	ROA
S&P (Full)	$190,775	767	54.37%	$248.73	$34,600	551.4
NASD (Full)	$219,400	775	50.71%	$283.10	$41,800	524.9
Russell (Full)	$132,825	817	52.51%	$162.58	$53,650	247.6
30-Yr. Bonds	$14,063	798	50.25%	$17.62	$10,875	129.3
10-Yr. Notes	$18,609	751	53.00%	$24.78	$8,297	224.3
5-Yr. Notes	$14,203	733	50.48%	$19.38	$3,766	377.1
Japanese Yen	$2,725	745	47.92%	$3.66	$9,088	30.0
Euro Currency	$13,075	745	50.74%	$17.55	$12,163	107.5
Swiss Franc	$16,888	769	52.15%	$21.96	$9,925	170.2

Six Signals Plus Non–Either-Or— Putting It All Together

The non–either-or indicators suggest extreme situations relative to the normal daily ones. There have been a slew of up closes in a row, for example. There is evidence of a bottom or at least short-term support (cup or three-day 20 percent support signal). Percentages will be against you if you're trying to day trade in a direction opposite these signals. If you get more than one, the simple majority points the way as we've demonstrated.

We've also seen impressive results with the six either-or indicators. What if we only trust that reading when it does not contradict the non–either-or majority? A shorthand for that would be if combined six signals are greater than zero and the other five total at least zero, then you take the buy signal. Vice versa for shorts (minus signal for six indicators, zero or less for other five). Table 44.1 shows the original six signal performance on the top lines. The second lines have us acting on the six indicator only when not contradicted by the five non–either-ors.

The total number of trials decreases as it inevitably will with filters—but in this case, not by much. With one exception, the percentage profit increases across the board. With two slight exceptions, the ROA also improves.

Can we nudge these results up even further? Let's add one final technique we explored earlier. The 66 percent stoploss (Table 44.2).

Again, we see overall improvements across the board—all the result of step-by-step testing that we validated from the basic elemental levels up. Not too shabby, if I do say so.

TABLE 44.1 Six Indicator with Five Non–Either-Or Qualifier—Version 1—
01-02-01 through 11-19-05

	Net Profit	# Trades	% Profit	Profit/ Trade	Max. DD	ROA
S&P (Full)						
Original 6 Signal	$259,237	666	57.81%	$389.25	$23,275	1114.0
With 5 Signal Qualifier	$286,688	522	60.73%	$549.21	$23,275	1232.0
NASD (Full)						
Original 6 Signal	$98,550	669	51.72%	$147.31	$74,050	133.1
With 5 Signal Qualifier	$121,100	513	52.05%	$236.06	$37,850	319.9
Russell (Full)						
Original 6 Signal	$106,625	632	51.27%	$168.71	$50,775	210.0
With 5 Signal Qualifier	$115,975	492	53.04%	$234.77	$44,175	262.5
30-Yr. Bonds						
Original 6 Signal	$56,062	685	54.60%	$81.84	$6,906	811.8
With 5 Signal Qualifier	$40,063	517	53.58%	$77.49	$5,875	681.9
10-Yr. Notes						
Original 6 Signal	$34,688	665	53.23%	$52.16	$5,063	685.1
With 5 Signal Qualifier	$33,797	519	55.49%	$65.12	$3,891	868.6
5-Yr. Notes						
Original 6 Signal	$27,641	675	55.26%	$40.95	$3,359	822.9
With 5 Signal Qualifier	$22,625	533	55.35%	$42.45	$2,828	800.0
Japanese Yen						
Original 6 Signal	($500)	712	50.14%	($0.70)	$9,513	NA
With 5 Signal Qualifier	$2,725	588	51.19%	$4.63	$9,875	27.6
Euro Currency						
Original 6 Signal	$14,700	701	52.07%	$20.97	$18,025	81.6
With 5 Signal Qualifier	$27,025	570	53.33%	$47.41	$11,775	229.5
Swiss Franc						
Original 6 Signal	$10,050	703	51.64%	$14.30	$14,950	67.2
With 5 Signal Qualifier	$10,188	575	52.52%	$17.72	$12,563	81.1

TABLE 44.2   Filtered Six Indicator with 66 Percent Stop—01-02-01
through 11-19-05

	Net Profit	# Trades	% Profit	Profit/Trade	Max. DD	ROA
S&P (Full)	$277,188	522	57.66%	$531.01	$18,975	1461.0
NASD (Full)	$160,000	513	48.93%	$311.89	$27,800	575.5
Russell (Full)	$131,225	494	50.20%	$265.64	$35,450	370.2
30-Yr. Bonds	$41,531	517	51.26%	$80.33	$5,250	791.1
10-Yr. Notes	$30,125	519	52.22%	$58.04	$5,813	518.2
5-Yr. Notes	$19,516	533	52.16%	$36.61	$3,016	647.1
Japanese Yen	$2,550	588	48.30%	$4.34	$8,213	31.1
Euro Currency	$21,325	570	49.65%	$37.41	$8,800	242.3
Swiss Franc	$15,725	575	49.57%	$27.35	$7,375	213.2

An alternate version would be to follow the above rules, and also enter in the direction of the non–either-or signals if the six basic indicators total zero. (Primary indicator tie throws the signal into the secondary group.) Table 44.3 shows those results.

The first version (Table 44.2) probably has better overall return on accounts. It's a close call though, which means you may want to weigh the fact that there are more trials (fortification) in Table 44.3. This one pretty much comes down to personal preference.

Which is a good note upon which to end our system presentation. From here, it's all up to you. May you churn out exciting theoretical numbers—and may your actual trading approximate them.

TABLE 44.3   Filter Indicator—66 Percent Stop—Version 2—01-02-01
through 11-19-05

	Net Profit	# Trades	% Profit	Profit/Trade	Max. DD	ROA
S&P (Full)	$303,538	897	54.07%	$338.39	$25,750	1,179.0
NASD (Full)	$241,300	882	48.75%	$273.58	$29,950	805.7
Russell (Full)	$249,800	904	49.67%	$276.33	$48,250	517.7
30-Yr. Bonds	$46,031	889	49.49%	$51.78	$9,438	487.7
10-Yr. Notes	$27,688	879	49.72%	$31.50	$6,953	398.2
5-Yr. Notes	$22,016	883	49.26%	$24.93	$3,219	683.9
Japanese Yen	$4,638	896	47.43%	$5.18	$8,325	55.7
Euro Currency	$21,963	891	48.26%	$24.65	$10,813	203.1
Swiss Franc	$20,100	907	49.06%	$22.16	$11,838	169.8

CHAPTER 45

Know It When You See It—What Is Mechanical, What Isn't—(A Quiz)

1. If yesterday's close is above the previous 20-day closing average, then buy the next open plus 75 percent of the previous day's range on a stop. Vice versa for sells. No exit stops, no profit targets . . . you're perpetually in the market.

   That's mechanical!

2. You're trading a 25-day high and low breakout system perfectly, until one day, you decide to get flat and take no signals for the next two sessions while the Fed meets on interest rates. You don't know how the decision would impact your data sample—you only know that it can't be imprudent to not trade in an uncertain, potentially threatening environment. After all, there's always tomorrow.

   Maybe you had a mechanical system, but now you don't!

3. You do the exact same thing as the above, only this time, getting flat on interest rate days is part of your program. You know which days historically were Fed days, and you researched accordingly. You determined that by sidestepping, your return-on-account figure decreased by 13 percent, but you're happy with the modification because it eliminates your two worst outliers. Besides, your numbers are still good overall, and you're grateful for being able to sleep better.

   Assuming you can find data that will give you accurate report dates and times, yes, this could well be a mechanical system!

198

The difference between 2 and 3 is simply a matter of how and why the rule was applied. In the latter, you made a decision based on the different ramifications of your testing. The Number 2 scenario, by contrast, was completely arbitrary.

4. Your totally mechanical support and resistance technique mandates that you profitably exit your soybean position at 723½. The rally off the opens peters out one quarter cent shy of that, and three minutes later, your trading buddy starts quacking in your ear about how stupid you would be to let this thing run against you for the sake of two measly cents away from the target you now find yourself. You decide that sounds logical, take your only slightly-diminished profit, and the two of you head down to the bar to toast your prudence and reasonability.

Not mechanical! If you do that often enough, it's as if you have a whole new parameter in place. Which parameter would be better? Didn't you already determine that in your research?

It is not the job of a mechanical technician to massage every trade in progress. It's his or her job to analyze a data universe in its totality and determine the best course of action from there. That includes living with just-misses as readily as you accept the "just-made-it-under-the-wire" scenarios.

5. Your mother calls, all atwitter because she knows you have a big long position on in the equities and they're talking on TV about raising the terrorist alert to orange.

Definitely not a mechanical move if you succumb to her anxiety, although it may be the best argument yet for disconnecting your phone during market hours!

Again, there is no intrinsic goodness to being mechanical, nor badness to being discretionary. It's just that you just don't want to embark on something this tough with a fuzzy concept. The bottom line is, you cease being mechanical whenever you—yourself—become part of the picture.

CHAPTER 46

Embrace Mechanical Trading in Your Gut on a 100 Percent All-or-Nothing Basis

That's the Only Way It Will Work

We've stressed the importance of adhering to a 100 percent mechanical approach. That means trading without violation. One detour from your game plan can skew your results in unimaginable ways, particularly if you're doing so because of scary volatility. You should have every contingency figured into your program in the calm, unemotional prebattle period. If your gut has not helped you in normal environments, it certainly won't be useful when the shells are flying all around you.

I shut my system down in the middle of Black Monday. I had already cashed in a $20,000 windfall coming in short on the opening—several times my biggest single day winner at the time. I didn't want that heady experience to get away from me. As a result, I left an additional $50,000 of unrealized profit on the table. As recently as 2002, my partner and I elected to arbitrarily get out of hemorrhaging S&P longs. We then watched from the sidelines as the market then roared back to recapture about three quarters of our losses—on paper only.

Take it from someone who has been there, done that . . . many, many times. An unrealized mechanical paper profit hurts most operators worse than an actual loss. The above two experiences literally made me sick. During the first one, I was working in a business I hated. That $50,000 might have given me a year of freedom. The second improvisation seriously impacted my trading partnership. It was hard for us to regain our bearings—to even know how to re-engage after skewing our projected results so horrendously. How do you regard additional losses, which, had you traded correctly, would only be representing the tail end of an equity recovery?

The unique thing about mechanical trading is that you always know exactly what you would have done had you been disciplined. Your idealized blueprint is always out there—indisputable, beyond subjectivity. It will constantly remind you of whenever you cost yourself because of improvisation.

I've stressed and I've stressed the mechanical approach. Most people are not going to listen. That's another truism I've gotten out of experience. Most won't use this book in the way it could best be used—as a springboard for personal commitment to mechanical trading. (Let me know that *you've* done it—I'll consider that fulfilling enough)!

I stand by my enclosed ideas—some I'm personally using in one form or another. Still, you'd be better off building on what's offered rather than blindly following it. You should get used to rejecting all gurus. You can't be fortified without your own hands-on step-by-step approach.

Initial financing is an essential part of this process. Trading is like any other business—the number one cause of failure is undercapitalization. I know I've said that already—some things you just can't hear enough. It's crucial that your startup funds be enough to cover your worst historic drawdowns and then some. (Again, at least one and a half times the worst case you've seen is a rough consensus among the luminaries.) Actual mechanical trade should be as close to the historic blueprint as possible. That means emotionless, for one thing. There is nothing in your historic testing that says, "And here, we cut the trade short because we were worried about losing more money." This all seems moronically obvious, and yet people who thoroughly understand the mechanical concept falter all the time. People on the floor. My friends. Me.

It's amazing how truly alone you can become pursuing a course like this, but I guess that defines a solitary trading approach. I can't get friends to stick with a system for more than three trades. I can't get people with talented programming skills to just sit down and definitively nail this stuff. Why? Isn't having ultimate control of your life worth any effort—more important than your ego and your fear and greed and blah blah? Isn't it all the reward you would need? I don't understand humans sometimes.

You have to adjust for limit orders that sometimes won't be filled in real life even though your model says they were. You have to know that a closing price can't be immediately determined from a closing range even though your software insists it can be. You have to know what is logistically different in the real world versus your theoretical one. The 2000 NASDAQ bubble we discussed earlier should also suggest cautionary red flags. Always understand your testing field as well as your signals. Optimize as you must, but don't overoptimize. It's a fine line, but you have to prudently navigate it.

Re-review the basics over and over again. Never trade on scared money. If you don't have enough to operate a money machine big enough to allow you to quit your day job, then don't quit your day job. You'll never get on top of this game without patience. If you accept the kind of returns your system can reasonably offer, you could conceivably one day bankroll yourself to higher echelons.

As you approach the trading-for-a-living level, take note of how the best mechanical traders ensure their continued survival. That element is built into their total approach as much as their entry and exit signals. They know exactly how much they need to run a given mix of systems. The amount tends to err on the conservative side—something well beyond reasonably conventional element of ruin parameters. They know their mandated allotments for each trade. They branch out in unique ways, often seeking obscure, widely ignored markets for the sake of diversification. (Baltic freight index or dried cocoon futures anyone?) Sometimes seemingly dissimilar systems can be shadowing each other more than we're bargaining for. System noncorrelation was a frequently cited priority among the people in *Market Beaters*.

Actual mechanical trading could be the most cut and dried, easiest thing in the world. It's the human element that makes it otherwise. If you've taught yourself how to handle it like second nature, you could have a potential lifelong pass to the golf course, or anywhere else that strikes your fancy. There's just such a big final hurdle between successful system development and ultimate psychological acceptance. The ultimate system blueprint says to do it the easy way.

CHAPTER 47

Final Observations

1. The average trader cannot succeed unless he or she is 100 percent mechanical. Most of us can't "hear what the markets are telling us" because for all practical purposes, the markets ain't saying sqaut.

2. Human psychology tends to be drastically out of synch with what is needed to trade successfully.

3. Market activity consists overwhelmingly of noise with a very small trend component. The latter is what makes mechanical trading possible, but it can't be perceived over one trial. It takes many trades—a numbers game universe—for an edge to manifest itself.

4. Spontaneous traders therefore have nothing to tune into other than noise. That is why it is so hard for such a trader to move forward or get better over time. There is no tangible reinforcement.

5. There is the occasional trader who proves the exception to the rule. He or she is born with the talent, and tends to discover it almost immediately after embarking on a trading career. If you've been losing money for several months, you are almost certainly not one of those people.

6. When one combines mechanical with discretionary trading, one tends to get the worst of both worlds.

7. Simple is best.

8. Basic elements can be combined to create greater wholes.

9. Day trading can work, but there are inherent problems compared to other types of trading. The main obstacle lies in the relatively small trading arcs compared to trading costs.

10. Ideas generally have to test well over a fairly wide array of markets and trading environments in order to be considered trustworthy.

11. If you're getting a buzz from your trading, you're not doing it right. Good trading should be boring.

12. Never act on anything you don't thoroughly understand. Understand every step and every aspect of your research.

13. Nobody has a magic informational pipeline. The most successful traders of all time are still going to be wrong roughly half the time. Never coat-tail anybody. Never trade on touts.

14. If you're praying, you're wrong. In fact, God loves to punish system violators.

15. If you're emotionally engaged at all, you're wrong.

16. If you think there's any wisdom in "yes, I know what the system says, but this time, it has to be wrong," *you're* wrong. Wrong wrong wrong—(should I stress it one more time?)—*wrong*.

And finally, you might want to frame this one and put it somewhere you can constantly reference it—like your bathroom mirror.

If you are not following your systems 100 percent exactly as mandated, then by definition you are not trading mechanically.

TradeStation Formulas

*T*he following formulas should produce results exactly as seen in the book or close to it. (There are occasional corrected ticks and other logistical issues that might result in different numbers for different times the tests were run. Sorry—these are just realities we're stuck with.)

One fine point—actual automated trade could be done in intraday trading—that is, any of the systems that work in 5, 10 minute bars, and so forth. When applied to daily bars, however, it is suggested you manually input the trades. Otherwise, the "set exit on close" function will fail to get you out on the close. It will work in historic testing since it can instantly equate a closing price with a trigger. In the real world, though, the close isn't decided until after the fact. There are ways you could work around it including inserting daily bars into intraday, but of course that would necessitate recoding the formulas. The most logical alternative would be to exit on a market order one or two minutes before the close.

TABLE 5.2 Close versus Simple Average

inputs: n(40);
if c > average(c,n) then buy next bar at market;
if c < average(c,n) then sell short next bar at market;
setexitonclose;

TABLE 6.1 Forever Long S&Ps

inputs: P(37);
if c < lowest(c,p)[1] then buy next bar at l limit;
setprofittarget (1250);

TABLE 7.1 Two-Day Five-Day Indicator

```
if average(c,2) < average(c,5) then buy next bar at market;
if average(c,2) > average(c,5) then sell short next bar at market;
setexitonclose;
```

TABLE 7.4 Fading Two Like Closes in a Row

```
if c < c[1] and c[1] < c[2] then buy next bar at market;
if c > c[1] and c[1] > c[2] then sell short next bar at market;
setexitonclose;
```

TABLE 8.2 Order of Extreme 50-Day Extreme Highest/Lowest Close

```
Input: m(50);
if highestbar(c,m) > lowestbar(c,m) then buy next bar at market;
if highestbar(c,m) < lowestbar(c,m) then sell short next bar at market;
setexitonclose;
```

TABLE 9.1 First Three Either-Or Indicators Combined

```
inputs:e(40),n(2),p(5),q(50);
variables: x(0),y(0),z(0);
if c > average(c,e) then x=1;
if c < average(c,e) then x=-1;
IF average(c,n) < average(c,p)then y=1;
if average(c,n) > average(c,p)then y=-1;
if highestbar(c,q) > lowestbar(c,q) then z=1;
if highestbar(c,q) < lowestbar(c,q) then z=-1;
if x+y+z > 0 then buy next bar at market;
if x+y+z < 0 then sell short next bar at market;
setexitonclose;
```

TABLE 10.5 Complete Range versus 10-Day Average Range Indicator

(Delete appropriate sides of the "or" equations to individually test each half of formula.)
```
inputs:n(10);
if (range < average(range,n) and c > c[1])or (range > average(range,n) and c < c[1])
    then buy next bar at market;
if (range < average(range,n) and c < c[1]) or (range > average(range,n) and c >
    c[1])then sell short next bar at market;
setexitonclose;
```

TABLE 11.1 15 Day High-Low Average

```
if c > (average(h,15)+average(l,15))/2 then buy next bar at market;
if c < (average(h,15)+average(l,15))/2 then sell short next bar at market;
setexitonclose;
```

TABLE 12.1 First Five Either-Or Indicators Combined

```
inputs:e(40),f(2),g(5),j(50),m(10),n(15);
variables: q(0),u(0),x(0),y(0),z(0);
if c > average(c,e) then q=1;
if c < average(c,e) then q=-1;
if average(c,f) < average(c,g) then u=1;
if average(c,f) > average(c,g) then u=-1;
if highestbar(c,j) > lowestbar(c,j) then x=1;
if highestbar(c,j) < lowestbar(c,j) then x=-1;
if (range < average(range,m) and c > c[1]) or (range > average(range,m) and c <
     c[1]) then y=1;
if (range < average(range,m) and c < c[1]) or (range > average(range,m) and c >
     c[1])then y=-1;
if c > (average(h,n)+average(l,n))/2 then z=1;
if c < (average(h,n)+average(l,n))/2 then z=-1;
if q+u+x+y+z > 0 then buy next bar at market;
if q+u+x+y+z < 0 then sell short next bar at market;
setexitonclose;
```

TABLE 12.2 Five Either-Or—+3/-3 Threshold

(Substitute following for last three lines in 12.1.)
```
if q+u+x+y+z > =3 then buy next bar at market;
if q+u+x+y+z < =-3 then sell short next bar at market;
setexitonclose;
```

TABLE 13.1 Various Three Out of Five Either-Or Combos

---

*To test various three out of five combos, select appropriate three variables to plug
into buy/sell command lines of Table 12.1 . q=1. u=2. x=3. y=4. z=5.*

TABLE 14.1 Fading Open-to-Close

```
if c < o then buy next bar at market;
if c > o then sell short next bar at market;
setexitonclose;
```

TABLE 14.2   Fading Two Same-Way Open-to-Closes

if c < o and c[1] < o[1] then buy next bar at market;
if c > o and c[1] > o[1] then sell short next bar at market;
setexitonclose;

TABLE 15.1   Cups and Caps (Day)

if l > l[1] and l[1] < lowest(l,3)[2] and c > c[1] and c[1] < c[2] then buy next bar at
    market;
if h < h[1] and h[1] > highest(h,3)[2] and c < c[1] and c[1] > c[2] then sell short
    next bar at market;
setexitonclose;

TABLE 15.2   Cups and Caps—Overnight

if l > l[1] and l[1] < lowest(l,3)[2] and c > c[1] and c[1] < c[2] then buy this bar on
    close;
sell next bar at market;
if h < h[1] and h[1] > highest(h,3)[2] and c < c[1] and c[1] > c[2] then sell short this
    bar on close;
buy to cover next bar at market;

TABLE 15.3   Cups-Caps—Overnight with Stops and Targets

if l > l[1] and l[1] < lowest(l,3)[2] and c > c[1] and c[1] < c[2] then buy this bar on
    close;
if marketposition=1 and barssinceentry=1 then sell next bar at market;
sell next bar at highest(h,3)+.25*average(range,3) limit;
sell next bar at lowest(l,3)-(minmove/pricescale) stop;
if h < h[1] and h[1] > highest(h,3)[2] and c < c[1] and c[1] > c[2] then sell short this
    bar on close;
if marketposition=-1 and barssinceentry=1 then buy to cover next bar at market;
buy to cover next bar at lowest(l,3)-.25*average(range,3) limit;
buy to cover next bar at highest(h,3)+(minmove/pricescale) stop;

TABLE 16.1   20 Percent Support-Resistance Indicator

inputs: n(.2);
if highest(l,3)-lowest(l,3) < =n*(highest(h,3)-lowest(l,3)) then buy next bar at
    market;
if highest(h,3)-lowest(h,3) < =n* (highest(h,3)-lowest(l,3))then sell short next bar
    at market;
setexitonclose;

TABLE 17.1 Eight Indicators Combined (Simple Majority)

```
variables: aa(0),bb(0),cc(0),dd(0),ee(0),ff(0),gg(0),hh(0);
if average(c,2) < average(c,5)then aa=1;
if average(c,2) > average(c,5)then aa=-1;
if c > average(c,40) then bb=1;
if c < average(c,40) then bb=-1;
if highestbar(c,50) > lowestbar(c,50) then cc=1;
if highestbar(c,50) < lowestbar(c,50) then cc=-1;
if (range < average(range,10)) and c > c[1] or (range > average(range,10)) and c <
    c[1] then dd=1;
if (range < average(range,10)) and c < c[1] or (range > average(range,10)) and c >
    c[1] then dd=-1;
if c > (average(h,15)+average(l,15))/2 then ee=1;
if c < (average(h,15)+average(l,15))/2 then ee=-1;
if c < o and c[1] < o[1] then ff=1 else ff=0;
if c > o and c[1] > o[1] then ff=-1;
if l > l[1] and l[1] < lowest(l,3)[2] and c > c[1] and c[1] < c[2] then gg=1 else
    gg=0;
if h < h[1] and h[1] > highest(h,3)[2] and c < c[1] and c[1] > c[2] then gg=-1;
if highest(l,3)-lowest(l,3) < =.2*(highest(h,3)-lowest(l,3)) then hh=1 else hh=0;
if highest(h,3)-lowest(h,3) < =.2* (highest(h,3)-lowest(l,3)) then hh=-1;
if aa+bb+cc+dd+ee+ff+gg+hh > 0 then buy next bar at market;
if aa+bb+cc+dd+ee+ff+gg+hh < 0 then sell short next bar at market;
setexitonclose;
```

TABLE 17.7 Eight Indicators—+/– 3 or Beyond

(Substitute following for last three lines in 17.4.)
```
if aa+bb+cc+dd+ee+ff+gg+hh > =3 then buy next bar at market;
if aa+bb+cc+dd+ee+ff+gg+hh < =-3 then sell short next bar at market;
setexitonclose;
```

TABLE 18.4 Eight Indicators—Simple Majority—33 Percent Entry Stop

(Substitute following for final command lines in 17.4.)
```
if aa+bb+cc+dd+ee+ff+gg+hh > 0 then buy next bar at o of
    tomorrow+.33*average(range,3) stop;
if aa+bb+cc+dd+ee+ff+gg+hh < 0 then sell short next bar at o of tomorrow-
    .33*average(range,3) stop;
setexitonclose;
```

TABLE 18.5 Eight Indicators—33 Percent Entry Stop—+3/–3 Qualifier

(Substitute following for final command lines in 17.4.)
if aa+bb+cc+dd+ee+ff+gg+hh > =3 then buy next bar at o of
    tomorrow+.33*average(range,3) stop;
if aa+bb+cc+dd+ee+ff+gg+hh < =-3 then sell short next bar at o of tomorrow-
    .33*average(range,3) stop;
setexitonclose;

TABLE 19.2 Eight Indicators—Simple Majority—25 Percent Limit Entry

(Substitute following for final command lines in 17.4.)
if aa+bb+cc+dd+ee+ff+gg+hh > 0 then buy next bar at o of tomorrow-
    .25*average(range,3) limit;
if aa+bb+cc+dd+ee+ff+gg+hh < 0 then sell short next bar at o of
    tomorrow+.25*average(range,3) limit;
setexitonclose;

TABLE 19.3 Eight Indicators—25 Percent Limit Entry—+3/–3 Qualifier

(Substitute following for final command lines in 17.4.)
if aa+bb+cc+dd+ee+ff+gg+hh > =3 then buy next bar at o of tomorrow-
    .25*average(range,3) limit;
if aa+bb+cc+dd+ee+ff+gg+hh < =-3 then sell short next bar at o of
    tomorrow+.25*average(range,3) limit;
setexitonclose;

TABLE 20.3 Eight Indicators (Simple Majority) with 66 Percent Stoploss

(Substitute following for final command lines in 17.4.)
if aa+bb+cc+dd+ee+ff+gg+hh > 0 then buy next bar at market;
sell next bar at o of tomorrow-.66*average(range,3) stop;
if aa+bb+cc+dd+ee+ff+gg+hh < 0 then sell short next bar at market;
buy to cover next bar at o of tomorrow+.66*average(range,3) stop;
setexitonclose;

TABLE 21.1 Second High-Low Exit Strategy

```
variables: hh(0),ll(0),q(0),u(0),x(0),y(0),z(0);
if marketposition=1 and barssinceentry=0 then hh=h;
if marketposition=-1 and barssinceentry=0 then ll=l;
if c > average(c,40) then q=1;
if c < average(c,40) then q=-1;
if average(c,2) < average(c,5) then u=1;
if average(c,2) > average(c,5) then u=-1;
if highestbar(c,50) > lowestbar(c,50) then x=1;
if highestbar(c,50) < lowestbar(c,50) then x=-1;
if (range < average(range,10) and c > c[1]) or (range > average(range,10) and c <
    c[1]) then y=1;
if (range < average(range,10) and c < c[1]) or (range > average(range,10) and c >
    c[1]) then y=-1;
if c > (average(h,15)+average(l,15))/2 then z=1;
if c < (average(h,15)+average(l,15))/2 then z=-1;
if q+u+x+y+z > 0 and c > average(c,20) then buy next bar at o of tomorrow-
    .33*average(range,3) limit;
if barssinceentry=2 and marketposition=1 and highest(h,2) > hh and
    nthhighest(2,h,2) > hh then sell next bar at highest(h,2) limit;
if barssinceentry=3 and marketposition=1 and highest(h,3) > hh and
    nthhighest(2,h,3) > hh then sell next bar at highest(h,3) limit;
if barssinceentry=4 and marketposition=1 and highest(h,4) > hh and
    nthhighest(2,h,4) > hh then sell next bar at highest(h,4) limit;
if barssinceentry=5 and marketposition=1 and highest(h,5) > hh and
    nthhighest(2,h,5) > hh then sell
next bar at highest(h,5) limit;
if barssinceentry=6 and marketposition=1 and highest(h,6) > hh and
    nthhighest(2,h,6) > hh then sell next bar at highest(h,6) limit;
if barssinceentry=7 and marketposition=1 and highest(h,7) > hh and
    nthhighest(2,h,7) > hh then sell next bar at highest(h,7) limit;
if barssinceentry=8 and marketposition=1 and highest(h,8) > hh and
    nthhighest(2,h,8) > hh then sell next bar at highest(h,8) limit;
if barssinceentry=9 and marketposition=1 and highest(h,9) > hh and
    nthhighest(2,h,9) > hh then sell next bar at highest(h,9) limit;
if barssinceentry=10 and marketposition=1 and highest(h,10) > hh and
    nthhighest(2,h,10) > hh then sell next bar at highest(h,10) limit;
if barssinceentry=11 and marketposition=1 and highest(h,11) > hh and
    nthhighest(2,h,11) > hh then sell next bar at highest(h,11) limit;
if barssinceentry=12 and marketposition=1 and highest(h,12) > hh and
    nthhighest(2,h,12) > hh then sell next bar at highest(h,12) limit;
if barssinceentry=13 and marketposition=1 and highest(h,13) > hh and
    nthhighest(2,h,13) > hh then sell next bar at highest(h,13) limit;
if barssinceentry=14 and marketposition=1 and highest(h,14) > hh and
    nthhighest(2,h,14) > hh then sell next bar at highest(h,14) limit;
```

(continues)

TABLE 21.1 *(Continued)*

if c < average(c,20) then sell next bar at market;
if q+u+x+y+z < 0 and c < average(c,20) then sell short next bar at o of
    tomorrow+.33*average(range,3) limit;
if barssinceentry=2 and marketposition=-1 and lowest(l,2) < ll and nthlowest(2,l,2)
    < ll then buy to
cover next bar at lowest(l,2) limit;
if barssinceentry=3 and marketposition=-1 and lowest(l,3) < ll and nthlowest(2,l,3)
    < ll then buy to cover next bar at lowest(l,3) limit;
if barssinceentry=4 and marketposition=-1 and lowest(l,4) < ll and nthlowest(2,l,4)
    < ll then buy to cover next bar at lowest(l,4) limit;
if barssinceentry=5 and marketposition=-1 and lowest(l,5) < ll and nthlowest(2,l,5)
    < ll then buy to cover next bar at lowest(l,5) limit;
if barssinceentry=6 and marketposition=-1 and lowest(l,6) < ll and nthlowest(2,l,6)
    < ll then buy to cover next bar at lowest(l,6) limit;
if barssinceentry=7 and marketposition=-1 and lowest(l,7) < ll and nthlowest(2,l,7)
    < ll then buy to cover next bar at lowest(l,7) limit;
if barssinceentry=8 and marketposition=-1 and lowest(l,8) < ll and nthlowest(2,l,8)
    < ll then buy to cover next bar at lowest(l,8) limit;
if barssinceentry=9 and marketposition=-1 and lowest(l,9) < ll and nthlowest(2,l,9)
    < ll then buy to cover next bar at lowest(l,9) limit;
if barssinceentry=10 and marketposition=-1 and lowest(l,10) < ll and
    nthlowest(2,l,10) < ll then buy to cover next bar at lowest(l,10) limit;
if barssinceentry=11 and marketposition=-1 and lowest(l,11) < ll and
    nthlowest(2,l,11) < ll then buy to cover next bar at lowest(l,11) limit;
if barssinceentry=12 and marketposition=-1 and lowest(l,12) < ll and
    nthlowest(2,l,12) < ll then buy to cover next bar at lowest(l,12) limit;
if barssinceentry=13 and marketposition=-1 and lowest(l,13) < ll and
    nthlowest(2,l,13) < ll then buy
to cover next bar at lowest(l,13) limit;
if barssinceentry=14 and marketposition=-1 and lowest(l,14) < ll and
    nthlowest(2,l,14) < ll then buy to cover next bar at lowest(l,14) limit;
if c > average(c,20) then buy to cover next bar at market;

TABLE 21.2 Second High-Low Exit Strategy with Added Two Tick Penalty. (See
                Table 21.2 for docking instructions.)

variables: hh(0),ll(0),q(0),u(0),x(0),y(0),z(0);
if marketposition=1 and barssinceentry=0 then hh=h;
if marketposition=-1 and barssinceentry=0 then ll=l;
if c > average(c,40) then q=1;
if c < average(c,40) then q=-1;
if average(c,2) < average(c,5)then u=1;
if average(c,2) > average(c,5)then u=-1;
if highestbar(c,50) > lowestbar(c,50) then x=1;

TABLE 21.2 *(Continued)*

if highestbar(c,50) < lowestbar(c,50) then x=-1;
if (range < average(range,10) and c > c[1])or (range > average(range,10) and c <
    c[1]) then y=1;
if (range < average(range,10) and c < c[1]) or (range > average(range,10) and c >
    c[1]) then y=-1;
if c > (average(h,15)+average(l,15))/2 then z=1;
if c < (average(h,15)+average(l,15))/2 then z=-1;
if q+u+x+y+z > 0 and c > average(c,20) then buy next bar at (o of tomorrow-
    (.33*average(range,3)))-
(minmove/pricescale) limit;
if barssinceentry=2 and marketposition=1 and highest(h,2) > hh and
    nthhighest(2,h,2) > hh then sell next bar at
    (highest(h,2))+(minmove/pricescale) limit;
if barssinceentry=3 and marketposition=1 and highest(h,3) > hh and
    nthhighest(2,h,3) > hh then sell next bar at (highest(h,3))
    +(minmove/pricescale) limit;
if barssinceentry=4 and marketposition=1 and highest(h,4) > hh and
    nthhighest(2,h,4) > hh then sell next bar at (highest(h,4))
    +(minmove/pricescale) limit;
if barssinceentry=5 and marketposition=1 and highest(h,5) > hh and
    nthhighest(2,h,5) > hh then sell next bar at (highest(h,5))
    +(minmove/pricescale) limit;
if barssinceentry=6 and marketposition=1 and highest(h,6) > hh and
    nthhighest(2,h,6) > hh then sell next bar at (highest(h,6))
    +(minmove/pricescale) limit;
if barssinceentry=7 and marketposition=1 and highest(h,7) > hh and
    nthhighest(2,h,7) > hh then sell next bar at (highest(h,7))
    +(minmove/pricescale) limit;
if barssinceentry=8 and marketposition=1 and highest(h,8) > hh and
    nthhighest(2,h,8) > hh then sell next bar at (highest(h,8))
    +(minmove/pricescale) limit;
if barssinceentry=9 and marketposition=1 and highest(h,9) > hh and
    nthhighest(2,h,9) > hh then sell next bar at (highest(h,9))
    +(minmove/pricescale) limit;
if barssinceentry=10 and marketposition=1 and highest(h,10) > hh and
    nthhighest(2,h,10) > hh then sell next bar at (highest(h,10))
    +(minmove/pricescale) limit;
if barssinceentry=11 and marketposition=1 and highest(h,11) > hh and
    nthhighest(2,h,11) > hh then sell next bar at (highest(h,11))
    +(minmove/pricescale) limit;
if barssinceentry=12 and marketposition=1 and highest(h,12) > hh and
    nthhighest(2,h,12) > hh then sell next bar at (highest(h,12))
    +(minmove/pricescale) limit;

(continues)

TABLE 21.2 *(Continued)*

if barssinceentry=13 and marketposition=1 and highest(h,13) > hh and
    nthhighest(2,h,13) > hh then sell next bar at (highest(h,13))
    +(minmove/pricescale) limit;
if barssinceentry=14 and marketposition=1 and highest(h,14) > hh and
    nthhighest(2,h,14) > hh then sell next bar at (highest(h,14))
    +(minmove/pricescale) limit;
if c < average(c,20) then sell next bar at market;
if q+u+x+y+z < 0 and c < average(c,20)then sell short next bar at (o of
    tomorrow+.33*average(range,3))+(minmove/pricescale) limit;
if barssinceentry=2 and marketposition=-1 and lowest(l,2) < ll and nthlowest(2,l,2)
    < ll then buy to cover next bar at lowest(l,2)-(minmove/pricescale) limit;
if barssinceentry=3 and marketposition=-1 and lowest(l,3) < ll and nthlowest(2,l,3)
    < ll then buy to cover next bar at lowest(l,3) -(minmove/pricescale) limit;
if barssinceentry=4 and marketposition=-1 and lowest(l,4) < ll and nthlowest(2,l,4)
    < ll then buy to cover next bar at lowest(l,4) -(minmove/pricescale) limit;
if barssinceentry=5 and marketposition=-1 and lowest(l,5) < ll and nthlowest(2,l,5)
    < ll then buy to cover next bar at lowest(l,5) -(minmove/pricescale) limit;
if barssinceentry=6 and marketposition=-1 and lowest(l,6) < ll and nthlowest(2,l,6)
    < ll then buy to cover next bar at lowest(l,6) -(minmove/pricescale) limit;
if barssinceentry=7 and marketposition=-1 and lowest(l,7) < ll and nthlowest(2,l,7)
    < ll then buy to cover next bar at lowest(l,7) -(minmove/pricescale) limit;
if barssinceentry=8 and marketposition=-1 and lowest(l,8) < ll and nthlowest(2,l,8)
    < ll then buy to cover next bar at lowest(l,8) -(minmove/pricescale) limit;
if barssinceentry=9 and marketposition=-1 and lowest(l,9) < ll and nthlowest(2,l,9)
    < ll then buy to
cover next bar at lowest(l,9) -(minmove/pricescale) limit;
if barssinceentry=10 and marketposition=-1 and lowest(l,10) < ll and
    nthlowest(2,l,10) < ll then buy to cover next bar at lowest(l,10) -
    (minmove/pricescale) limit;
if barssinceentry=11 and marketposition=-1 and lowest(l,11) < ll and
    nthlowest(2,l,11) < ll then buy to cover next bar at lowest(l,11) -
    (minmove/pricescale) limit;
if barssinceentry=12 and marketposition=-1 and lowest(l,12) < ll and
    nthlowest(2,l,12) < ll then buy to cover next bar at lowest(l,12) -
    (minmove/pricescale) limit;
if barssinceentry=13 and marketposition=-1 and lowest(l,13) < ll and
    nthlowest(2,l,13) < ll then buy to cover next bar at lowest(l,13) -
    (minmove/pricescale) limit;
if barssinceentry=14 and marketposition=-1 and lowest(l,14) < ll and
    nthlowest(2,l,14) < ll then buy to cover next bar at lowest(l,14) -
    (minmove/pricescale) limit;
if c > average(c,20) then buy to cover next bar at market;

TABLE 22.1 Second High/Low #2

variables: hh(0),ll(0),q(0),u(0),x(0),y(0),z(0);
if marketposition=1 and barssinceentry=0 then hh=h;
if marketposition=-1 and barssinceentry=0 then ll=l;
if c > average(c,25) then buy next bar at o of tomorrow+.5*average(range,3) stop;
if barssinceentry=2 and marketposition=1 and highest(h,2) > hh and
    nthhighest(2,h,2) > hh then sell next bar at highest(h,2) limit;
if barssinceentry=3 and marketposition=1 and highest(h,3) > hh and
    nthhighest(2,h,3) > hh then sell
next bar at highest(h,3) limit;
if barssinceentry=4 and marketposition=1 and highest(h,4) > hh and
    nthhighest(2,h,4) > hh then sell next bar at highest(h,4) limit;
if barssinceentry=5 and marketposition=1 and highest(h,5) > hh and
    nthhighest(2,h,5) > hh then sell next bar at highest(h,5) limit;
if barssinceentry=6 and marketposition=1 and highest(h,6) > hh and
    nthhighest(2,h,6) > hh then sell next bar at highest(h,6) limit;
if barssinceentry=7 and marketposition=1 and highest(h,7) > hh and
    nthhighest(2,h,7) > hh then sell next bar at highest(h,7) limit;
if barssinceentry=8 and marketposition=1 and highest(h,8) > hh and
    nthhighest(2,h,8) > hh then sell next bar at highest(h,8) limit;
if barssinceentry=9 and marketposition=1 and highest(h,9) > hh and
    nthhighest(2,h,9) > hh then sell next bar at highest(h,9) limit;
if barssinceentry=10 and marketposition=1 and highest(h,10) > hh and
    nthhighest(2,h,10) > hh then sell next bar at highest(h,10) limit;
if barssinceentry=11 and marketposition=1 and highest(h,11) > hh and
    nthhighest(2,h,11) > hh then sell next bar at highest(h,11) limit;
if barssinceentry=12 and marketposition=1 and highest(h,12) > hh and
    nthhighest(2,h,12) > hh then sell next bar at highest(h,12) limit;
if barssinceentry=13 and marketposition=1 and highest(h,13) > hh and
    nthhighest(2,h,13) > hh then sell next bar at highest(h,13) limit;
if barssinceentry=14 and marketposition=1 and highest(h,14) > hh and
    nthhighest(2,h,14) > hh then sell next bar at highest(h,14) limit;
if c < average(c,25) then sell next bar at market;
if c < average(c,25) then sell short next bar at o of tomorrow-(.5*average(range,3))
    stop;
if barssinceentry=2 and marketposition=-1 and lowest(l,2) < ll and nthlowest(2,l,2)
    < ll then buy to cover next bar at lowest(l,2) limit;
if barssinceentry=3 and marketposition=-1 and lowest(l,3) < ll and nthlowest(2,l,3)
    < ll then buy to cover next bar at lowest(l,3) limit;
if barssinceentry=4 and marketposition=-1 and lowest(l,4) < ll and nthlowest(2,l,4)
    < ll then buy to cover next bar at lowest(l,4) limit;
if barssinceentry=5 and marketposition=-1 and lowest(l,5) < ll and nthlowest(2,l,5)
    < ll then buy to cover next bar at lowest(l,5) limit;
if barssinceentry=6 and marketposition=-1 and lowest(l,6) < ll and nthlowest(2,l,6)
    < ll then buy to cover next bar at lowest(l,6) limit;

(continues)

TABLE 22.1 *(Continued)*

if barssinceentry=7 and marketposition=-1 and lowest(l,7) < ll and nthlowest(2,l,7)
 < ll then buy to cover next bar at lowest(l,7) limit;
if barssinceentry=8 and marketposition=-1 and lowest(l,8) < ll and nthlowest(2,l,8)
 < ll then buy to cover next bar at lowest(l,8) limit;
if barssinceentry=9 and marketposition=-1 and lowest(l,9) < ll and nthlowest(2,l,9)
 < ll then buy to cover next bar at lowest(l,9) limit;
if barssinceentry=10 and marketposition=-1 and lowest(l,10) < ll and
 nthlowest(2,l,10) < ll then buy to cover next bar at lowest(l,10) limit;
if barssinceentry=11 and marketposition=-1 and lowest(l,11) < ll and
 nthlowest(2,l,11) < ll then buy to cover next bar at lowest(l,11) limit;
if barssinceentry=12 and marketposition=-1 and lowest(l,12) < ll and
 nthlowest(2,l,12) < ll then buy to cover next bar at lowest(l,12) limit;
if barssinceentry=13 and marketposition=-1 and lowest(l,13) < ll and
 nthlowest(2,l,13) < ll then buy to cover next bar at lowest(l,13) limit;
if barssinceentry=14 and marketposition=-1 and lowest(l,14) < ll and
 nthlowest(2,l,14) < ll then buy to cover next bar at lowest(l,14) limit;
if c > average(c,25) then buy to cover next bar at market;

TABLE 22.2 Second High/Low Exit #3

variables: hh(0),ll(0),q(0),u(0),x(0),y(0),z(0);
if marketposition=1 and barssinceentry=0 then hh=h;
if marketposition=-1 and barssinceentry=0 then ll=l;
if c > h[1] and c > average(c,40) then buy next bar at o of
 tomorrow+.5*average(range,3) stop;
if barssinceentry=2 and marketposition=1 and highest(h,2) > hh and
 nthhighest(2,h,2) > hh then sell next bar at highest(h,2) limit;
if barssinceentry=3 and marketposition=1 and highest(h,3) > hh and
 nthhighest(2,h,3) > hh then sell next bar at highest(h,3) limit;
if barssinceentry=4 and marketposition=1 and highest(h,4) > hh and
 nthhighest(2,h,4) > hh then sell next bar at highest(h,4) limit;
if barssinceentry=5 and marketposition=1 and highest(h,5) > hh and
 nthhighest(2,h,5) > hh then sell next bar at highest(h,5) limit;
if barssinceentry=6 and marketposition=1 and highest(h,6) > hh and
 nthhighest(2,h,6) > hh then sell
next bar at highest(h,6) limit;
if barssinceentry=7 and marketposition=1 and highest(h,7) > hh and
 nthhighest(2,h,7) > hh then sell next bar at highest(h,7) limit;
if barssinceentry=8 and marketposition=1 and highest(h,8) > hh and
 nthhighest(2,h,8) > hh then sell next bar at highest(h,8) limit;
if barssinceentry=9 and marketposition=1 and highest(h,9) > hh and
 nthhighest(2,h,9) > hh then sell next bar at highest(h,9) limit;
if barssinceentry=10 and marketposition=1 and highest(h,10) > hh and
 nthhighest(2,h,10) > hh then sell next bar at highest(h,10) limit;

TABLE 22.2 *(Continued)*

if barssinceentry=11 and marketposition=1 and highest(h,11) > hh and
nthhighest(2,h,11) > hh then sell next bar at highest(h,11) limit;
if barssinceentry=12 and marketposition=1 and highest(h,12) > hh and
nthhighest(2,h,12) > hh then sell next bar at highest(h,12) limit;
if barssinceentry=13 and marketposition=1 and highest(h,13) > hh and
nthhighest(2,h,13) > hh then sell next bar at highest(h,13) limit;
if barssinceentry=14 and marketposition=1 and highest(h,14) > hh and
nthhighest(2,h,14) > hh then sell next bar at highest(h,14) limit;
if c < average(c,40) then sell next bar at market;
if c < l[1] and c < average(c,40) then sell short next bar at o of tomorrow-
(.5*average(range,3)) stop;
if barssinceentry=2 and marketposition=-1 and lowest(l,2) < ll and nthlowest(2,l,2)
< ll then buy to cover next bar at lowest(l,2) limit;
if barssinceentry=3 and marketposition=-1 and lowest(l,3) < ll and nthlowest(2,l,3)
< ll then buy to
cover next bar at lowest(l,3) limit;
if barssinceentry=4 and marketposition=-1 and lowest(l,4) < ll and nthlowest(2,l,4)
< ll then buy to cover next bar at lowest(l,4) limit;
if barssinceentry=5 and marketposition=-1 and lowest(l,5) < ll and nthlowest(2,l,5)
< ll then buy to cover next bar at lowest(l,5) limit;
if barssinceentry=6 and marketposition=-1 and lowest(l,6) < ll and nthlowest(2,l,6)
< ll then buy to cover next bar at lowest(l,6) limit;
if barssinceentry=7 and marketposition=-1 and lowest(l,7) < ll and nthlowest(2,l,7)
< ll then buy to cover next bar at lowest(l,7) limit;
if barssinceentry=8 and marketposition=-1 and lowest(l,8) < ll and nthlowest(2,l,8)
< ll then buy to cover next bar at lowest(l,8) limit;
if barssinceentry=9 and marketposition=-1 and lowest(l,9) < ll and nthlowest(2,l,9)
< ll then buy to cover next bar at lowest(l,9) limit;
if barssinceentry=10 and marketposition=-1 and lowest(l,10) < ll and
nthlowest(2,l,10) < ll then buy to cover next bar at lowest(l,10) limit;
if barssinceentry=11 and marketposition=-1 and lowest(l,11) < ll and
nthlowest(2,l,11) < ll then buy to cover next bar at lowest(l,11) limit;
if barssinceentry=12 and marketposition=-1 and lowest(l,12) < ll and
nthlowest(2,l,12) < ll then buy to cover next bar at lowest(l,12) limit;
if barssinceentry=13 and marketposition=-1 and lowest(l,13) < ll and
nthlowest(2,l,13) < ll then buy to cover next bar at lowest(l,13) limit;
if barssinceentry=14 and marketposition=-1 and lowest(l,14) < ll and
nthlowest(2,l,14) < ll then buy
to cover next bar at lowest(l,14) limit;
if c > average(c,40) then buy to cover next bar at market;

TABLE 22.3   Second High/Low Exit #4—Enter On Limits

```
variables: hh(0),ll(0),q(0),u(0),x(0),y(0),z(0);
if marketposition=1 and barssinceentry=0 then hh=h;
if marketposition=-1 and barssinceentry=0 then ll=l;
if c > h[1] and c > average(c,40) then buy next bar at o of tomorrow-
      .5*average(range,3) limit;
if barssinceentry=2 and marketposition=1 and highest(h,2) > hh and
      nthhighest(2,h,2) > hh then sell next bar at highest(h,2) limit;
if barssinceentry=3 and marketposition=1 and highest(h,3) > hh and
      nthhighest(2,h,3) > hh then sell next bar at highest(h,3) limit;
if barssinceentry=4 and marketposition=1 and highest(h,4) > hh and
      nthhighest(2,h,4) > hh then sell next bar at highest(h,4) limit;
if barssinceentry=5 and marketposition=1 and highest(h,5) > hh and
      nthhighest(2,h,5) > hh then sell next bar at highest(h,5) limit;
if barssinceentry=6 and marketposition=1 and highest(h,6) > hh and
      nthhighest(2,h,6) > hh then sell next bar at highest(h,6) limit;
if barssinceentry=7 and marketposition=1 and highest(h,7) > hh and
      nthhighest(2,h,7) > hh then sell next bar at highest(h,7) limit;
if barssinceentry=8 and marketposition=1 and highest(h,8) > hh and
      nthhighest(2,h,8) > hh then sell next bar at highest(h,8) limit;
if barssinceentry=9 and marketposition=1 and highest(h,9) > hh and
      nthhighest(2,h,9) > hh then sell next bar at highest(h,9) limit;
if barssinceentry=10 and marketposition=1 and highest(h,10) > hh and
      nthhighest(2,h,10) > hh then sell next bar at highest(h,10) limit;
if barssinceentry=11 and marketposition=1 and highest(h,11) > hh and
      nthhighest(2,h,11) > hh then sell next bar at highest(h,11) limit;
if barssinceentry=12 and marketposition=1 and highest(h,12) > hh and
      nthhighest(2,h,12) > hh then sell next bar at highest(h,12) limit;
if barssinceentry=13 and marketposition=1 and highest(h,13) > hh and
      nthhighest(2,h,13) > hh then sell next bar at highest(h,13) limit;
if barssinceentry=14 and marketposition=1 and highest(h,14) > hh and
      nthhighest(2,h,14) > hh then sell next bar at highest(h,14) limit;
if c < average(c,40) then sell next bar at market;
if c < l[1] and c < average(c,40) then sell short next bar at o of
      tomorrow+(.5*average(range,3)) limit;
if barssinceentry=2 and marketposition=-1 and lowest(l,2) < ll and nthlowest(2,l,2)
      < ll then buy to cover next bar at lowest(l,2) limit;
if barssinceentry=3 and marketposition=-1 and lowest(l,3) < ll and nthlowest(2,l,3)
      < ll then buy to cover next bar at lowest(l,3) limit;
if barssinceentry=4 and marketposition=-1 and lowest(l,4) < ll and nthlowest(2,l,4)
      < ll then buy to cover next bar at lowest(l,4) limit;
if barssinceentry=5 and marketposition=-1 and lowest(l,5) < ll and nthlowest(2,l,5)
      < ll then buy to cover next bar at lowest(l,5) limit;
if barssinceentry=6 and marketposition=-1 and lowest(l,6) < ll and nthlowest(2,l,6)
      < ll then buy to cover next bar at lowest(l,6) limit;
```

TABLE 22.3 *(Continued)*

if barssinceentry=7 and marketposition=-1 and lowest(l,7) < ll and nthlowest(2,l,7)
    < ll then buy to cover next bar at lowest(l,7) limit;
if barssinceentry=8 and marketposition=-1 and lowest(l,8) < ll and nthlowest(2,l,8)
    < ll then buy to cover next bar at lowest(l,8) limit;
if barssinceentry=9 and marketposition=-1 and lowest(l,9) < ll and nthlowest(2,l,9)
    < ll then buy to cover next bar at lowest(l,9) limit;
if barssinceentry=10 and marketposition=-1 and lowest(l,10) < ll and
    nthlowest(2,l,10) < ll then buy to cover next bar at lowest(l,10) limit;
if barssinceentry=11 and marketposition=-1 and lowest(l,11) < ll and
    nthlowest(2,l,11) < ll then buy to cover next bar at lowest(l,11) limit;
if barssinceentry=12 and marketposition=-1 and lowest(l,12) < ll and
    nthlowest(2,l,12) < ll then buy to cover next bar at lowest(l,12) limit;
if barssinceentry=13 and marketposition=-1 and lowest(l,13) < ll and
    nthlowest(2,l,13) < ll then buy to cover next bar at lowest(l,13) limit;
if barssinceentry=14 and marketposition=-1 and lowest(l,14) < ll and
    nthlowest(2,l,14) < ll then buy to cover next bar at lowest(l,14) limit;
if c > average(c,40) then buy to cover next bar at market;

TABLE 23.1 Optimizing Original Five Either-Or Indicators

(Use Table 9.1.)

TABLE 24.1 The One-Minute "Mega System"

variables:e(0),f(0),g(0),j(0);
e=(h-o);
f=(o-l);
g=average(e,5);
j=average(f,5);
if time > =845 and time < 1455 then buy next bar at o of tomorrow-j limit;
if time=1500 then sell next bar at market;
if time > =845 and time < 1455 then sell short next bar at o of tomorrow+g limit;
if time=1500 then buy to cover next bar at market;

TABLE 25.1 Yen Weekly Range Expansion

buy next bar at o of tomorrow+range stop;
sell short next bar at o of tomorrow-range stop;

TABLE 25.4 1.5 Daily Range Expansion

inputs: q(1.5),n(25);
if c > average(c,n) then buy next bar at o of tomorrow+(q*range) stop;
sell next bar at o of tomorrow-(q*range) stop;
if c < average(c,n) then sell short next bar at o of tomorrow-(q*range) stop;
buy to cover next bar at o of tomorrow+(q*range) stop;

TABLE 26.5 Days of the Week Indicator (Complete)

(Delete appropriate lines to test individual days of week.)
variables: e(0),f(0),j(0);
if c > o then e=c-o;
if c < o then f=o-c;
if c > o then j=1;
if c < o then j=-1;
if dayofweek(date)=5 and c > c[1] then buy next bar at market;
if dayofweek(date)=1 and c < c[1] then buy next bar at market;
if dayofweek(date)=2 and highest(e,2) < highest(f,2) then buy next bar at
    market;
if dayofweek(date)=3 and highest(e,3) < highest(f,3) then buy next bar at
    market;
if dayofweek(date)=4 and highest(e,4) < highest(f,4) then buy next bar at
    market;
if dayofweek(date)=5 and c < c[1] then sell short next bar at market;
if dayofweek(date)=1 and c > c[1] then sell short next bar at market;
if dayofweek(date)=2 and highest(e,2) > highest(f,2) then sell short next bar at
    market;
if dayofweek(date)=3 and highest(e,3) > highest(f,3) then sell short next bar at
    market;
if dayofweek(date)=4 and highest(e,4) > highest(f,4) then sell short next bar at
    market;
setexitonclose;

TABLE 27.1 Perennially Short S&Ps

inputs:n(21),p(6);
if dayofmonth(date) > =p and dayofmonth(date) < =(p+3) then sell short next bar
    at market;
if dayofmonth(date) > =n and dayofmonth(date) < =(n+3) then buy to cover next
    bar at market;

TABLE 27.3 Days of Month Indicator (Full)

```
inputs:n(21),p(6);
if dayofmonth(date) > =n and dayofmonth(date) < =(n+3) then buy next bar at
    market;
if dayofmonth(date) > =p and dayofmonth(date) < =(p+3) then sell short next bar
    at market;
```

TABLE 27.4 Days of Month—Day Trades

```
inputs:n(21),p(6);
if dayofmonth(date) > =n or dayofmonth(date) < p then buy next bar at market;
if dayofmonth(date) > =p and dayofmonth(date) < n then sell short next bar at
    market;
setexitonclose;
```

TABLE 27.5 Days of Month—Buying after Lower Closes, Selling after
Higher—Day

```
inputs:n(21),p(6);
if c < c[1] and dayofmonth(date) > =n or dayofmonth(date) < p then buy next bar
    at market;
if c > c[1] and dayofmonth(date) > =p and dayofmonth(date) < n then sell short
    next bar at market;
setexitonclose;
```

TABLE 28.1 Index Month of the Year Indicator

```
inputs:n(10),p(4);
variables: e(0),m(0);
m=month(date);
if m < > m[1] and m[1]=n then e=1;
if m < > m[1] and m[1]=p then e=-1;
if e=1 then buy next bar at market;
if e=-1 then sell short next bar at market;
```

TABLE 28.3 Month of Year and Day of Month Combined

```
inputs:n(10),p(4);
variables: e(0),f(0),m(0);
m=month(date);
if m < > m[1] and m[1]=n then e=1;
if m < > m[1] and m[1]=p then e=-1;
if (dayofmonth(date) > =21 or dayofmonth(date) < 6) then f=1;
if (dayofmonth(date) > =6 and dayofmonth(date) < 21) then f=-1;
if e+f=2 then buy next bar at market;
if e+f < 2 then sell next bar at market;
if e+f=-2 then sell short next bar at market;
if e+f > -2 then buy to cover next bar at market;
```

TABLE 28.4 Month of Year—Day of Month Combined—Day System

```
(Substitute following for final command lines in Table 28.3.)
if o of tomorrow < c and e+f=2 then buy next bar at market;
if o of tomorrow > c and e+f=-2 then sell short next bar at market;
setexitonclose;
```

TABLE 28.5 Three Calendar Indicators Agree

```
inputs:n(10),p(4);
variables: e(0),f(0),x(0),u(0),g(0),m(0);
if c > o then e=c-o;
if c < o then f=o-c;
if (dayofweek(date)=5 and c > c[1]) or
(dayofweek(date)=1 and c < c[1]) or
(dayofweek(date)=2 and highest(e,2) < highest(f,2)) or
(dayofweek(date)=3 and highest(e,3) < highest(f,3)) or
(dayofweek(date)=4 and highest(e,4) < highest(f,4)) then g=1;
if (dayofweek(date)=5 and c < c[1]) or
(dayofweek(date)=1 and c > c[1]) or
(dayofweek(date)=2 and highest(e,2) > highest(f,2)) or
(dayofweek(date)=3 and highest(e,3) > highest(f,3)) or
(dayofweek(date)=4 and highest(e,4) > highest(f,4)) then g=-1;
m=month(date);
if m < > m[1] and m[1]=n then x=1;
if m < > m[1] and m[1]=p then x=-1;
if (dayofmonth(date) > =21 or dayofmonth(date) < 6) then u=1;
if (dayofmonth(date) > =6 and dayofmonth(date) < 21) then u=-1;
if x+u+g=3 then buy next bar at market;
if x+u+g < 3 then sell next bar at market;
if x+u+g=-3 then sell short next bar at market;
if x+u+g > -3 then buy to cover next bar at market;
```

TABLE 28.6 Two of Three Calendar Signals—Day System

(Substitute following for final command lines in Table 28.5.)
if o of tomorrow < c and x+u+g > 0 then buy next bar at market;
if o of tomorrow > c and x+u+g < 0 then sell short next bar at market;
setexitonclose;

TABLE 29.1 Monthly Dates, Day of Week, Eight Indicators Combined

---

variables: aaa(0),bbb(0),ccc(0),e(0),f(0),g(0),xx(0),j(0),x(0),uuu(0);
if c > o then e=c-o else e=0;
if c < o then f=o-c else f=0;
if (dayofweek(date)=5 and c > c[1]) or
(dayofweek(date)=1 and c < c[1]) or
(dayofweek(date)=2 and highest(e,2) < highest(f,2)) or
(dayofweek(date)=3 and highest(e,3) < highest(f,3)) or
(dayofweek(date)=4 and highest(e,4) < highest(f,4)) then aaa=1;
if (dayofweek(date)=5 and c < c[1]) or
(dayofweek(date)=1 and c > c[1]) or
(dayofweek(date)=2 and highest(e,2) > highest(f,2)) or
(dayofweek(date)=3 and highest(e,3) > highest(f,3)) or
(dayofweek(date)=4 and highest(e,4) > highest(f,4)) then aaa=-1;
if (dayofmonth(date) > =21 or dayofmonth(date) < 6) then bbb=1;
if (dayofmonth(date) > =6 and dayofmonth(date) < 21) then bbb=-1;
if average(c,2) < average(c,5)then g=1;
if average(c,2) > average(c,5)then g=-1;
if c > average(c,40) then xx=1;
if c < average(c,40) then xx=-1;
if highestbar(c,50) > lowestbar(c,50) then j=1;
if highestbar(c,50) < lowestbar(c,50) then j=-1;
if (range < average(range,10)) and c > c[1] or (range > average(range,10)) and c <
    c[1] then x=1;
if (range < average(range,10)) and c < c[1] or (range > average(range,10)) and c >
    c[1] then x=-1;
if c > (average(h,15)+average(l,15))/2 then uuu=1;
if c < (average(h,15)+average(l,15))/2 then uuu=-1;
if g+xx+j+x+uuu > 0 then ccc=1;
if g+xx+j+x+uuu < 0 then ccc=-1;
if aaa+bbb+ccc > 0 then buy next bar at market;
if aaa+bbb+ccc < 0 then sell short next bar at market;

TABLE 30.1 Dow-Spoo Perpetual

```
variables: g(0);
if c/closed(1) > (c of data(2)/(closed(1) of data(2)))then g=1;
if c/closed(1) < (c of data(2)/(closed(1) of data(2)))then g=-1;
if g > 0 then buy next bar at market;
if g < 0 then sell short next bar at market;
```

TABLE 30.2 Dow-Spoo Basic Day Trade Version

```
variables: g(0);
if c/closed(1) > (c of data(2)/(closed(1) of data(2)))then g=1;
if c/closed(1) < (c of data(2)/(closed(1) of data(2)))then g=-1;
if time > =845 and time < =1445 and g > 0 then buy next bar at market;
if time=1500 then sell next bar at market;
if time > =845 and time < =1445 and g < 0 then sell short next bar at market;
if time=1500 then buy to cover next bar at market;
```

TABLE 30.5 Dow-Spoo with Three Bar Requirement

```
inputs:u(3);
variables: g(0);
if c/closed(1) > (c of data(2)/(closed(1) of data(2)))then g=1;
if c/closed(1) < (c of data(2)/(closed(1) of data(2)))then g=-1;
if time > =930 and time < =1445 and lowest(g,u) > 0 then buy next bar at market;
if time=1500 then sell next bar at market;
if time > =930 and time < =1445 and highest(g,u) < 0 then sell short next bar at
    market;
if time=1500 then buy to cover next bar at market;
```

FIGURE 30.8 Dow-Spoo with 50-Day Average

```
inputs:e(50);
variables: g(0);
if c/closed(1) > (c of data(2)/(closed(1) of data(2)))then g=1;
if c/closed(1) < (c of data(2)/(closed(1) of data(2)))then g=-1;
if time > =900 and time < =1445 and c > average(c,e) and c[1] < =average(c,e)[1]
    and g > 0 then buy next bar at market;
if time > =900 and time < =1445 and c < average(c,e) and c[1] > =average(c,e)[1]
    and g < 0 then sell short next bar at market;
```

TABLE 30.10 Dow-Spoo—Six Bar High/Low Stop—Day

```
inputs:n(.5),u(6);
variables: g(0);
if c/closed(1) > c of data(2)/(closed(1) of data(2))then g=1;
if c/closed(1) < c of data(2)/(closed(1) of data(2))then g=-1;
if time > =900 and time < =1430 and lowest(g,u) > 0 then buy next bar at
    highest(h,6) stop;
if time=1500 then sell next bar at market;
if time > =900 and time < =1430 and highest(g,u) < 0 then sell short next bar at
    lowest(l,6) stop;
if time=1500 then buy to cover next bar at market;
```

TABLE 30.11 Dow-Spoo—Six Bar High/Low Limit—Day

```
variables: g(0);
if c/closed(1) > (c of data(2)/(closed(1) of data(2))) then g=1;
if c/closed(1) < (c of data(2)/(closed(1) of data(2))) then g=-1;
if time > =845 and time < =1445 and c > average(h,6) and g > 0 then buy next bar
    at c-.5*range limit;
if time=1500 then sell next bar at market;
if time > =845 and time < =1445 and c < average(l,6) and g < 0 then sell short
    next bar at c+.5*range limit;
if time=1500 then buy to cover next bar at market;
```

TABLE 30.12 Dynamic Dow-Spoo—Day

```
variables: g(0);
if c/(closed(1)) > c of data(2)/(closed(1) of data(2))then g=1;
if c/(closed(1)) < c of data(2)/(closed(1) of data(2))then g=-1;
if ((time > =930 and time < 1000 and average(g,12) > 0) or
(time > =1000 and time < 1030 and average(g,18) > 0) or
(time > =1030 and time < 1100 and average(g,24) > 0) or
(time > =1100 and time < 1130 and average(g,30) > 0) or
(time > =1130 and time < 1200 and average(g,36) > 0) or
(time > =1200 and time < 1230 and average(g,42) > 0) or
(time > =1230 and time < 1300 and average(g,48) > 0)) then buy next bar at market;
if time=1500 then sell next bar at market;
if ((time > =930 and time < 1000 and average(g,12) < 0) or
(time > =1000 and time < 1030 and average(g,18) < 0) or
(time > =1030 and time < 1100 and average(g,24) < 0) or
(time > =1100 and time < 1130 and average(g,30) < 0) or
(time > =1130 and time < 1200 and average(g,36) < 0) or
(time > =1200 and time < 1230 and average(g,42) < 0) or
(time > =1230 and time < 1300 and average(g,48) < 0)) then sell short next bar at
    market;
if time=1500 then buy to cover next bar at market;
```

TABLE 31.2   Entering Re Daily Opening—Index Version

(For bond-currency versions, substitute following for first line—
    inputs:x(8.2),y(14.00);)
inputs:x(9.3),y(15.15);
if time=(x*100) and c > opend(0) then buy next bar at market;
if time=(y*100) then sell this bar on close;
if time=(x*100) and c < opend(0) then sell short next bar at market;
if time=(y*100) then buy to cover this bar on close;

TABLE 31.3   Two Bar in Row versus Open—60-Minute Bars—Index Version

(For bond-currency versions, substitute following for first line—
    inputs:b(9.2),x(13.20);)
inputs:b(10.3),x(14.3);
if time > =(b*100) and time < (x*100) and c > opend(0) and c[1] > opend(0) and c
    > c[1] then buy next bar at market;
if time=(x*100) then sell next bar at market;
if time > =(b*100) and time < (x*100)and c < opend(0) and c[1] < opend(0) and c <
    c[1] then sell short next bar at market;
if time=(x*100) then buy to cover next bar at market;

TABLE 31.4   Final Third of Day System—Index Version

(For bond-currency versions, substitute following for first line—
    inputs:x(11.5),y(14.00);)
inputs:x(13),y(15.15);
if time=(x*100) and c > opend(0) and c[1] > opend(0) then buy next bar at market;
if time=(y*100) then sell this bar on close;
if time=(x*100) and c < opend(0) and c[1] < opend(0) then sell short next bar at
    market;
if time=(y*100) then buy to cover this bar on close;

TABLE 32.1	Soybean Switch 1

```
inputs:q(2),n(20),y(.5),z(.4),u(.1);
variables:x(0),mp(0),rr(0),xx(0);
if average(range,5) > =q*average(range,n)[5] then x=1 else x=0;
mp=marketposition;
rr=highest(h,n)-lowest(l,n);
if highest(h,n)-c < =u*rr then xx=1 else xx=0;
if x+xx > =1 then buy next bar at o of tomorrow+range stop;
if mp=1 then sell next bar at o of tomorrow+y*rr limit;
if mp=1 then sell next bar at o of tomorrow-z*rr stop;
if mp=1 then sell next bar at l-range stop;
if x+xx > =1 then sell short next bar at o of tomorrow-range stop;
if mp=-1 then buy to cover next bar at o of tomorrow-y*rr limit;
if mp=-1 then buy to cover next bar at o of tomorrow+z*rr stop;
```

TABLE 33.1	Range Expansion with "Two Same-way" Filter

```
inputs:u(.6),n(20);
variables: x(0);
if (c > c[1] and c[1] > c[2])or (c < c[1] and c[1] < c[2]) then x=1 else x=0;
if average(x,n) > =u then buy next bar at o of tomorrow+(.5*average(range,3))
    stop;
sell next bar at o of tomorrow-(.5*average(range,3)) stop;
if average(x,n) > =u then sell short next bar at o of tomorrow-
    (.5*average(range,3)) stop;
buy to cover next bar at o of tomorrow+(.5*average(range,3)) stop;
```

TABLE 34.1	12:30 Entry System—Index Version

```
(For bond-currency versions, substitute following for first line— inputs:x(13.5);
inputs: x(15.05);
variables:hh(0),ll(0),hhh(0),lll(0);
if time=930 then hh=highd(0);
if time=930 then ll=lowd(0);
if time=1130 then hhh=highd(0);
if time=1130 then lll=lowd(0);
if time=1230 and opend(0)-lowd(0) < =.25*(highd(0)-lowd(0))and highd(0) > hhh
    and hhh > hh then buy next bar at market;
if time=(x*100) then sell next bar at market;
if time=1230 and highd(0)-opend(0) < =.25*(highd(0)-lowd(0))and lowd(0) < lll and
    lll < ll then sell short next bar at market;
if time=(x*100) then buy to cover next bar at market;
```

TABLE 35.1   Majority Direction of 9 Open-Closes (5 Min)

variables:e(0);
if c > o then e=1 else e=0;
if c < o then e=-1;
if time > =915 and time < =1445 and average(e,9) > 0 then buy next bar at
    market;
if time=1500 then sell next bar at market;
if time > =915 and time < =1445 and average(e,9) < 0 then sell short next bar at
    market;
if time=1500 then buy to cover next bar at market;

TABLE 35.2   Daily Midpoint as Demarcation Line

if time > =915 and time < =1445 and c > (highd(0)+lowd(0))/2 then buy next bar
    at market;
if time=1500 then sell next bar at market;
if time > =915 and time < =1445 and c < (highd(0)+lowd(0))/2 then sell short next
    bar at market;
if time=1500 then buy to cover next bar at market;

TABLE 35.3   Four Indicator System

inputs:n(9);
variables:aa(0),bb(0),cc(0),dd(0),x(0);
if c > o then x=1 else x=0;
if c < o then x=-1;
if c/closed(1) > (c of data(2)/(closed(1) of data(2)))then aa=1;
if c/closed(1) < (c of data(2)/(closed(1) of data(2)))then aa=-1;
if c > opend(0) then bb=1;
if c < opend(0) then bb=-1;
if average(x,n) > 0 then cc=1;
if average(x,n) < 0 then cc=-1;
if c > (highd(0)+lowd(0))/2 then dd=1;
if c < (highd(0)+lowd(0))/2 then dd=-1;
if time > =915 and time < =1445 and aa+bb+cc+dd=4 then buy next bar at
    market;
if time=1500 then sell next bar at market;
if time > =915 and time < =1445 and aa+bb+cc+dd=-4 then sell short next bar at
    market;
if time=1500 then buy to cover next bar at market;

TABLE 35.6 Four Indicator with Exit Qualifier

```
inputs:n(9);
variables:aa(0),bb(0),cc(0),dd(0),x(0),u(0);
if c > o then x=1 else x=0;
if c < o then x=-1;
u=aa+bb+cc+dd;
if c/closed(1) > (c of data(2)/(closed(1) of data(2))) then aa=1;
if c/closed(1) < (c of data(2)/(closed(1) of data(2))) then aa=-1;
if c > opend(0) then bb=1;
if c < opend(0) then bb=-1;
if average(x,n) > 0 then cc=1;
if average(x,n) < 0 then cc=-1;
if c > (highd(0)+lowd(0))/2 then dd=1;
if c < (highd(0)+lowd(0))/2 then dd=-1;
if time > =915 and time < =1445 and aa+bb+cc+dd=4 then buy next bar at
     market;
if u < 0 and u[1] < 0 then sell next bar at market;
if time=1500 then sell next bar at market;
if time > =915 and time < =1445 and aa+bb+cc+dd=-4 then sell short next bar at
     market;
if u > 0 and u[1] > 0 then buy to cover next bar at market;
```

TABLE 36.1 Going with First Contrary Close after Five Same Directional
in Row

```
if c > c[1] and c[1] < c[2] and c[2] < c[3] and c[3] < c[4] and c[4] < c[5] and c[5] <
     c[6] then buy next bar
at market;
if c < c[1] and c[1] > c[2] and c[2] > c[3] and c[3] > c[4] and c[4] > c[5] and c[5] >
     c[6] then sell short next bar at market;
setexitonclose;
```

TABLE 36.2 Going with Five Same-way Closes in Row—Long Term Perpetual

```
if c < c[1] and c[1] > c[2] and c[2] > c[3] and c[3] > c[4] and c[4] > c[5] and c[5] >
     c[6] then buy next bar at market;
if c > c[1] and c[1] < c[2]and c[2] < c[3] and c[3] < c[4] and c[4] < c[5] and c[5] <
     c[6] then sell short next bar at market;
```

TABLE 36.3   Five One-way Closes, One Opposite, One Irrelevant—Perpetual

---

(Type "setexitonclose" at the end for day version.)

if c[1] < c[2] and c[2] > c[3] and c[3] > c[4] and c[4] > c[5] and c[5] > c[6] and c[6] >
     c[7] then buy next bar at market;

if c[1] > c[2] and c[2] < c[3] and c[3] < c[4] and c[4] < c[5] and c[5] < c[6] and c[6] <
     c[7] then sell short next bar at market;

TABLE 37.1   Third Day Fade

---

if marketposition < 1 and c < l[1] and c[1] < l[2] then buy next bar at o of
     tomorrow-.33*average(range,3) limit;

if marketposition=1 then sell next bar at h limit;

if marketposition=1 then sell next bar at l-(minmove/pricescale)stop;

if marketposition=1 then setexitonclose;

if marketposition > -1 and c > h[1] and c[1] > h[2] then sell short next bar at o of
     tomorrow+.33*average(range,3) limit;

if marketposition=-1 then buy to cover next bar at l limit;

if marketposition=-1 then buy to cover next bar at h+(minmove/pricescale)stop;

if marketposition=-1 then setexitonclose;

TABLE 37.2   Closes Beyond Five-Day Low/High Averages

---

variables:x(0),y(0);

inputs:n(5);

if c < average(l,5) then x=1 else x=0;

if c > average(h,5) then y=1 else y=0;

if marketposition < 1 and lowest(x,3)=1 and c < c[1] and c[1] < c[2] then buy next
     bar at market;

if marketposition=1 and barssinceentry > 0 then sell next bar at h limit;

if marketposition=1 and barssinceentry > 0 then sell next bar at l-
     (minmove/pricescale)stop;

if marketposition=1 and barssinceentry > 1 then setexitonclose;

if marketposition > -1 and lowest(y,3)=1 and c > c[1] and c[1] > c[2] then sell short
     next bar at market;

if marketposition=-1 and barssinceentry > 0 then buy to cover next bar at l limit;

if marketposition=-1 and barssinceentry > 0 then buy to cover next bar at
     h+(minmove/pricescale)stop;

if marketposition=-1 and barssinceentry > 1 then setexitonclose;

TABLE 38.1 20 Day N-Day System

buy next bar at highest(h,20) stop;
sell short next bar at lowest(l,20) stop;

TABLE 38.3 N Day with 10-Day Stops

if marketposition < 1 then buy next bar at highest(h,20) stop;
if barssinceentry > =10 and (c[10] > highest(c,10) or h[10] > highest(h,10))
then sell next bar at market;
if marketposition > -1 then sell short next bar at lowest(l,20) stop;
if barssinceentry > =10 and (c[10] < lowest(c,10) or l[10] < lowest(l,10))
then buy to cover next bar at market;

TABLE 39.1 Five-Minute RSI Go-with System—Index Version

(For bond-currency versions, substitute following for first line—
inputs: Length(9),n(15),b(8.35),x(13.3),z(13.55);)
inputs: Length(9),n(15),b(9.15),x(14.45),z(15.1);
variables: e(0);
e = RSI(Close, Length);
if time > =(b*100) and time < =(x*100) and e > (100-n) then buy next bar at
    market;
if time=(z*100) then sell next bar at market;
if time > =(b*100) and time < =(x*100) and e < n then sell short next bar at
    market;
if time=(z*100) then buy to cover next bar at market;

TABLE 40.1 Fading Reversals

inputs:p(2);
variables:hh(0),ll(0);
if marketposition=1 and barssinceentry=0 then hh=h;
if marketposition=-1 and barssinceentry=0 then ll=l;
if marketposition < 1 and h > h[1] and c < c[1] then buy next bar at market;
if(h < =h[1] or c > =c[1]) then sell next bar at hh limit;
if barssinceentry > 0 then sell next bar at ll-minmove/pricescale stop;
if marketposition > -1 and l < l[1] and c > c[1] then sell short next bar at market;
if (l > =l[1] or c < =c[1]) then buy to cover next bar at ll limit;
if barssinceentry > 0 then buy to cover next bar at hh+minmove/pricescale stop;

TABLE 41.1 Four-Day Range Expansion

```
buy next bar at o of tomorrow+2*average(range,3) stop;
if barssinceentry=2 then sell next bar at h limit;
if barssinceentry=2 then sell next bar at l stop;
if barssinceentry=2 then setexitonclose;
sell short next bar at o of tomorrow-(2*average(range,3))stop;
if barssinceentry=2 then buy to cover next bar at l limit;
if barssinceentry=2 then buy to cover next bar at h stop;
if barssinceentry=2 then setexitonclose;
```

TABLE 41.3 9 Day 66 Percent Momentum System

```
variables:mp(0),hc(0),lc(0),xx(0);
hc=highest(h,9)-c;
lc=c-lowest(l,9);
if hc > lc then xx=hc;
if hc < lc then xx=lc;
mp=marketposition;
if mp < 1 and hc > lc then buy next bar at o of tomorrow+(.66*lc) stop;
if mp=1 and barssinceentry > 0 then sell next bar at entryprice-(1.32*xx) stop;
if mp > -1 and lc > hc then sell short next bar at o of tomorrow-(.66*hc) stop;
if mp=-1 and barssinceentry > 0 then buy to cover next bar at
      entryprice+(1.32*xx) stop;
```

TABLE 41.6 Contracting Range—Fade Close on Momentum

```
if (average(range,10) < average(range,25)) and (c < c[1] and c < average(c,5)) then
      buy next bar (o of tomorrow+(.2*range)) stop;
if (c > average(c,10) and c > average(c,25)) then sell next bar at (o of tomorrow-
      (.2*range)) stop;
if barssinceentry > 0 then sell next bar at entryprice-average(range,25) stop;
if (average(range,10) < average(range,25)) and (c > c[1] and c > average(c,5)) then
      sell short next bar (o of tomorrow-(.2*range)) stop;
if (c < average(c,10) and c < average(c,25)) then buy to cover next bar (o of
      tomorrow+(.2*range)) stop;
if barssinceentry > 0 then buy to cover next bar at entryprice+average(range,25)
      stop;
```

TABLE 41.7 5 vs 15-Day Closing Averages

---

if average(c,5) > average(c,15) and average(c,5)[1] > average(c,15)[1] and
    average(c,5)[2] > average(c,15)[2]and average(c,5)[3] < average(c,15)[3] then
    buy next bar at market;
if average(c,5) < average(c,15) and average(c,5)[1] < average(c,15)[1] and
    average(c,5)[2] < average(c,15)[2] and average(c,5)[3] > average(c,15)[3] then
    sell short next bar at market;

TABLE 41.8 Soybean Seasonal—Buy in March

---

variables: e(0);
e=month(date);
if e=3 and e < > e[1] then buy next bar at market;
if month(date)=7 then sell next bar at market;
setprofittarget(2000);
setstoploss (4000);

TABLE 41.10 Soybean Seasonal—Sell in July

---

variables: e(0);
e=month(date);
if e=7 and e < > e[1]then sell short next bar at market;
if month(date)=11 then buy to cover next bar at market;
setprofittarget(4000);
setstoploss (5000);

TABLE 41.11 Three-Day 30-Day Crossover

---

if average(c,3)[3] < average(c,30)[3] and average(c,3)[2] > average(c,30)[2] and
    average(c,3)[1] > average(c,30)[1] and average(c,3) > average(c,30) then buy
    next bar at market;
if average(c,3) < average(c,30) then sell next bar at market;
if average(c,3)[3] > average(c,30)[3] and average(c,3)[2] < average(c,30)[2] and
    average(c,3)[1] < average(c,30)[1] and average(c,3) < average(c,30)then sell
    short next bar at market;
if average(c,3) > average(c,30) then buy to cover next bar at market;

TABLE 41.12 15 and 30 Days Back Indicator

```
if c > c[15] and c > c[30] then buy next bar at market;
if c < c[15] or c < c[30] then sell next bar at market;
if c < c[15] and c < c[30] then sell short next bar at market;
if c > c[15] or c > c[30] then buy to cover next bar at market;
```

TABLE 41.14 Bond-Index

```
if time=1000 and c > opend(0)and c of data2 > opend(0)of data2 and highd(0)of
    data2-c of data2 < =.25*(highd(0)of data2-lowd(0)of data2) then buy next bar
    at market;
if time=1000 and c > opend(0)and c of data2 < opend(0) and c of data2-lowd(0)of
    data2 < =.25*(highd(0)of data2-lowd(0)of data2) then buy next bar at market;
if time=1510 then sell next bar at market;
if time=1000 and c < opend(0)and c of data2 < opend(0) and c of data2-lowd(0)of
data2 < =.25*(highd(0)of data2-lowd(0)of data2) then sell short next bar at
    market;
if time=1000 and c < opend(0)and c of data2 > opend(0) and highd(0)of data2-c of
    data2 < =.25*(highd(0)of data2-lowd(0)of data2) then sell short next bar at
    market;
if time=1510 then buy to cover next bar at market;
```

TABLE 42.1 Fading Two Out of Three Open-To-Closes

```
variables: e(0);
if c > o then e=1;
if c < o then e=-1;
if average(e,3) < 0 then buy next bar at market;
if average(e,3) > 0 then sell short next bar at market;
setexitonclose;
```

TABLE 42.2 6 Indicator (Simple Majority)

```
variables: e(0),aa(0),bb(0),cc(0),dd(0),ee(0),ff(0),gg(0);
if c > o then e=1;
if c < o then e=-1;
if average(c,2) < average(c,5)then aa=1;
if average(c,2) > average(c,5)then aa=-1;
if c > average(c,40) then bb=1;
if c < average(c,40) then bb=-1;
if highestbar(c,50) > lowestbar(c,50) then cc=1;
if highestbar(c,50) < lowestbar(c,50) then cc=-1;
```

TABLE 42.2 *(Continued)*

---

if (range < average(range,10)) and c > c[1] or (range > average(range,10)) and c <
    c[1] then dd=1;
if (range < average(range,10)) and c < c[1] or (range > average(range,10)) and c >
    c[1] then dd=-1;
if c > (average(h,15)+average(l,15))/2 then ee=1;
if c < (average(h,15)+average(l,15))/2 then ee=-1;
if average(e,3) < 0 then ff=1;
if average(e,3) > 0 then ff=-1;
if aa+bb+cc+dd+ee+ff > 0 then buy next bar at market;
if aa+bb+cc+dd+ee+ff < 0 then sell short next bar at market;
setexitonclose;

TABLE 42.3 Six Indicator with 66 Percent Stoploss

(Substitute following for final command lines in Table 42.2.)
if aa+bb+cc+dd+ee+ff > 0 then buy next bar at market;
sell next bar at o of tomorrow-.66*average(range,3) stop;
if aa+bb+cc+dd+ee+ff < 0 then sell short next bar at market;
buy to cover next bar at o of tomorrow+.66*average(range,3) stop;

TABLE 43.1 Five Combined Non-Either-or Indicators

---

variables:aa(0),bb(0),cc(0),dd(0),ee(0);
if c[1] < c[2] and c[2] > c[3] and c[3] > c[4] and c[4] > c[5] and c[5] > c[6] then aa=1
    else aa=0;
if c[1] > c[2] and c[2] < c[3] and c[3] < c[4] and c[4] < c[5] and c[5] < c[6] then aa=-
    1;
if c[1] < c[2] and c[2] > c[3] and c[3] > c[4] and c[4] > c[5] and c[5] > c[6] and c[6] >
    c[7] then bb=1 else bb=0;
if c[1] > c[2] and c[2] < c[3] and c[3] < c[4] and c[4] < c[5] and c[5] < c[6] and c[6] <
    c[7] then bb=-1;
if l > l[1] and l[1] < lowest(l,3)[2] and c > c[1] and c[1] < c[2]then cc=1 else cc=0;
if h < h[1] and h[1] > highest(h,3)[2] and c < c[1] and c[1] > c[2]then cc=-1;
if highest(l,3)-lowest(l,3) < =.2*(highest(h,3)-lowest(l,3)) then dd=1 else dd=0;
if highest(h,3)-lowest(h,3) < =.2* (highest(h,3)-lowest(l,3))then dd=-1;
if c < o and c[1] < o[1] then ee=1 else ee=0;
if c > o and c[1] > o[1] then ee=-1;
if aa+bb+cc+dd+ee > 0 then buy next bar at market;
if aa+bb+cc+dd+ee < 0 then sell short next bar at market;
setexitonclose;

TABLE 44.1   Six Indicator with Five Non–Either-or Qualifier—Version 1

```
variables:e(0),aa(0),bb(0),cc(0),dd(0),ee(0),ff(0),aaa(0),bbb(0),ccc(0),ddd(0),eee(0);
if c > o then e=1 else e=0;
if c < o then e=-1;
if c[1] < c[2] and c[2] > c[3] and c[3] > c[4] and c[4] > c[5] and c[5] > c[6] then
     aaa=1 else aaa=0;
if c[1] > c[2] and c[2] < c[3] and c[3] < c[4] and c[4] < c[5] and c[5] < c[6] then
     aaa=-1;
if c[1] < c[2] and c[2] > c[3] and c[3] > c[4] and c[4] > c[5] and c[5] > c[6] and c[6] >
     c[7] then bbb=1 else bbb=0;
if c[1] > c[2] and c[2] < c[3] and c[3] < c[4] and c[4] < c[5] and c[5] < c[6] and c[6] <
     c[7] then bbb=-1;
if l > l[1] and l[1] < lowest(l,3)[2] and c > c[1] and c[1] < c[2]then ccc=1 else ccc=0;
if h < h[1] and h[1] > highest(h,3)[2] and c < c[1] and c[1] > c[2]then ccc=-1;
if highest(l,3)-lowest(l,3) < =.2*(highest(h,3)-lowest(l,3)) then ddd=1 else ddd=0;
if highest(h,3)-lowest(h,3) < =.2* (highest(h,3)-lowest(l,3))then ddd=-1;
if c < o and c[1] < o[1] then eee=1 else eee=0;
if c > o and c[1] > o[1] then eee=-1;
if average(c,2) < average(c,5)then aa=1;
if average(c,2) > average(c,5)then aa=-1;
if c > average(c,40) then bb=1;
if c < average(c,40) then bb=-1;
if highestbar(c,50) > lowestbar(c,50) then cc=1;
if highestbar(c,50) < lowestbar(c,50) then cc=-1;
if (range < average(range,10)) and c > c[1] or (range > average(range,10)) and c <
     c[1] then dd=1;
if (range < average(range,10)) and c < c[1] or (range > average(range,10)) and c >
     c[1] then dd=-1;
if c > (average(h,15)+average(l,15))/2 then ee=1;
if c < (average(h,15)+average(l,15))/2 then ee=-1;
if average(e,3) < 0 then ff=1;
if average(e,3) > 0 then ff=-1;
if aa+bb+cc+dd+ee+ff > 0 and aaa+bbb+ccc+ddd+eee > =0 then buy next bar at
     market;
if aa+bb+cc+dd+ee+ff < 0 and aaa+bbb+ccc+ddd+eee < =0 then sell short next
     bar at market;
setexitonclose;
```

TABLE 44.2 Filtered Six Indicator with 66 Percent Stop

(Substitute following for last three lines in 44.1.)

```
if aa+bb+cc+dd+ee+ff > 0 and aaa+bbb+ccc+ddd+eee > =0 then buy next bar at
    market;
sell next bar at o of tomorrow-.66*average(range,3) stop;
if aa+bb+cc+dd+ee+ff < 0 and aaa+bbb+ccc+ddd+eee < =0 then sell short next
    bar at market;
buy to cover next bar at o of tomorrow+.66*average(range,3) stop;
setexitonclose;
```

TABLE 44.3 Filter Indicator—66 Percent Stop—Version 2

(Substitute following for last three lines in 44.1.)

```
if (aa+bb+cc+dd+ee+ff > 0 and aaa+bbb+ccc+ddd+eee > =0) or
    (aa+bb+cc+dd+ee+ff=0 and aaa+bbb+ccc+ddd+eee > 0) then buy next bar at
    market;
sell next bar at o of tomorrow-.66*average(range,3) stop;
if (aa+bb+cc+dd+ee+ff < 0 and aaa+bbb+ccc+ddd+eee < =0) or
    (aa+bb+cc+dd+ee+ff=0 and aaa+bbb+ccc+ddd+eee < 0) then sell short next
    bar at market;
buy to cover next bar at o of tomorrow+.66*average(range,3) stop;
setexitonclose;
```

Index

Averages, *see* Close versus 40-day closing average; Fifteen-day high/low averages; Fifty-day average; Five-day low/high averages; Five versus 15-day closing averages; Three-day average; Two-day versus five-day averages

Bonds:
  contracts, 108–109
  indexes and, 187–189
    formula, 234

Calendar signals, *see* Days of the month; Days of the week; Months of the year
Close versus 40-day closing average, 14–15
  combined with other indicators, 31–34, 39–46, 58–64
  formula, 205
  second high/low exit system and, 77
  virgin data and, 88–95
Coiling, 35–37
Commodities, 103–104
Continuous 66 percent momentum system, 177–179
  formula, 232

Contracting ranges, *see* Ranges, contracting
Cups and caps, 49–55
  combined with other indicators, 58–64
  day formula, 208
  overnight formula, 208
  overnight with stops and targets formula, 208
Currencies, 104–108

Daily midpoint as demarcation line formula, 228
Daily opening price, 138–142
Days of the month, 115–119, 124–126
  buying after lower closes, selling after higher formula, 221
  day trade formula, 221
  eight indicators combined formula, 223
  indicator formula, 221
  month of year and day of month combined formulas, 222
  three calendar indicators agreement formula, 222
  two of three calendar indicators agreement formula, 223

Days of the week, 111–114
eight indicators combined
formula, 223
indicator formula, 220
three calendar indicators
agreement formula, 222
two of three calendar indicators
agreement formula, 223
Dennis, Richard, 165
Dow Jones Average, characteristics
of, 131. *See also* Dow-Spoo
spread
Dow-Spoo spread, 127–137
formulas, 224–225
Drivers, 18, 23–24
Dynamic stops, 72

Fading open to close formula, 207
Fading reversals formula, 231
Fading two like closes in a row
formula, 206
Fading two out of three open-to-
closes formula, 234
Fifteen-day high/low averages, 38
combined with other indicators,
39–46, 58–64
formula, 207
second high/low exit system and,
77
Fifteen–30 day close indicator,
186–187
Fifteen and 30 days back indicator
formula, 234
Fifty-day average, Dow-Spoo with,
formula, 224
Fifty-day order of extreme
highest/lowest closes, 29–30
combined with other indicators,
31–34, 39–46, 58–64
formula, 206
second high/low exit system and,
77
virgin data and, 88–95

Final third system, 140–142
Financial markets, value of testing
with nine, 85–86
Financial switch, 151–152
Five closes in same direction,
158–162
formula, 229
Five-day low/high averages,
164
formula, 230
Five one-way closes, one opposite,
one irrelevant formula,
230
Five versus 15-day closing
averages, 181
formula, 233
Forever Long strategy, 19–20
Forever Long S&P formula,
205
optimization rules and, 20–24
Four combined entry signals in
indexes, 153–157
Four-day range expansion, 176–177
Friday bias, 111, 113

Indexes:
advantages of trading, 103,
110–111
bond-index formula, 234
combining biases with
indicators, 124–126
days of the month and, 115–119
days of the week and, 111–114
entering re daily opening
formula, 226
final third of day system formula,
226
four combined entry signals in,
153–157
month of the year and, 120–123
sixty-minute bars formula, 226
switch and, 148–150
12:30 entry system formula, 227

Indicators, 10–13. *See also specific indicators*
  five indicators combined, 39–42
    formula, 207
    optimizing formula, 219
  four indicator system formula, 228
  four indicator with exit qualifier formula, 229
  eight indicators combined, 58–64
    formulas, 209–210
  index biases combined, 124–126
  other combinations of, 43–46
  six indicator formula, 234–235
  six indicator with five combined formula, 236
  six indicator with 66 percent stoploss formula, 235, 237
  three indicators combined, 31–34
    formula, 206
  three indicators out of five (various) formula, 207
Intraday trading:
  daily opening price, 138–142
  financial switch, 151–152
  four combined entry signals in indexes, 153–157
  index switch and, 148–150
  threshold levels switch, 143–147
  window hours of, 138

Limits:
  entering on, 69–71
  price targets and, 76
  second high/low exit system and, 83–84

Majority direction of nine open-closes formula, 228
Market drift, reoptimization/virgin data and, 85–95

Market Rap: The Odyssey of a Still-Struggling Commodity Trader (Collins), 10
Mechanical trading:
  advantages over non-mechanical, 1–4
  dual realities of, 143–144
  identifying, 198–199
  importance of believing in, 200–204
  numbers game and, 5–6
Mega System:
  formula, 219
  pros and cons of, 96–102
Monday bias, 111–113
Money management stops, 72
Months of the year, 120–126. *See also* Days of the month
  days of the month formulas combined with, 222
  eight indicators formula combined with, 223
  indicator formula, 221
  three calendar indicators agreement formula, 222
  two of three calendar indicators agreement formula, 223

N Day, 165–170
  ten-day stops formula, 231
  twenty-day system formula, 231
Neighboring numbers, optimization and, 17, 20, 21–22
Non–either-or indicators, 193–194
  five combined, formulas, 235–236
  six signals plus, 195–197
Non-mechanical trading:
  numbers game and, 5–6
  problems with, 1–4
  spontaneity and, 7–9
Numbers games, 5–6

One-minute bars, trading off (Mega System), 96–102
  formula, 219
Opening price, daily, 138–142
Open-to-close indicators:
  combined with other indicators, 58–64
  two same directional, 47–48
  yesterday's, 47–48
Optimization, 16–17
  reoptimization, 85–95
  rules of, 17–18
  rules of, applied to Forever Long strategy, 19–24
Outliers, 62–63
Overnight sessions, cups and caps and, 49–53

Perennially short S&Ps formula, 220
Price targets, pros and cons of, 76–81
Profits and losses, even disbursement of, 18, 23

Ranges. *See also* Ten-day range indicator
  contracting, 179–181
    fade to close on momentum formula, 232
  cuing off relative range sizes, 35–37
  expanding:
    four days in trade, 200 percent, 176–177
    four days in trade formula, 232
    1.5 daily formula, 220
    two same-way filter formula, 227
  weekly yen formula, 219
Related fields, optimization and, 17, 20, 22–23

Reoptimization, market drift/virgin data and, 85–95
Return on account (ROA), as performance gauge, 39–40, 88–95, 96
Reversal day indicator, 174–175
Reverse signals, stops and, 72–73
RSI indicator, 171–173
  five-minute go-with system formula, 231
Ruggiero, Murray, 17

S&P 500, *see* Dow-Spoo spread
Second high/low exit system, 77–81
  formulas, 211–219
  other applications of, 82–84
Sector analysis, 103–109. *See also* Indexes
  bond contracts, 108–109
  commodities, 103–104
  currencies, 104–108
Six bar high/low stop Dow-Spoo formulas, 225
66 percent (continuous) momentum system, 177–179
  formula, 232
66 percent stop, 191
  filtered indicators with, formulas, 237
Soybeans:
  buy in March formula, 233
  seasonal buys of, 181–186
  sell in July formula, 233
  switch and, 144–147
    formula, 227
Steidlmayer, Peter, 56
Stops:
  basic types of, 72–73
  dynamic, not static, 73–75
  entering on, 65–68
  N Day and, 166–170
  price targets and, 77, 81

Switches:
  financial switch, 151–152
  index switch, 148–150
  soybeans and, 144–147
    formula, 227
  between threshold levels,
    143–147

Ten-day range indicator, 35–37
  combined with other indicators,
    39–42, 58–64
  formula, 206
  second high/low exit system and,
    77
Third day fade, 163–164
  formula, 230
Three-day average:
  entering stop orders and, 65–68
  limits and, 69–71
Three-day 30-day crossover, 186
  formula, 233
Three-day 20 percent support-
    resistance, 56–57
  combined with other indicators,
    58–64
Thursday bias, 113
Trade in progress, as focus of gut
    traders, 2, 5
TradeStation, xxiv–xxv
  formulas, 205–237
  steps for calculating RSI, 171
  tips on using formulas, 205
Trading, advantages of mechanical
    over non-mechanical, 1–9

Trailing stops, 72
Tuesday bias, 113
Turtle System, 165
12:30 entry system formula,
    227
20 percent support-resistance
    formula, 208
Two bar in row versus open
    system, 139–141
Two-day versus five-day averages,
    25–28
  combined with other indicators,
    31–34, 39–46, 58–64
  formula, 206
  second high/low exit system and,
    77
  virgin data and, 88–95
200 percent range expansion,
    176–177
Two same-way filter, range
    expansion formula, 227
Two same-way open-to-closes,
    fading, 47–48
  formula, 208

Vegas numbers game, 6
Virgin data, reoptimization/market
    drift and, 85–95

Wednesday bias, 113
Weekday, *see* Days of the week

Yen weekly range expansion
    formula, 219

About the Author

Art Collins has been developing and successfully trading mechanical commodity systems since 1986. He is a Chicago Board of Trade member, lecturer, and author. His most recent book, *Market Beaters*, was a collection of interviews with 13 renowned mechanical trading experts. Art also regularly contributes to *Futures Magazine* and other investment periodicals. He welcomes reader response: artcollins@ameritech.net.